ON WINGS OF SONG

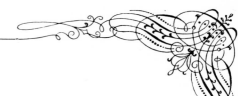

WILFRID BLUNT

ON WINGS OF SONG

A Biography of Felix Mendelssohn

Hamish Hamilton · London

This book was designed and produced by
George Rainbird Ltd
Marble Arch House
44 Edgware Road
London W2

Published in Great Britain in 1974 by
Hamish Hamilton Ltd
90 Great Russell Street
London WC1

House editor: Ellen Crampton
Design: Margaret Thomas

Colour plates printed by
Westerham Press Ltd, Westerham, Kent
Text printed and bound by
Jarrold & Sons Ltd, Norwich

ISBN: 0241–02455–2

Other books by Wilfrid Blunt:

The Art of Botanical Illustration
Pietro's Pilgrimage
A Persian Spring
Of Flowers and a Village
Cockerell
Isfahan
The Dream King
The Compleat Naturalist
John Christie of Glyndebourne
The Golden Road to Samarkand

Permission to quote from copyright material has been granted
by the following:

The Free Press of Glencoe (Macmillan Publishing Co., Inc.).
Mendelssohn: A New Image of the Composer and His Age.
© 1963 by Eric Werner. Translated by Dika Newlin.

Robert Hale & Company. Funk and Wagnalls *Gentle Genius* by George Marek, 1972.

London Management. *The Memoirs of Hector Berlioz.* © 1969 by
David Cairns. Victor Gollancz.

Oxford University Press. *Mendelssohn and his Friends in Kensington.*
Edited by Rosamund Brunel Gotch, 1934.

To Louise

MENDELSSOHN: FICTION AND FACT

'Since contented nations and contented
men have no history, one should on principle
abandon the idea of writing a life of
Mendelssohn, for indeed no one was ever
more consistently and entirely happy than
the composer of *A Midsummer Night's Dream*.'
EMILE VUILLERMOZ

'I knew and loved the man too well to
like to see him so absurdly idealized.'
WILLIAM STERNDALE BENNETT

Acknowledgments

I have to acknowledge with gratitude the help of many friends. Dr Hugo von Mendelssohn Bartholdy, a descendant of the composer and Director of the Internationale Felix-Mendelssohn-Gesellschaft at Basel, Dr Rudolf Elvers, Curator of the Mendelssohn-Archiv in Berlin, and Miss Margaret Crum of the Department of Western Manuscripts at the Bodleian Library, Oxford, all allowed me to draw freely on their wide knowledge of Mendelssohn. Miss Sandra Raphael, Mr Philip and Miss Susan Radcliffe, and Mr John Holmstrom are among those who were so kind as to read my typescript and offer valuable suggestions.

I am also indebted to the following for advice of various kinds: Mr Douglas Botting, Mr Ray Desmond, Miss Herma Fiedler, Professor Sir Ernst Gombrich, Mr Eric Hawksley, Dr A. S. Herington, Mr Frank Hussey, Professor Arthur Hutchings, Mr Richard Jefferies, Dr Otto Kurz, Mr R. C. Mackworth-Young, Sir Oliver Millar, Sir John Pope-Hennessy, The Lady Redcliffe-Maud, Mrs A. W. Sale, Mr F. R. Thompson, Mr Harry Wilton, Mrs Oliver Woods and, last but not least, my brother Anthony.

Those in charge of the Royal Archives at Windsor Castle facilitated my researches in the Journal of Queen Victoria, from which, by gracious permission of H.M. the Queen, I have been enabled to quote certain passages. The staff of the London Library were also, as always, extremely helpful. My picture researcher and house editor at Rainbird's, Mrs Ellen Crampton, has done a splendid job, as has the designer, Miss Margaret Thomas. I am indebted to Mr Eric Prince for suggesting the title that was ultimately adopted for the book.

Finally I would like to express my gratitude to an artist not known to me personally. Herr Dietrich Fischer-Dieskau, by his impeccable recordings of forty of Mendelssohn's lovely but for the most part too rarely heard songs, opened up a new world for me, making me regret that I, a one-time Lieder singer, then included so few of them in my programmes. But when I reflect on the perfection of his interpretation, perhaps I should be glad that I did not.

W.J.W.B.

Contents

Colour Plates

Between 1809 and 1813
six great composers were born

3 February 1809: Mendelssohn
22 February 1810: Chopin
8 June 1810: Schumann
22 October 1811: Liszt
22 May 1813: Wagner
10 October 1813: Verdi

Between 1826 and 1828
three great composers died

6 June 1826: Weber
26 March 1827: Beethoven
19 November 1828: Schubert

Foreword

It was, I think, Alfred Bacharach who, echoing E. C. Bentley, once wrote:

> The art of Biography
> Is different from Musicography.
> Musicography is about 'Cellos,
> But Biography is about Fellows.

Thus defined, this book is very definitely a biography – a work primarily about Mendelssohn the Man. It is written for the reader who instinctively recoils from those musical 'quotes' so liberally scattered through the text when the professional musician presents a great composer to the world. In it will be found nothing about sonata form, plagal cadences or dissolving tritones. When Wilfrid Mellers writes of 'the use of the second inversion of the neutral diminished seventh' in a book[1] that has been described as 'invariably illuminating', Wilfrid Blunt freely confesses to remaining unilluminated and he suspects that he does not stand alone in that outer darkness.

Though Mendelssohn was a German, and though he died only ten years after Queen Victoria's accession, he was so revered in England in the middle and latter part of the nineteenth century that it is perhaps permissible to think of him for a moment as a Victorian composer. Now although there is a remarkable revival of interest today in Victorian architecture, painting, and bric-à-brac of every kind, the works of Victorian composers are still largely neglected. Alfred Gaul's *The Holy City*, for example, which was once standard fare for every choral society in this country, today is heard no more; yet it is no less (and no more) worthy of reappraisal than is many a 'Betjeman' church or Landseer painting. (Perhaps it is partly because of his name that Gaul appears to be more honoured in France than in England; at all events, the museum at Rouen is said proudly to display his gift of the pencil and indiarubber he used while composing his cantata *Joan of Arc*.)

Towering above these lesser Victorian composers – many of whom were knighted, while several others (wrote Ernest Newman) 'were such manifest mediocrities that to us today it is a mystery how they escaped knighthood' – is Felix Mendelssohn; yet it is still customary in certain quarters to dismiss him as just another purveyor of saccharine. E. M. Forster once said that every artist had the right to be judged by his *best* work, and Mendelssohn's best is fit to stand in most musical company. By the age of seventeen he had produced compositions such as the Octet for Strings (1825) and the overture to *A Midsummer Night's Dream* (1826)

---

[1] 'Man and his Music', vol. III, *The Sonata Principle*.

which are of a quality and an originality that no other youthful prodigy – not even Mozart or Schubert – had achieved at the same age. His *Hebrides* Overture (*Fingal's Cave*), 'Italian' Symphony and Violin Concerto in E minor are masterpieces.

Then why is Mendelssohn still despised and rejected by some who ought to know better? Possibly one reason may be that he was rich and charming and successful; a good son, a devoted husband and an affectionate father. If a composer is a homosexual (Tchaikovsky), a womanizing priest (Liszt), a super-cad (Wagner), a consumptive exile (Chopin) or a Bohemian (Schubert), he is at once appropriate material for novels or films or television; Mendelssohn was none of these things. Only by his early death – for the public, like the gods, loves those who die young – does he invite popular sympathy.

Yet it seems to me that in this permissive age it may be pleasant for a change to read about a composer who thought music more important than sex and who found his own wife more attractive than his neighbour's. His life was interesting if undramatic, and his voyage through it not always quite so calm as his earlier biographers, by their well-intentioned but foolish suppression of certain passages in his letters, would have us believe. He knew Weber, Berlioz, Schumann, Chopin, Liszt and Wagner; and as a child he was much hugged by the aged Goethe. He described in delightful letters the musical and social life of London, Rome, Paris, and the principal cities of Germany, and illustrated the accounts of his many travels with competent and sometimes amusing sketches. In 1829, when he was only twenty, he was responsible for the first performance of Bach's *St Matthew Passion* since its composer's death in 1750 – a revival that was to have far-reaching repercussions. As a virtuoso pianist he fell little short of Liszt and Thalberg, and he was generally acknowledged to have been the finest organist of his day. He was a brilliant improviser, and he had a prodigious musical memory, astonishing his London audiences by conducting without a score and, incidentally, by using a baton – both then novelties in English concert halls.

So surely the time is ripe to persuade all but the irredeemably prejudiced and the totally unmusical that Mendelssohn, at his best, was a superb Classical-Romantic composer. Indeed there are already signs that a Mendelssohn revival may soon be on its way: and in this both the gramophone companies and the radio have played an important part. In addition to the records of his songs made by Dietrich Fischer-Dieskau, we now have fine recordings, by the Academy of St Martin-in-the-Fields and other ensembles and soloists of all of his twelve early string symphonies and many more worthwhile juvenile works that were not previously available. If my book plays even the smallest part in reawakening an interest in Mendelssohn the Man, which must inevitably create an interest in Mendelssohn the Composer, I shall feel that I have not laboured in vain.

W.J.W.B.

OPPOSITE *Felix Mendelssohn. Pencil drawing by Wilhelm Hensel, c. 1822*

PART ONE

Youth 1809-1829

CHAPTER ONE

Moses and Abraham Mendelssohn

'Once I was the son of my father; now I am the father of my son.' So said Abraham Mendelssohn, son of the great German philosopher Moses Mendelssohn and father of the composer Jakob Ludwig Felix Mendelssohn, who with unnecessary modesty once dismissed himself as 'a mere dash' between the names of these two famous men.

To most English readers of this book the name Mendelssohn will mean one thing only: music; to some it may also recall the great banking house, which judiciously ceased activities during Hitler's régime but has since risen phoenix-like from the ashes; and probably no more than a handful will even have heard of Moses Mendelssohn, the friend of Lessing and in his day one of the foremost scholars and philosophers in all Germany.

Few great men have entered upon life more gravely handicapped than did this Moses, son of a poor Jewish scribe named Mendel of Dessau, whose acquaintance we may make on an October day of the year 1743. A little, ugly, stammering, hunchbacked fourteen-year-old Jewish boy has arrived at one of the gates of Berlin. He has walked all the way from Dessau, a distance of seventy or eighty miles, and he is hungry, ragged, wretched, exhausted, frightened; he carries no pass and is therefore liable to arrest. He knows hardly a word of German, but the guards manage to make him understand that Jews are admitted only at the Rosenthaler Gate. Wearily he continues on his way there, and it is said that in the records of the watch there occurs this simple entry: 'Today there passed through the Rosenthaler Gate six oxen, seven swine and one Jew.'

Moses had gone to Berlin because his much-loved Talmud teacher at Dessau, Rabbi David Fränkel, had been appointed Chief Rabbi there. The boy sought him out, was warmly welcomed and continued his rabbinical studies with him; but Fränkel was in no position to support him, and he was obliged to scrape a living by doing various menial jobs. He tells of the weekly loaf marked with a pencil into six equal parts; on the Sabbath he fasted. Yet neither crushing poverty, nor the intolerance of many Jewish elders who forbade the learning of German and made access to Christian sources of information perilous, was ever for a moment allowed to interfere with this brilliant boy's almost obsessional pursuit of knowledge. By the time he was twenty he had secretly added German, French, English, Latin and Greek to his Hebrew, and was already beginning to study mathematics, literature and philosophy. A year later he became tutor to the children of a rich Jewish silk merchant named Isaac Bernhard, then an accountant in Bernhard's office, and finally a partner in the firm. Though

LEFT *Moses Mendelssohn – Felix's grandfather. Engraving after a portrait by J. C. Frisch, 1787*

BELOW *The Rosenthaler Gate, Berlin. Lithograph, 1824. In the eighteenth century this was the only gate by which Jews might enter the city*

the work was often to be deplored as time-consuming and futile, at least it provided him with a living wage. The worst of his tribulations were now over.

Jews in the Prussia of Frederick the Great were perpetually harassed by petty restrictions, extortions and humiliations of various kinds, punctuated by the occasional pogrom; but a number of successful financiers and outstanding scholars among them were beginning to surmount social and legal barriers, and it was only a matter of time before they were able to mix with the highest families in the land. It was Moses' intellectual brilliance, his integrity, and an irresistible charm which made all who had dealings with him forget his physical disabilities, that lifted him from the ghetto into the accepted world of international scholarship. Then in 1754 came his meeting, over a game of chess, with the poet Lessing, who in his play *The Jews* (1749) had vehemently pleaded for religious toleration. This casual encounter proved the beginning of one of the immortal friendships of eighteenth-century Germany, and in his drama *Nathan the Wise* (1778–9), dedicated to Moses Mendelssohn, Lessing drew an unforgettable portrait of his friend.

The most influential of Moses Mendelssohn's many philosophical works was his *Phädon* (1767), a treatise on the immortality of the soul, written in emulation of Plato's *Phaedo* and soon translated into more than thirty languages. But from philosophy and criticism he turned to his true life's work, the emancipation of the Jews, and in his *Jerusalem* (1783) gave what Kant described as 'irrefutable' proof that the State had no right to interfere in the religion of its citizens. He himself believed that Judaism was 'revealed legislation' rather than a religion, and that all monotheistic religions were no more than different interpretations of one eternal truth. This 'German Plato', 'German Socrates', 'Luther of the German Jews' and 'third Moses' (the second being the twelfth-century Jewish philosopher Moses Maimonides[1] of Cordoba) – as he was variously called – was in the last years of his life universally venerated and acclaimed; how sad that one so famous in his day should now be almost forgotten!

In 1762 Moses Mendelssohn had married Fromet Gugenheim, a young Jewess who had been sufficiently impressed by his writings to overcome the initial shock of her first meeting with their author. One of the gratuitous insults imposed by Frederick the Great on all Jews in Prussia at this time was the compulsory purchase on marriage of a stipulated quantity of reject china from the newly established royal china factory; thus the young couple found themselves lumbered, and at huge expense, with twenty unwanted life-sized china apes.

Though, as Moses frankly informed Lessing, his bride 'had no property, and was neither clever nor pretty', he was, he confessed, 'infatuated' with her. Fortunately she proved to have other qualities, being a shrewd manager who even, we are told, counted the raisins and almonds put out when guests came to the house, 'so as to prevent waste in trifles lest the household should want in more essential things'.

The marriage proved both a happy and a fruitful one, and six of their eight children – three sons and three daughters – lived to reach maturity. Of these the second, Abraham, born in 1776, was to become the father of the composer. The eldest daughter, Dorothea – masculine, emancipated and a bluestocking – after an unhappy marriage forced upon her

---

[1] Moses Mendelssohn's excessive study in childhood of Maimonides' *Guide for the Perplexed* had occasioned a nervous disorder, the neglect of which led to a spinal deformity.

by her father, set up house with, and finally married *en secondes noces*, the poet Friedrich Schlegel – brother of August, famous as the translator of Shakespeare into German; she became a Lutheran, but eventually with her second husband joined the Church of Rome. Her letters (wrote her great-nephew, Sebastian Hensel) reveal 'a fine vein of bright, irrepressible humour, to which she gave vent in droll sallies, innocent badinages, and mischievous innuendoes'.

The second daughter, Henriette, plain and slightly deformed – yet apparently a spinster by inclination rather than of necessity – was for some years headmistress of a select finishing school for girls in Paris, where she moved in literary circles. Later she led a 'life of brilliant misery' as governess to the beautiful daughter of General Sebastiani, but soon after the girl's marriage[1] in 1824 returned to Berlin where until her death in 1831 she was in close contact with her brother Abraham and his family. After many heart-searchings she too became a Roman Catholic. She figures as 'Tante Jette' in the family letters.

A year after his marriage – and thanks to the good offices of a French nobleman, the marquis d'Argens, who while in Berlin made a personal appeal to Frederick the Great – Moses had been made a *Schutz-Jude* (Protected Jew) and was thereafter spared some of the humiliations that continued to come the way of his less fortunate co-religionists. But he was so unmistakably a Jew – almost the Jew of the caricature – that nothing could protect him and his family from the crude insults of guttersnipes when they walked in the streets of Berlin. How could he explain to his sons why these urchins shouted 'Jew-boy' after them and threw stones at them, how answer the inevitable question, 'Father, is it shameful to be a Jew?'

Abraham was only ten years old at the time of his father's death in 1786. He continued to live at home until he was twenty, when he obtained the post of clerk in the banking-house of Fould & Co. in Paris.

The son of Moses was far from being 'a mere dash'. Though he had neither the qualities which made his father a philosopher nor those which made his son a musician, he was a man of considerable general ability and financial shrewdness, and though not a creative artist he had an instinctive understanding of music which was more than once to astonish Felix. He was, wrote Sebastian Hensel, 'a harmonious, independent, vigorous character', who stood 'between the firm adherence to Judaism of Moses and the sincere Christian faith of Felix and Fanny [Felix's elder sister], between the philosophical views of his father and the aesthetic views of his children.'

It was while Abraham was living in Paris that he heard from his sister Henriette of her great friend Lea Salomon, the brilliant daughter of wealthy Berlin Jews. Indeed Henriette saw to it that the girl's name should crop up with growing frequency in their conversations because, as at last she confessed, she had decided that Lea would make her brother an ideal wife. Wares heralded with much advertisement are apt to disappoint when finally produced; but not Lea: in 1803 or 1804 Abraham met her – on the journey from Paris to Berlin, it is said – immediately fell in love with her, proposed, and was accepted.

Then a difficulty arose. Abraham hated Berlin and loved Paris where, thanks to Napoleon,

---

[1] An error of judgment: she was murdered by her husband, the son of the duc de Praslin. See *A Crime of Passion* by Stanley Loomis, Philadelphia, 1967.

LEFT *Abraham Mendelssohn – Felix's father, and* RIGHT *Lea Mendelssohn – Felix's mother. Pencil drawings by Wilhelm Hensel*

Jews were no longer persecuted. But Lea's mother would not hear of her daughter living in France; nor was Lea, who if she had a fault was something of a snob, prepared to marry a mere clerk. For a time it seemed as if an impasse had been reached, Abraham telling Henriette that he would rather 'eat dry bread in Paris' than cake in Berlin. But at last his sister persuaded him to surrender on most points, and it was agreed that he should go into partnership with his elder brother, Joseph, who had founded a banking-house in Berlin. The proposal was that Abraham should start a branch in the free Hanseatic city of Hamburg, Lea's dowry providing the necessary capital. The marriage took place in Berlin on 26 December 1804.

Sebastian Hensel thus describes his grandmother, Lea Mendelssohn, the mother of Felix:

> She was not handsome, but her eloquent black eyes, her sylph-like figure, her gentle, modest behaviour, and the power of her lively conversation, full of accurate judgment and striking but never malicious wit, made her most attractive. She was acquainted with every branch of fashionable information; she played and sang with expression and grace – but seldom, and only for her friends; she drew exquisitely; she spoke and read French, English, Italian, and – secretly – Homer, in the original. . . . Her taste, formed by the classic authors of so many languages, was exact and refined, but she seldom ventured to pass a judgment. A most speaking trait of her character was this: by the legacy of some relation she was in the possession of a considerable fortune, but her dress was always as simple as it was elegant, whilst she allowed her [widowed] mother, who was not nearly so rich, a liberal income, and carefully kept house for her. . . .

In general the description will pass, though it may well seem doubtful whether Lea's wit was always free of malice. But she was *not*, or at all events not always, sylph-like. In 1819 Abraham, writing to his fourteen-year-old daughter Fanny, said, 'Don't worry about being fat; it's one more point of resemblance to your mother (and you can never be too like her, for she hasn't her equal). When she was young she too was very plump. . . .' It seems to have been a family failing on the female side, for Heine later wrote of Fanny's younger sister, Rebecka, that she was 'every pound an angel'.

For seven years the young Mendelssohns lived and prospered mightily in Hamburg, where the first three of their four children were born: Fanny in 1805, Felix in 1809 and Rebecka in 1811; the fourth, Paul, followed in 1813 – he was always late for everything, his father once said – after the family had had to flee by night in disguise to Berlin. This hasty exodus was the outcome of Napoleon's Continental blockade. Hamburg had been occupied in 1806 by the French, and four years later incorporated into the French Empire. All trade with England was forbidden; but for a time, thanks to the corruptibility of successive French governors, the city became a vast smugglers' camp, and running the blockade with ships flying neutral flags a patriotic and profitable pastime in which Abraham very successfully joined. For all his love of Paris he was a true German at heart, and in any case the behaviour of the army of occupation was such as to have undermined the loyalty of the most ardent Francophile.

But the arrival in 1811 of a new governor, the dreaded Marshal Davoût, put an immediate stop to this sport, and anyone suspected of having been involved in it now went in danger of his life. That Abraham was wise in deciding to escape with his family is testified by the inscription on a sarcophagus in one of the cemeteries, commemorating the fate of one thousand one hundred and thirty-eight citizens of Hamburg 'who, having been banished by Marshal Davoût together with many thousands of their fellow-citizens during the severe winter of 1813–14, fell victims to grief, starvation and disease'. This revolt so savagely crushed in Hamburg was of course part of a general uprising, a German war of liberation against the French after their ignominious retreat from Moscow, and conditions in Berlin were also for a time unpleasant; but at last the French were ejected, life returned to normal, and the Mendelssohns, comfortably established in Fromet Mendelssohn's house in the Neue Promenade, could turn their attention to their young family.

Two Clever Children 1805-1820

Abraham, in announcing the birth of Fanny to his mother-in-law, had added, 'Lea says that the child has Bach-fugue fingers.' She was right: both Fanny and Felix showed precocious musical talent almost from the cradle, and both were to become passionate admirers of Bach. Of Felix we are told that as an infant he registered the strongest dislike of brass instruments and military music, but listened enraptured to anything of 'a softer and more refined character'. At first the two children were taught by their parents, Lea making herself responsible for the piano.

In 1816, when Abraham was obliged to go to Paris on business, he took his family with him. On their way through Weimar, Abraham, who carried a letter of introduction from the distinguished Berlin musician and friend of Goethe, Karl Friedrich Zelter, called on the poet in a business capacity, Zelter thinking that the banker might advise Goethe about investments. Goethe, who was at this time in his middle sixties, regretted that the Mendelssohns' visit was too short for him to be able to make the acquaintance of Lea and the children whom, he told Zelter, he would gladly have invited to breakfast.

While in Paris Fanny and Felix, now eleven and seven years old respectively, had lessons for several months from a distinguished professional pianist, Marie Bigot. Back in Berlin their education was soon taken seriously in hand. Ludwig Berger (a disciple of Clementi and John Field) was engaged to teach them the piano, Karl Heyse (subsequently father of the novelist Paul von Heyse) literature and the humanities, and Zelter harmony and composition. Nor were drawing, dancing, swimming and physical training neglected, and in 1819 the boy also joined the singing classes of the Singakademie. At the same time he began to learn the violin from a man named Henning, to surprise his father on his return from another visit to Paris; and subsequently he studied under the famous violinist Eduard Rietz. Felix was indeed *felix* – 'fortunate'! His grandfather Moses had won success in the face of what might have seemed insuperable odds; Felix started life with every advantage that money could buy, and the wise guidance of intelligent and devoted (though very domineering) parents.

In 1818 the nine-year-old child made his first appearance as a pianist at a small private concert of chamber music, and his sister Fanny, as another surprise for Abraham, learned twenty-four of Bach's preludes by heart and played them to him. Henriette, when told of Fanny's feat of memory, wrote to Lea that the news had left her 'speechless with astonishment' but that she doubted the wisdom of such exertion. 'The extraordinary talent of your children wants direction, not forcing. Papa Abraham, however, is insatiable, and the best appears to him only just good enough.'

The character of Abraham is revealed in his letters to his children. They were full of admonitions, and those that he received from them were 'marked out of ten' in kindly but schoolmasterly fashion. To Fanny (aged fourteen) he wrote from Amsterdam:

Of your two letters, my dear Fanny, the second, with your tragi-comic complaints of having nothing to write about, was more correctly and more carefully written than the first, in which you speak only about the theatre. You are now old enough to find subjects to write to me about, not only in the daily happenings but also in what you are thinking. . . . For instance, while I was at home your mother told me a great deal about your lessons with the clergyman; you should now do that yourself, so that I can see . . . what influence his teaching is having on your heart and mind. . . .

There is a delightful letter to his younger son, Paul. He begins by urging him to press less heavily on his pen, to keep his fingers loose and to sit upright, then continues: 'I haven't

LEFT *Felix's sisters, Fanny and Rebecka. Pencil drawing by Wilhelm Hensel, 1828*
RIGHT *Felix playing the piano. After a pencil drawing by Wilhelm Hensel, 1821*

Felix, with Paul acting Rumpelstiltzkin. *Pencil drawing by Felix,* c. *1822*

given an immediate answer to your question about marrying Mieke, because I wanted to think it over. I feel that we had better wait till I come home, so that I can see Mieke first. If I find her nice and clean, and if you are a good boy for a fortnight, then we can discuss it.' Paul, it should be explained, was six years old and Mieke, the gardener's daughter, was four.

But that Felix needed little epistolary guidance is proved by a charming letter which he wrote at the age of ten and a half to a young friend:[1]

My dear Signore Rudolph,

'I really don't know what to think of you' – 'You call me a good-for-nothing scoundrel, and you, you rascal – what about you then?? –' '– I write to him twice but get no reply, so shouldn't I get even with him?' And reproaches? Unworthy friend! Well! Pax! That was a joke. Well! Pax! Now I'm being serious. I often remember

[Three bars of music follow]

and how the great oaf stood there and puffed away on a horn twice as big as himself.

But really, I didn't answer because I've been so busy lately that I was simply made of Latin, French and arithmetic. There was also a double sonata that I was composing, with the result that I was rarely through before half past eight. . . .

Le cor et la paresse se disputent mon cœur. And believe me, had you remained here (and still been my friend) I would have come to you from time to time with a handful of work, just as you used to come to me with a handful of work. . . . Our little sofa is very well and sends its kindest regards, and Herr Berger too; he told me that you are coming back to Berlin soon, so let me know if this is settled. I am finishing this letter at 7 p.m., and it also

[1] Quoted by Jacob, and see Rudolf Elvers, 'Ein Jugendbrief von Felix Mendelssohn,' Berlin (1963), p. 95ff.

brings greetings to your father. Don't forget my kisses, my Rudölphchen, wet though they
may have been; but here I send some drier ones and remain very firmly
your friend
F. Mendelssohn

★   ★   ★

Like all German Jews at this time, the Mendelssohns were faced with the great decision:
should they become Christians, or should they at least bring up their children as Christians?
The matter is of sufficient importance to warrant its consideration in some detail.

Though his two sisters had been converted to Christianity, Abraham had remained a Jew
and, though a sceptic, he still took Judaism very seriously. In 1812 German Jews had been
given legal emancipation, conversion being rewarded by full civil equality, and Lea wanted
their children to be brought up as Lutheran Christians. Her brother Jakob had been
converted and, to replace the Jewish-sounding Salomon, had adopted the name of Bartholdy,
after the former owner of family estates. For his apostasy he had been cursed and cast off
by his mother. In 1816, after much discussion, it was decided that the four Mendelssohn
children should be baptized, thereby purchasing what Heine called 'tickets of admission to
European culture'; but the news of this apostasy was carefully kept from the ears of old Frau
Salomon.

Abraham and Lea still hesitated to take this drastic step themselves, and it would seem
that he eventually consulted his brother-in-law on the subject. Only Bartholdy's reply
survives. He was not at all convinced by Abraham's arguments in favour of retaining his
Jewish faith and his Jewish name, these arguments being in his opinion no longer valid:

> You say you owe it to the memory of your father; but do you think that you have done
> something bad in giving your children the religion which appears to you to be the best? It is
> the justest homage you or any of us could pay to the efforts of your father to promote light
> and knowledge, and he would have acted like you for his children, and perhaps like me for
> himself. You may remain faithful to an oppressed, persecuted religion; you may leave it to
> your children as a prospect of lifelong martyrdom, as long as you believe it to be absolute
> truth. But when you have ceased to believe that, it is barbarism. I advise you to adopt the
> name of Mendelssohn Bartholdy to distinguish you from the other Mendelssohns. At the
> same time you would please me very much, because it would be the means of preserving my
> memory in the family. Thus you would gain your point without doing anything unusual,
> for in France and elsewhere it is the custom to add the name of one's wife's relations as a
> distinction.

Abraham took his advice and he and his wife were baptized in 1822. At the same time he
adopted the name Mendelssohn Bartholdy,[1] which was retained by Felix.

It must not be imagined that conversion to Christianity protected Jews from the occasional
hostility of the rabble. In 1819 there was a little pogrom in Berlin – the so-called *Judensturm*,
the last real pogrom in Germany before the days of Hitler – and the industrious Werner has
unearthed, in the ninth volume of an obscure collection of memoirs of the period, an account
of the ten-year-old Felix being stopped in the street by a Prussian prince who spat at his feet
and cried, '*Hep hep*, Jew-boy!'[2] Indeed Abraham at this time very seriously considered leaving

---

[1] *Without* a hyphen (but often wrongly written). The descendants of Felix's brother Paul, however, added a hyphen.
[2] *Hep* – the war-cry of German Jew-baiters, said to be an abbreviation of *Hierosolyma est perdita*, 'Jerusalem is lost'.

Germany for ever and settling in Paris. Five years later, when the Mendelssohns were on holiday at a Baltic health resort, Felix and Fanny were baited and stoned by hooligans. Felix showed much courage in defending his sister, but broke down and wept bitterly when he got home. These and other similar incidents deeply scarred the sensitive boy. Anti-Semitism was particularly in evidence in Berlin – a city which, for this and other reasons, Felix gradually came to detest.

There is, incidentally, a pleasant sequel to the story of the cursing and casting off of poor Bartholdy by old Bella Salomon. Fanny, who was a great favourite with her grandmother and often went to her to play, was one day rewarded by the invitation to choose anything she liked. Fanny immediately replied, 'Forgive Uncle Bartholdy!' Frau Salomon, who had expected the request of a new bonnet or other piece of finery, was touched and became reconciled to her son – 'for Fanny's sake', as she wrote to him. Bartholdy, after an unsettled life, finally became Prussian Consul-General in Rome and a distinguished collector and patron of the arts; he was also a capable historian and the author of several books. He died unmarried in 1825 in the Casa Bartholdy, which can be seen in Felix's drawing of the Spanish Steps (reproduced on page 123).

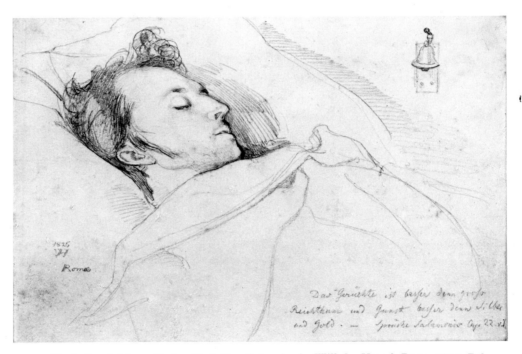

ABOVE *Uncle Bartholdy on his deathbed. Pencil drawing by Wilhelm Hensel, Rome, 1825. Below is written, 'A good name is rather to be chosen than great riches, and loving favour rather than silver and gold.' Proverbs 22, v. 1*

OPPOSITE *Felix Mendelssohn at the age of twelve. Oil sketch by Carl Begas, 1821*
OVERLEAF *The Pont-Neuf, Paris. Watercolour by Turner, c. 1830*

In 1820, when Fanny was confirmed, her father wrote her a long and very self-revealing letter from Paris, where he had been sent on business connected with the war indemnity to be paid by France to Prussia, discussing the implications of this 'important step' that she was taking. He begins by asking:

Does God exist? What is God? Is He a part of ourselves, and does He continue to live after the other part has ceased to be? And where? And how? All this I do not know, and therefore I have never taught you anything about it. But I know that there exists in me and you and in all human beings an everlasting inclination towards all that is good, true and right, and a conscience which warns and guides us when we go astray. I know it, I believe it, I live in this faith, and this is my religion. This I could not teach you, and nobody can learn it; but everybody has it who does not intentionally and knowingly cast it away. . . .

The outward form of religion your teacher has given you is historical, and changeable like all human ordinances. Some thousands of years ago the Jewish form was the reigning one, then the heathen form, and now it is the Christian. We, your mother and I, were born and brought up by our parents as Jews, and without being obliged to change the form of our religion have been able to follow the divine instinct in us and in our conscience. We have educated you and your brothers and sister in the Christian faith, because it is the creed of most civilized people, and contains nothing that can lead you away from what is good, and much that guides you to love – obedience, tolerance and resignation – even if it offers nothing but the example of its Founder, understood by so few and followed by still fewer.

By pronouncing your confession of faith you have fulfilled the claims of *society* on you and obtained the name of a Christian. Now *be* what your duty as a human being demands of you: *true, faithful, good*; obedient and devoted till death to your mother, and may I also say to your father, unremittingly attentive to the voice of your conscience, which may be suppressed but never silenced, and you will gain the highest happiness that is to be found on earth – harmony and contentedness with yourself. . . .

Closely associated with a change of religion was the matter of the changed surname. That Abraham came to feel very strongly about the use of the name Bartholdy is revealed in an enormously long letter which he wrote to Felix in July 1829, when his twenty-year-old son was paying his first visit to England. Four years before this he had had visiting-cards engraved 'Felix M. Bartholdy' made for the boy, but Felix had refused to use them. He now, he said, observed with the gravest disapproval that in concert programmes and newspaper articles Felix's name was always given as 'Mendelssohn' not 'Mendelssohn Bartholdy'. If Felix was responsible for this, then he had committed 'a huge wrong'. Admittedly a name was only a name, but so long as Felix was under his jurisdiction it was his 'plain and indisputable duty' to bear the same name as his father.

It was also, he continued, Felix's duty to take for granted that any decision his father made had been taken only after the most careful consideration. He had eventually adopted Christianity because he felt it right to do for himself what he recognized as best for his children. But he now bitterly regretted that he had not at the same time discarded the name Mendelssohn altogether. 'You cannot,' he said, 'you *must* not use the name Mendelssohn. Felix Mendelssohn Bartholdy is too long and too unpractical. You must use the name Felix

Goethe. Oil painting by Karl Stieler, given to Mendelssohn in 1838 by Goethe's son Walther. The poem on the sheet was originally inscribed by Goethe beneath a silhouette by Adele Schopenhauer given by her to Mendelssohn

Bartholdy. There can no more be a Christian Mendelssohn than there can be a Jewish Confucius. If Mendelssohn is your name, then you are *ipso facto* a Jew. . . . Dear Felix, take this to heart and do as I say.' The letter is signed, 'your Father and Friend'.

Few young men today would allow themselves to be ordered about in this way, and it is satisfactory to find that Felix, devoted son though he was, felt that at the age of twenty there were decisions that he must make for himself; many English Victorian fathers were equally dictatorial, as readers of Gosse's *Father and Son* will know. Werner (who reproduces Abraham's letter in full) writes that Felix defied his father by conducting his four concerts that summer under the name Felix Mendelssohn, but in fact these concerts had taken place before Abraham's letter can have reached him. However, though 'Mendelssohn Bartholdy' is to be found on the covers of many of his published works, Felix saw to it that he was known to the world as Mendelssohn, thus unwittingly associating himself with Mozart rather than with the 'five great Bs' – Bach, Beethoven, Berlioz, Brahms and Bruckner.

Meanwhile Felix was living day and night for his music.

His earliest dated composition was written on 11 December (1819?) for his father's birthday[1]; he was not yet eleven. By September of the same year he had filled a whole exercise book with Mozartian and Bachian pieces including two songs and a choral work for four-part mixed choir, and before the end of the year his total output had reached sixty pieces, including his *magnum opus* to date: a little comic opera entitled *Die Soldatenliebschaft* ('Soldiers in Love'). Soon afterwards came another, *Die beiden Pädagogen* ('The Two Schoolmasters'). The libretti of these and two further operas were provided by a clever young doctor, Johann Ludwig Casper, who had visited Paris and there encountered the *Comédies de vaudeville* of Scribe; he also sang the *buffo* tenor roles in them. These innocent little trifles were first produced in the home circle and then long forgotten; but in 1960 the libretti came to light in Oxford,[2] so enabling professional performances to be given in Germany and Austria of *Die Soldatenliebschaft* (Wittenberg, 1962) and *Die beiden Pädagogen* (Berlin, 1962 and Vienna, 1964).

One is inevitably led to compare and contrast the early careers and juvenile *œuvres* of Mendelssohn and Mozart (and we soon find Goethe and his friends doing just this). Both showed prodigious musical talent at the earliest age; both produced little operas (Mozart wrote *Bastien und Bastienne* at the age of twelve); both were in other respects normal, lively, fun-loving little boys, and each had a highly talented sister four years older than himself. But how different was their upbringing! Whereas the infant Wolfgang was dragged round the courts of Europe and put through his musical paces almost as if he had been a circus animal, Felix was carefully shielded from the dangers of exploitation. While Wolfgang and his sister were advertised in London as 'Miss Mozart of Eleven and Master Mozart of Seven years of age, Prodigies of Nature', infinite trouble was taken by Abraham Mendelssohn and Zelter to prevent Felix from having his head turned by publicity and flattery.

As a pianist, Wolfgang was probably the more prodigious; but in the opinion of most people the compositions of neither of the twelve-year-olds shows much originality, and whereas Felix's were largely his own unaided work, those of Wolfgang were undoubtedly

---

[1] See Martin Jacobi, *Felix Mendelssohn Bartholdy*, Bielefeld, (1915), p. 6, Facs.
[2] Among the papers of Miss Margaret Deneke.

'touched up' by his father. But by the age of sixteen the advantage, where composition was concerned, is with Felix, for his Octet for Strings of 1825 was of an individuality and a maturity far outstripping anything that Wolfgang had produced by 1772. The octet, and the overture to *A Midsummer Night's Dream* written a year later, are without any doubt the most astonishing achievements of any composer of the same age. Had Mozart and Mendelssohn both died at seventeen, the former would be remembered today as a prodigy performer on the piano, the latter as the composer of two masterpieces.

It was in the summer of 1820, even before the composition of *Die Soldatenliebschaft*, that there is for the first time mention of the possibility of Felix becoming a professional musician. Abraham, writing to Fanny from Paris, says of Felix:

> Music will perhaps become his profession, whilst for *you* it can and must only be an ornament, never the root of your being and doing. We may therefore forgive him some ambition and desire to be acknowledged in a pursuit which appears very important to him, because he feels a vocation for it, whilst it does you credit that you have always shown yourself good and sensible in these matters. . . . Remain true to these sentiments and to this line of conduct; they are feminine, and only what is truly feminine is an ornament to your sex.

Bartholdy, on the other hand, whose opinion may perhaps have been often sought by Abraham but was at all events often given, came down firmly against Felix becoming a professional. The boy never forgave his uncle for offering advice which, happily, Abraham on this occasion did not take, and Bartholdy's interference may well have been the reason why Felix took a dislike to the name. Music, said Bartholdy, was 'no career, no life, no aim; in the beginning you are just as far as at the end, and with full consciousness of its being so; as a rule you are even better off at first than at last. Let the boy go through a regular course of schooling, and then prepare for a state-career by studying law at the university. His art will remain his friend and companion. . . . If you intend him to become a merchant, let him enter a counting-house early.'

It is kindest to believe that Bartholdy did not realize the extent to which Felix's life was already dominated by music. This utter dedication and the boy's extraordinary talent are revealed in a delightful little sketch from the pen of Julius Benedict, a youth only five years older than Felix. Benedict, who was also the son of a German Jewish banker, was the favourite pupil of Weber and later his biographer. After a successful career in Vienna and Naples he became conductor at the Lyceum, Drury Lane, and at His Majesty's, and settled in London, where he died in 1885 at the age of eighty; of his innumerable compositions, his opera *The Lily of Killarney* (1863) is alone (if at all) remembered today. In his *Sketch of the Life and Works of the late Felix Mendelssohn Bartholdy* (1850) Benedict wrote:

> It was the beginning of May, 1821, when, walking in the streets of Berlin with my master and friend, Carl Maria von Weber, he directed my attention to a boy, apparently about eleven or twelve years old, who, on perceiving the author of *Freyschütz*, ran towards him, giving him a most hearty and friendly greeting.
>   ''Tis Felix Mendelssohn,' said Weber; introducing me at once to the prodigious child, of whose marvellous talent and execution I had already heard so much at Dresden. I shall never forget the impression of that day on beholding that beautiful youth, with his auburn hair clustering in ringlets round his shoulders, the look of his brilliant clear eyes, and the smile of innocence and candour on his lips. He would have it that we should go with him at once

to his father's house; but as Weber had to attend a rehearsal, he took me by the hand, and made me run a race till we reached his home. Up he went briskly to the drawing-room, where, finding his mother, he exclaimed, 'Here is a pupil of Weber's, who knows a great deal of his music of the new opera. Pray, Mama, ask him to play for us'; and so, with an irresistible impetuosity, he pushed me to the pianoforte and made me remain there until I had exhausted all the store of my recollections. . . .

Then Mendelssohn was persuaded to 'play from MEMORY such of Bach's fugues or Cramer's exercises as I could name'.

A second visit followed, when Benedict found Mendelssohn 'gravely' at work on his latest composition, a piano quartet[1] – a score 'as beautiful as if it had been written by the most skilful copyist':

But whilst I was lost in admiration and astonishment at beholding the work of a master written by the hand of a boy, all at once he sprang up from his seat, and, in his playful manner, ran to the pianoforte, performing note for note all the music from *Freyschütz*, which three or four days previously he had heard me play, and asking 'How do you like this chorus?' 'What do you think of this air?' 'Do you not admire this overture?' and so on. Then, forgetting quartets and Weber, down we went into the garden, he clearing high hedges with a leap, running, singing, or climbing the trees like a squirrel – the very image of health and happiness.

It was 'the perfect moral and physical education' that Felix received from his parents and carefully chosen teachers, who prevented him from being conceited or losing 'the childlike simplicity of his manners', that so impressed Benedict. 'Favoured thus by Providence with an independent, and even brilliant social position, surrounded by men eminent for science and mental attainments, kept from the contact of all that was vulgar and mean, the tender plant was carefully fostered, and soon unfolded its blossoms'.

[1] Benedict identifies it as his Piano Quartet in C minor (op. 1), but Mendelssohn mentions elsewhere that this was *begun* at Sécheron in the following year.

Carl Maria von Weber

CHAPTER THREE

A Visit to Weimar 1821

It was Karl Zelter (1758–1832) – Felix's teacher of harmony, counterpoint and composition and general director of his musical studies – who, even more than Abraham, was responsible for the boy's favourable development and saw to it that this 'tender plant', though 'carefully fostered', was hardened off and not cosseted. Of Fanny and Felix he wrote that they hovered round him 'like bees around flowers'. And it was Zelter who was about to introduce his most talented pupil to the man whom Felix was later to call 'the imperial sun of my life' – Goethe, the septuagenarian sage who had ruled like a king in Weimar for nearly half a century.

Abraham had given much thought to the choice of a musical mentor for his gifted child, and he could not have reached a better decision. The son of a mason and himself for a while an apprentice in the same trade, Zelter had risen by sheer ability to become (in 1800) Director of the Singakademie in Berlin and in time the city's most illustrious teacher of musical theory. This 'loutish bear from the north' (as a Bavarian called him) was a rough diamond; though notorious for rudeness which was in part derived from his peasant origin, in part assumed as a protective shell, he was a man of complete integrity and free from all servility. Many stories are told of his tactlessness: there was, for example, that of the terrified young soprano who was ordered, 'Sing away! I can stand as much as most people', and then immediately stopped in mid-flight to be told not to open her mouth like that as she hadn't the face for it.

Goethe, whose close friend and musical counsellor Zelter became and whose famous Thursday concerts he organized, saw his virtues and forgave – perhaps even enjoyed – his boorishness: 'Zelter's talk', he said, 'is robust as a mason's, but his feelings are sensitive and musical.' He belonged spiritually to the eighteenth century and was especially devoted to the music of Haydn, but mocked Weber, 'had strong reservations about Beethoven's greatness, and ignored Schubert entirely'. Since no musician had access to Goethe without 'having a haircut' (as it was called) by Zelter or his rival Johann Friedrich Reichardt of the Weimar Court Orchestra, these two men controlled his musical taste; and Zelter in particular has been much blamed, and justly, for keeping Goethe from advancing in this field into the nineteenth century. In 1816 the poet had received, together with a covering letter of recommendation from a friend in Vienna, a packet of songs by 'a nineteen-year-old composer named Franz Schubert'. He read (though he never acknowledged) the letter but did not even open the packet, which in fact contained some of Schubert's finest Goethe settings including '*Erlkönig*', '*Heidenröslein*' and '*Gretchen am Spinnrade*'. Many years later Goethe did hear Schubert's '*Erlkönig*', sung by the great Wilhelmine Schröde-Devrient; he much admired the skill of the singer but was baffled by the music. Both Zelter and Reichardt composed innumerable pedestrian settings of Goethe's lyrics.[1]

On 26 October 1821 Zelter wrote to Goethe saying that he was just about to leave with his daughter and a young pupil of his, Herr Mendelssohn's son, for Wittenberg, for a festival at which Schadow's new statue of Luther was to be unveiled; then he was returning to Weimar and, knowing that Goethe's house was full, would put up at the Elephant. 'I would like', he continued, 'to show my Doris and my best pupil your face before I quit this world (in which, however, I intend to remain as long as possible). He is a good and pretty boy, vivacious and obedient. Admittedly he is the son of a Jew, though not one himself.' And he added what today may sound strange, 'How odd it would be if the son of a Jew turned out to be an artist!' But in fact, before this time hardly a single Jew had made a name for himself in the German musical world.

'Just fancy,' wrote Lea to her sister-in-law Henriette in Paris – 'the little brat is lucky enough to be going with Zelter to Weimar. He wants to show him to Goethe. . .'. Of course she will miss him dreadfully, she says, but it is a chance not to be lost. And the break will do him good, because he gets so carried away by his music that he tends to work too hard for a boy of his age.

From Leipzig Felix wrote to his parents describing an uncomfortable night spent as the guests of old Professor Chladni[2] at Remberg: 'Prof. Z. complained that his bed was too short, Doris that hers had bugs [*Bevölkerung*], while I cursed the wretched eiderdown on mine. Before day had dawned I felt a hand gently touching me and pulling my eiderdown a bit off me. It was Herr Prof. . . . I asked him if he wanted something – a glass of water, or anything else. He replied, "Oh no! I'd been dreaming – dreaming that you'd been stolen from me – and I wanted to see whether you were still there!!!"'

The family, too, were busy with their pens, exhorting the child to do them credit in Weimar. His father tells him to remember to behave nicely and to sit properly at table, to speak clearly and to the point, to be modest and to be obedient. His mother wishes she could be a little mouse to watch how he manages for the first time on his own, and begs him 'to snap up every word that Goethe utters'. His sister Fanny writes in much the same vein, telling him to keep his eyes and ears wide open and threatening to have nothing more to do with him if, on his return, he can't repeat *verbatim* everything the great man has said.

They need not have worried; the child did magnificently, and in the letter he wrote home on 6 November he paints a charming picture of his first meeting with Goethe:

. . . Now listen, all of you! Today is Tuesday. On Sunday the Sun of Weimar, Goethe, arrived. In the morning we went to church and heard half of Handel's 100th Psalm. The organ, though big, is weak; that of the Marienkirche [in Berlin] is smaller but much more powerful. [Technical details follow.] Then I went to the Elephant and made a drawing of Lukas Cranach's house.[3] Two hours later Professor Zelter appeared and said, 'Goethe has arrived, the old gentleman has arrived!' We ran at once down the steps to Goethe's house and found him in the garden, just coming round the hedge. . . .

He is extremely friendly, but I don't think that any of his portraits are at all like him. Then he went to examine his interesting collection of fossils which his son had just arranged,

---

[1] Tennyson similarly had praise only for Edward Lear's trite settings of his poems.
[2] Ernst Chladni (1756–1824), German physicist.
[3] Goethe was directly descended from Lukas Cranach the Elder (1472–1553).

Karl Zelter. Lithograph after a painting by Carl Begas, c. 1826

and said repeatedly, 'Hm, hm, I'm perfectly satisfied.' After that I walked for half an hour in the garden with him and Professor Zelter. Then we went in to luncheon.

He doesn't look seventy-three – more like a man in his fifties. After luncheon Fräulein Ulrike, Frau Ottilie's[1] sister, asked him for a kiss, and I did the same. Every morning I get a kiss from the author of *Faust* and *Werther*, and every afternoon two kisses from my Father and Friend Goethe. Just think of it!

In the afternoon I played to Goethe for more than two hours, partly Bach fugues and partly improvisations. In the evening there was whist, and Professor Zelter, who took a hand, said, 'Whist means "shut up" . . .' We all had supper together – even Goethe who doesn't generally eat anything at night. Now, my coughing Fanny,[2] here's something for you. Yesterday morning I showed your songs to Frau Goethe, who has a good voice and is going to sing them to the old gentleman. . . . She likes them very much indeed.

[1] Ottilie von Goethe (*née* von Pogwisch), Goethe's daughter-in-law. Her marriage had broken down, and after Goethe had been left a widower she helped to look after him.
[2] When Felix submitted his latest compositions to his sister, she used to mark any disapproval by coughing.

Warum stehen sie davor?   Kämen sie getrost herein
Ist nicht Thüre da und Thor?   Würden wohl empfangen seyn
                                          Goethe 1828

Goethe's house in Weimar. Engraving after a drawing by Otto Wagner, 1827. Below it Goethe has written four lines of verse begging visitors to enter

Four days later he writes again. He has been playing his G minor Sonata to the Hereditary Grand Duke at the palace, and has heard Wranitzky's *Oberon* at the theatre. 'Then on Thursday morning the Grand Duke and Duchess[1] and the Hereditary Grand Duke came to us, and I was made to play from eleven in the morning till ten at night with only a two-hour break, finishing up with Hummel's Fantasia. . . . I play much more here than I do at home – seldom for less than four hours and sometimes six or even eight.' This information can hardly have pleased his mother, who had hoped that Weimar would be a rest cure.

Every afternoon Goethe opens his piano – a Streicher – and says, 'I haven't yet heard you today; now make a little noise for me.' Then he generally sits down beside me and when I have finished (mostly extemporizing) I ask for a kiss or take one. You can't imagine how good and kind he is, or have any idea of the treasures – all the minerals, busts, engravings little statuettes and big drawings – that the Pole Star among poets possesses.

His figure doesn't strike me as imposing; he isn't much taller than Father; but his bearing his speech, his name – *these* are imposing! He has a tremendously resonant voice and he can shout like ten thousand warriors. His hair is not yet white; his step is firm and his way of speaking gentle.

[1] Russian royalty visiting Weimar.

Zelter was proposing to take Felix with him to Jena; but when the house-party learnt of this there was a general outcry, and Zelter, summoned by Goethe, was peremptorily ordered to go to 'that old dump' alone and leave the boy behind. Whereupon 'Goethe was beset on all sides. They kissed his mouth and his hands, and those who could not gain access to them caressed him and kissed his shoulders. I really believe that if he had not been in his own house we would have carried him home in triumph as the Romans carried Cicero after the first Catiline oration. Incidentally, Fräulein Ulrike had also thrown her arms around his neck, and since he is paying her court (she is extremely pretty) the whole effect was charming.' The precocious child did not miss much!

Such was Goethe's life at Weimar. He was worshipped and kissed like today's pop stars and goal-scorers. His house was an Olympus ruled by *Jupiter tonans*, with a constantly changing bevy of goddesses at his beck and call and now this Ganymede (disguised as Orpheus) come to charm the aged god with his beauty and his music. It would, however, be rash to see in Goethe a Gustav von Aschenbach and in Felix a Tadzio.[1] Goethe turned to the Bible to find a parallel for his relationship with this 'precious boy': 'I am Saul,' he told him, 'and you are my David. When I am sad, come and cheer me with your playing.'

It so happens that we have two other first-hand accounts of Felix's visit to Goethe in 1821.

Ludwig Rellstab, musician and critic, had been invited by Goethe to an evening party at which Felix was to play; he had already heard the boy in the Mendelssohn house in Berlin, and so knew what to expect. He was amused to observe that Zelter, who when in Berlin was careless about dress, now wore old-fashioned breeches, silk stockings, and black patent-leather shoes with big silver buckles – pre-French Revolution Court costume which contrasted strangely with his gruff plebeian speech.

'My friend Zelter,' said Goethe to the assembled company, 'has brought his young pupil to see me. He is going to give us a sample of his musical gifts, but I am told that he is extraordinarily talented in other ways as well. . . .'

The boy took his seat at the piano and said to Zelter, 'What shall I play?' 'Whatever you can,' replied his master. 'At all events nothing that's too hard for you.' Since there was no possible piece that Felix couldn't have managed, commented Rellstab, this seemed quite gratuitously offensive.

After some discussion it was decided that the boy should improvise on a theme provided by Zelter, who with even greater lack of tact proposed a trite little tune called '*Ich träumte einst von Hannchen*' ('Once I dreamed of little Hann'). Felix said he did not know it. 'Then I'll play it to you,' replied Zelter, and proceeded to do so with his stiff, arthritic fingers.

Felix played it through after him . . . then plunged without more ado into the wildest allegro. The simple tune was transformed into a passionate figure which he took first in the bass, then in the treble, developing it with lovely contrasts. In short, he created a torrential fantasia that poured out like liquid fire. . . .
     The whole company was thunderstruck. The boy's small hands worked away at the great chords, mastering the most difficult combinations. The notes rushed headlong, dropping like pearls, flying in ethereal whispers. Surprising contrapuntal passages were evolved out

[1] Thomas Mann, *Death in Venice*.

of a stream of harmonies, though the banal melody played but a small part in this brilliant concourse of sound.

Zelter took care to conceal his pride in his pupil's triumph. 'What a wild ride!' he said. 'You must have been dreaming of dragons and hobgoblins.' Goethe rose to his feet and hugged the happy, proud but rather embarrassed boy, 'taking his head between his hands, roughly but kindly caressing him' and calling for more.

Goethe loved Bach, so Felix played one of the fugues. 'And why,' asked Zelter, 'did you leave out the trill?' 'Because it can't be played,' replied Felix. 'I see, I see. You mean because *you* can't play it?' 'Professor,' said the boy, 'I don't believe *anyone* can play it. Perhaps it oughtn't to be there.' The applause of the audience showed clearly enough where its sympathy lay.

Goethe then demanded a minuet, and Felix guessed what he had in mind. 'There is only one,' he said, and played the minuet from *Don Giovanni*. But he stubbornly refused to attempt the overture to the opera; it was, he maintained, impossible to do justice to it on the piano.[1] The overture to *Figaro*, however, was another matter, and he proceeded to play it with such mastery that Rellstab was almost persuaded that it gave him more pleasure than any orchestral performance he had ever heard.

While Goethe went to another room to fetch some music, Felix, at Rellstab's request, played a rondo by Cramer during which he touched a wrong note. 'Shouldn't it be a C sharp?' Rellstab asked as Felix hesitated. 'Yes – C or C sharp; it can be either.' The boy didn't want to admit his mistake.

Then Goethe returned with a sheet of manuscript whose neat script was unmistakable: an adagio by Mozart. It was a memorable moment: nearly sixty years earlier, when a boy of fourteen, Goethe had heard the seven-year-old Mozart play at Frankfurt; now the boy Mendelssohn was playing Mozart to him. But Goethe had a far more exacting task for Felix, and he next produced what seemed at first sight to be 'a sheet of ruled paper that had been sprayed with ink and then smudged'. It was Zelter who recognized it as Beethoven's hand: 'You could tell it a mile off,' he said. 'He always writes as if he were using a broomstick and then rubbed his sleeve over the page.'

It seems rather surprising that Goethe possessed a Beethoven manuscript. The two giants had met at Töplitz in 1812, and Goethe had neither liked the man nor, then or later, liked or understood his music. Writing soon afterwards to Zelter he had admitted the composer's talent but had been more particularly struck by his boorishness. 'He is perfectly entitled to think the world a detestable place,' he added, 'but that doesn't make it any more enjoyable for himself or anyone else.' The manuscript was, however, a setting of one of Goethe's poems.

Felix stared at the almost illegible scrawl. 'Now you're stumped!' cried Goethe, seeing his perplexity. Yet at his second attempt the boy managed to master the essentials of the chaotic manuscript and even to add the voice part. At one point he stopped his playing to exclaim, 'That's pure Beethoven! I'd have recognized him just from that bit alone.'

The other account comes from the pen of Johann Christian Lobe, a member of the Weimar Court Orchestra, who was summoned one day to Goethe's house with two colleagues to play

---

[1] Ten years later he did in fact play this overture in Milan to Karl Mozart, the composer's son.

chamber music with Felix. His recollections, which originally appeared in a German periodical, *Der Gartenlaube*, in 1867, throw an interesting light on Zelter's attitude towards his pupil.

Lobe, who arrived before Felix, noticed on the piano a number of manuscript scores, one entitled 'Studies in double counterpoint', another 'Fugues', and another 'Canons'. There was also 'Quartets for piano, violin, viola and cello'. All were inscribed in a firm and elegant hand with the name of the composer – Felix Mendelssohn Bartholdy. As the three string-players were taking their places there entered a man who looked like a retired sergeant-major; this was Zelter. Addressing the audience, Zelter said:

> I have come on ahead, gentlemen, in order to ask a favour of you. You are about to meet a twelve-year-old boy, my pupil. His talent as a pianist, and perhaps even more his brilliance as a composer, will amaze you. Now the boy has this peculiarity: while the flattery of amateurs leaves him quite unmoved, he listens eagerly to the opinions of professionals and, since the young innocent is too inexperienced to distinguish between well-intentioned encouragement and merited praise, takes them at their face value. So, gentlemen, if you feel like singing his praises, which I both hope and fear, please do so *moderato*, with not too much noisy instrumentation, and in that most colourless of all keys – C major. For I have so far managed to keep him from conceit and swollen-headedness – those damnable enemies of all artistic progress.

As Zelter finished speaking there entered precipitately 'an extraordinarily beautiful boy, slim and agile and of a decidedly southern type. A tumble of black [*sic*] curly hair hung down to his shoulders, and his eyes were lively and sparkling.' He was followed immediately by Goethe.

While Felix played, Goethe, also no doubt forewarned by Zelter, confined himself to an occasional 'Good!' or 'Bravo!' at the end of a piece, but he could not conceal his excitement. The recital at an end, Felix 'jumped up from the music-stool and looked around at each of us in turn with questioning eyes, obviously wanting to hear what we thought of his performance. But Goethe, apparently still bearing Zelter's warning in mind, said only, "You can see clearly enough that these gentlemen enjoyed your playing. Now run into the garden . . . and cool down; you look as if you were on fire."'

As soon as Felix had left the room the company was free to speak. Everyone was amazed – and not least the three string-players, who maintained that the boy's own compositions showed far greater originality than those of Mozart at the same age. Mozart at twelve, said Lobe, 'had turned out nothing but clever imitations of his models. So it looked as though in this boy the world had been blessed with a second Mozart, and what made it seem all the more probable was that he was so healthy and so fortunately placed.'

'Let us hope so indeed,' said Goethe.

So passed, and all too quickly, those never-to-be-forgotten sixteen days at Weimar. Though music filled much of the day, Felix also found time to enjoy himself as ordinary children do. He played with Goethe's two little grandsons, Walther[1] and Wolfgang (aged four and two), and romped with the ladies-in-waiting at Court, teasing one of them by snatching a pair of bellows from the grate and blowing her immaculate coiffure into disarray. ('These women', Goethe complained to Zelter, 'are doing all they can to spoil the boy.') Then, too, there

---

[1] Walther (d. 1885) later studied with Mendelssohn.

were paper games such as *bouts rimés*, where Goethe was often called in to adjudicate. Among the regular visitors to the house was Adele Schopenhauer, the younger sister of the philosopher, who had a talent for cutting paper silhouettes. She cut several for Felix, one of which, with a poem written by Goethe beneath it, was sent to him later in Berlin.

Felix certainly kept his eyes open and his wits about him at Weimar. Of a Polish pianist, Mlle Szymanowska, whose playing Goethe praised immoderately, he commented, 'People put the Szymanowska above Hummel. They confuse her pretty face with her not-so-pretty playing'; and of Goethe's close friend the classical scholar Friedrich Wilhelm Riemer, at this time librarian at Weimar, he noted that 'he seems to thrive on making lexicons. He is short and fat and shines like a priest or a full moon.' Goethe was right when he told Eckermann[1] that the Berliners in general were very sharp, that delicacy was wasted on them and that one had to be 'even a little bit rude' to hold one's own in their company. Zelter had long since shown him that.

Felix returned to Berlin in a fever of excitement. 'On his first day at home,' wrote Lea, 'he was a veritable volcano, erupting with fun and high spirits. Zelter had told him to speak slowly and distinctly, but you can imagine how little effect this had on his tremendous excitability.' Meanwhile at Weimar the old poet felt quite lost without his young charmer. Early in the new year he wrote to Zelter, 'Give greetings to Felix and his parents. Since you left, my piano remains dumb; a single attempt to awaken it was almost a disaster. Meanwhile there has been plenty of talk about music, which is always a poor subject of conversation.'

[1] Johann Peter Eckermann – Goethe's Boswell and author of *Conversations with Goethe*.

Silhouette, 'Jacob's Ladder', by Adele Schopenhauer. Given by her to Felix at Weimar in 1821

CHAPTER FOUR

❦ 1822 ❦

One of the greatest friendships of Felix's life was that with the German opera-singer and actor Eduard Devrient (1801–77), who published in 1868 his recollections of the composer, together with the letters he had received from him.

Devrient had often noticed the curly-headed child, trudging through the streets in his big boots, hand in hand with his father, or playing marbles outside the door of the Mendelssohns' house in the Neue Promenade, but it was not until January 1822 that they first got to know one another.

> Felix was a boy of thirteen, I a young man of over twenty who had been for almost three years a baritone with the Berlin Royal Opera Company. . . .
>
> I had heard much talk in musical circles of the boy's extraordinary talent, had seen him in the Singakademie and at Zelter's Friday concerts, and had met him at a musical tea-party where he appeared among the grown-ups dressed in a child's so-called '*Habit*' – a tight-fitting jacket, cut very low at the neck, over which the wide trousers were buttoned. Into the slanting pockets of these trousers the youngster loved to thrust his hands, rocking his curly head from side to side and shifting restlessly from one foot to the other. His brown eyes sparkled beneath half-lowered eyelids as, almost defiantly and with a slight lisp, he jerked out his answer to the searching questions that people usually put to infant prodigies.

Devrient found the boy's piano technique and musicianship astonishing, though at this time still inferior to Fanny's. He was told that Felix had already composed a great deal of music, including several little operas. His fiancée Therese, like Felix a pupil of Zelter's, took part in the informal concerts which began this year to be held regularly at the Mendelssohns' house, and on one occasion, when the bass (Felix's violin teacher, Henning) was unable to take part in the boy's latest operetta, Devrient was invited to stand in for him:

> This proved the first of many visits, during which Felix's two earlier operettas, *The Two Schoolmasters* and *Soldiers in Love*, were revived and his latest, *Die Wandernden Komödianten* ['The Strolling Players'], rehearsed. Considering the reputed wealth of Felix's father, the furnishing of the house seemed almost affectedly austere. Carpets and furniture were of the simplest; but the walls of the salon were hung with engravings after Raphael's frescoes in the *Loggie* [of the Vatican]. The singers sat round the big dining-table, near the grand piano at which Felix, perched on a stool provided with a thick cushion, conducted and controlled us without a trace of shyness, earnestly and eagerly and with as little ado as if he had been playing games with a handful of his playmates. That so many adults were giving time and trouble to his compositions seemed no more to make him conceited than did the fact that he had already written his third little opera and was hard at work on a bigger one.

The rehearsal at an end, Felix collected the parts and stacked them neatly before modestly accepting the congratulations of the performers; and even then he was more eager for criticism than for praise. He struck Devrient as being completely unspoilt.

Soon Devrient and his fiancée found themselves regular visitors at the Mendelssohns. Felix became as fond of Devrient as Fanny of Therese, and the parents gave these friendships their blessing. There was music-making and play-reading (Shakespeare mostly), and the regular Sunday morning concerts which Devrient and Therese attended either as performers or as members of the audience. Thanks to his wealth, Abraham Mendelssohn could afford to engage a small orchestra; this gave Felix the inestimable advantage of being able to familiarize himself with the various instruments and of hearing his own compositions performed. The boy would stand on a stool at the conductor's desk, looking the complete infant prodigy beside the seated players (especially the giant double-bass player): a tiny field-marshal calmly and competently conducting his little force with his baton. Of course other music besides his own was played at these concerts, and both he and Fanny took part in trios and piano concertos.

Devrient observed the parents as carefully as he did the children. Frau Mendelssohn he found intelligent, sensitive, and never for a moment idle; it was from her that Felix had learnt the importance of application and hard work. Sometimes Devrient called on her in the middle of the morning, when Felix would join them with the slice of bread and butter which entitled him to take a break. If, however, he went on talking a moment after he had finished it, she would shoo him out of the room and back to his studies. Some idea of the way in which the children were driven may be gathered from the fact that on Sunday mornings they were, for a treat, allowed to sleep on until six o'clock.

Where the girls were concerned the mother's authority was paramount, as Fanny was soon to discover if she did not know it already. But the boy was even more influenced by his father, who taught him that life must be lived in ceaseless striving after a goal and in the service of others. Devrient had, however, noticed Abraham's Achilles' heel: 'Abraham Mendelssohn's contentious disposition, which increased with his years and became more and more acrid, and at last intolerable, is strangely anomalous with so much wisdom, and may have arisen from physical causes. Had this excessive irritability anything to do with his sudden death, and was it to descend upon Felix?'

Felix and Fanny were passionately fond of one another; indeed, it may well seem doubtful whether he was ever to love another woman, even his wife, as deeply. Their mutual attachment was so marked and so obvious that as Felix approached manhood family friends began crudely joking that the brother and sister 'really ought to marry'. Even on her wedding-day in 1829 Fanny was to see fit to write to her brother, 'I have your portrait before me, and ever repeating your dear name, and thinking of you as if you stood at my side, I weep. . . . Every morning and every moment of my life I shall love you from the bottom of my heart, and I am sure that in doing so I shall not wrong Hensel [her husband].'

So it may well have been with a pang of jealousy that, about 1822, Felix, though still a boy, learned that the hand of his seventeen-year-old sister was being sought in marriage by a very talented but still struggling artist nine years older than herself. Wilhelm Hensel, a Gentile and the son of a poor Protestant clergyman, had had a hard fight to become a painter. After

Eduard Devrient. Pencil drawing by Wilhelm Hensel, 1831

taking part with distinction in the War of Liberation, during which he was several times wounded, and spending some time in Paris, he had arrived penniless in Berlin, where he scored a considerable success with an allegorical painting showing Tsar Alexander I of Russia as the Archangel Michael and Napoleon as Lucifer. It was, therefore, only appropriate that when, in January 1821, the Hereditary Grand Duke Nicholas of Russia and his wife visited the Prussian Court, Hensel should have been invited to design the costumes for the royal *tableaux vivants* of scenes from Thomas Moore's new Oriental romance, *Lalla Rookh*, which were to constitute the climax of the festivities.

Wilhelm Hensel, self-portrait. Pencil drawing, 1829

The performance over, the Grand Duchess, who had herself taken the part of Lalla Rookh, asked King Friedrich Wilhelm III whether she might have some permanent record of this happy occasion, whereupon His Majesty, who spoke mostly in verbs, is reported to have replied, '*Sollen haben*' ('must have') and commissioned Hensel to make an album of paintings of the twenty-seven scenes. These pictures, for which the royal actors and actresses consented to give individual sittings, were exhibited by Hensel before being sent to Russia, and it was in his studio that Fanny first met her future husband.

It was love (at all events on Hensel's side) at first sight, and his affection was certainly not rejected. He wanted, of course, to become officially engaged at once; but Lea would not agree. It was all so sudden; could he be sure that this was not just a passing infatuation? Then there were his financial prospects to be considered. True, he had scored a great success, which had led to his being awarded a Government scholarship to study for five years in Rome (together with a commission to make a full-sized copy[1] of Raphael's *Transfiguration*);

[1] Now in the Raphael Gallery of the Orangery at Sans Souci.

Design for the pantomime 'Lalla Rookh' by Wilhelm Hensel, 1821

but the public was notoriously fickle, and this might well prove to be no more than a flash in the pan. Further, though Lea had not the slightest objection to her daughter marrying a Gentile, she had an almost pathological mistrust of the Church of Rome. Wilhelm's sister had become a Roman Catholic; he himself would be going straight into the hornets' nest, and those wicked priests would surely get him. . . . So the decision was made – and one that today sounds cruel enough: Hensel was to go to Rome, and while there was not to correspond with Fanny. Lea would, however, write regularly and give him the family news; if, after five years, he and Fanny were still of the same mind, their engagement would be sanctioned.

Poor Wilhelm was clearly both indignant and distressed and must have said as much, for we find Lea writing to him to justify herself. The letter, which is very long, throws much light on the character of the mother of Felix:

. . . Seriously, dear Herr Hensel, you mustn't be angry with me for not allowing you and Fanny to write to one another. You are probably now pronouncing my attitude utterly

> barbarous; but in all fairness, put yourself for a moment in the position of a mother . . . and it will appear to you natural, just and sensible. . . . You know that I esteem you highly, have a real affection for you and have no objection to you whatever on personal grounds. The real reasons why I have not yet decided in your favour are the difference of age and the uncertainty of your position; a man may not think of marrying before his prospects in life are reasonably assured.

She goes on to point out the charming life of a bachelor artist, welcome everywhere, with no cares and no responsibilities; she does not add 'and probably no money' – which even for a bachelor has its drawbacks:

> He steps lightly over the rocks which difference of rank has piled up in the world; he works at what he likes and how he likes, choosing his favourite subjects in art and roving poetically in other regions, the most delighted, happy being in the whole of creation. But as soon as domestic cares take hold of him, all this magic vanishes; the lovely colouring fades, and he has to work to support his family.

She had, she said, brought up her children simply, so that they would not be obliged to make rich marriages:

> but in the eyes of parents a competency, a moderate but *fixed* income, is a necessary condition for a happy life. . . . Fanny is very young and, heaven be praised! has so far had no worries and no passion. I will not have you sending love-letters which will transport her for years into a state of consuming passion and a yearning frame of mind quite alien to her character, when I have her now before me blooming, healthy, happy and free.

She may perhaps have thought that Hensel was an opportunist, for, as she told a cousin at this time, 'Fanny isn't pretty'; she also had one shoulder rather higher than the other and was extremely short-sighted.

So Hensel left for Rome. Lea kept her word and wrote regularly, while the young artist, though debarred from writing to Fanny, plied her mother with memory drawings of the children (what Lea called 'spiritualized likenesses idealized, *à la Hensel*') and other sketches which he knew would be shown to the family. But five whole years were to pass before he again saw the girl he still desired and who was still waiting for him.

The student of Mendelssohn owes Wilhelm Hensel a debt of gratitude for his portraits of the Mendelssohn family and their whole circle. To Wilhelm and Fanny's son, Sebastian, the biographer of Mendelssohn is even more indebted for his invaluable work, *The Mendelssohn Family*, first published in Berlin in 1879 and shortly afterwards in an English translation that ran to a number of editions. Here gratitude is, however, qualified since the discovery by Eric Werner, who was given access to much of the original Mendelssohn correspondence now in New York, of the extent to which Sebastian Hensel trimmed the letters in order to present a sunnier picture of the uncle he hero-worshipped. 'The idol of the Victorian parlor,' writes Werner, 'adored by the German and English bourgeoisie alike, the ever-virtuous, angelic, sentimental Mendelssohn of our grandparents' day is a popular fiction, engendered by that once equally popular, yet very inaccurate book *The Mendelssohn Family*.' 'Inaccurate' is a harsh word; 'misleading' would be both truer and kinder to Hensel.

Though it had suited Lea's book to stress to Wilhelm the precariousness of a banking-house, prosperous one day and bankrupt the next, the fact was that Abraham was by now a very rich man in a Europe where an assured peace seemed likely to keep him so. At the beginning of July 1822 he decided to take his entire family, together with Heyse (the children's tutor), a Dr Neuburg and several servants on a prolonged tour of southern Germany and Switzerland. Abraham had been overworking and was badly in need of a holiday, but another reason for this costly undertaking may have been to get Fanny away from Wilhelm. A letter to Fanny from her Aunt Henriette in Paris, who was to follow the tour with the greatest interest, would seem to confirm this; for in it she urges her niece to enjoy herself, but adds, 'If you cannot actually be cheerful, remember Goethe's words, "Life also needs dark leaves in its wreath."'

In those days a holiday of such a kind and of such duration – for they were away from home for three months – was most unusual and not entirely to the liking of Lea, who hated travelling but who in the event climbed mountains with the best of them. At the very start there was a little *contretemps*: Felix got left behind at Potsdam, the occupants of each carriage believing him to be in one of the others. But Heyse, sent in search of the boy, soon came upon him walking briskly in pursuit and having already covered nearly ten of the fifteen miles to Grosskreutz, where his absence had first been noticed.

At Frankfurt-am-Main the 'dear caravan' (as Henriette called it) was enlivened by the addition of 'two very intelligent and amusing young ladies' – Marianne and Julie Saaling – the latter of whom was one day to become Heyse's wife. At Kassel the Mendelssohns met Louis Spohr, for whom they carried a letter of introduction from Zelter. Spohr – once overrated, then later absurdly neglected – was conductor of the famous Kassel Orchestra; he gave his visitors a warm welcome and there was much music-making which included a work – probably a piano or a string quartet – by Felix. At Frankfurt they looked up Schelble, the conductor of the fine Cäcilienverein, who was just beginning to perform small works by J. S. Bach, and Aloys Schmitt, a distinguished piano teacher whose *Exercises* have over the years tormented many thousands of the aspiring young. Again there was music, but the visit was memorable chiefly for the fact that Felix now first met a boy who was to become a lifelong[1] friend: Ferdinand Hiller (1811–85), later famous as a pianist and conductor. Fanny describes him as 'Schmitt's favourite pupil – a good-looking ten-year-old boy, open-hearted and frank in appearance'; he was known locally as 'the little pianist with the long hair'.

In his biography of Mendelssohn, published in Köln in 1874, Hiller recalls the occasion. He had already heard from Schmitt of the Berlin wonder-child who was to be brought to meet him, and watched patiently at the window to see him arrive. He was rewarded at last by the sight of Schmitt 'and behind him a boy, not much bigger than myself, who kept jumping up till he succeeded in getting his hands on Schmitt's shoulders so as to be carried pick-a-back for a few paces. . . . "He's jolly enough", I thought, and ran off to the sitting-room to tell my parents that the eagerly-awaited visitor had come. But I was amazed when I saw this same wild boy make a very dignified entry and, though lively and talkative, preserve a certain formality. . . .'

Next day Ferdinand was taken to the Swan, where the Mendelssohns and their party were staying. Various musicians had assembled there, with three of whom Felix played a piano

---

[1] Or almost lifelong. There appears to have been something of a rift between them a year or two before Felix died.

quartet of his own; but Ferdinand was more impressed by Fanny's 'truly masterly' performance of Hummel's Rondo Brillante in A flat. Curiously enough, Fanny mentions in a letter
written at the time that she was so nervous that at one point she broke down; she adds that
neither she nor Felix formed a very favourable opinion of the general level of musicianship.
Among those present was Devrient, whom Ferdinand describes as 'a young singer who
pleased me very much, not only by his good looks and graceful ways, but also by the exquisite
manner in which he sang an aria of Mozart's'. Ferdinand saw Felix again the following day,
when the latter made a much greater impression on him by very competently playing at sight
the violin part in a sonata by Schmitt, 'though inevitably the *bravura* passages were a bit
sketchy'.

From Frankfurt the caravan continued southwards by way of Darmstadt and Stuttgart to
Schaffhausen, the two Saaling girls, 'who overflowed with fun and humour, contributing no
small amount of the necessary travelling spirits'. Both Fanny and Felix were overwhelmed
by the majesty of Switzerland, and most of all by the approach to the St Gotthard – so
temptingly near to the Italy of which they dreamed but which their parents could not be
persuaded to enter. Fanny wrote ecstatically to her cousin Marianne Mendelssohn (Joseph's
daughter-in-law), 'I have seen God's grand nature, my heart has trembled with emotion and
veneration. . . . Never have I felt such a sensation!' Her heart swelled, her bosom heaved,
till she 'found relief in a flood of tears'. This kind of reaction was, of course, expected of
a well-brought-up girl in the Romantic era.

At the Devil's Bridge – the old wooden one, for the modern granite bridge was not built
until 1830 – the mountain torrent of the Reuss reached its most spectacular. Fanny reported,
'You find yourself completely closed in by the rocks; in front of you, in several breaks, rushes
down the immense flood of water; high above is the slender but safe bridge. The cutting
wind, which blows here towards evening and is called the glacier-wind, the snowy peaks here
and there standing forth, the oncoming twilight in this "mountain valley", and every other
surrounding feature, contributed to increase the feeling of awe.' Then, at the Urner Loch,
she gazed 'almost petrified with wonder' at the peaceful valley and lush green meadows
spread at her feet.

They went everywhere that was then fashionable: to Tell's chapel and to Interlaken; to
the Wengern-Alp, the Haslital and the Staubbach; to Ferney in honour of Voltaire, and
finally to Vevey, where the possibility of ascending the Rhône Valley and crossing the
Simplon to Lake Maggiore and the Borromean Islands was discussed, but finally rejected.
Meanwhile Felix, who had 'quite fallen in love with this divine country', was sketching and
counting the waterfalls, and filling his head with musical ideas, and writing to Zelter about
yodelling and mountain huts and peasant singing and the organs (including that in Bern
Cathedral) which he sampled. He even found time to compose: at Sécheron, near Lake
Geneva, he began his Piano Quartet in C minor (op. 1) which was finished after his return
to Berlin, and at Lausanne he completed the first act of his latest opera, *Die beiden Neffen,
oder der Onkel aus Boston* ('The Two Nephews, or the Uncle from Boston').

On the way home another stop was made at Frankfurt.[1] And then, as a *bonne bouche*, came
a visit to Goethe at Weimar, where Frau Mendelssohn saw with motherly pride 'how
immensely beloved Felix had made himself among these superior people. . . . Goethe talked

---

[1] According to Devrient, Felix first met Hiller now, and not on the outward journey. It is a matter of small importance.

for hours with my husband about him, and earnestly begged to have him again for a still longer visit; he gazed at him with obvious pleasure, and his face lit up when the boy's improvisations had pleased him.' Fanny in her turn played Bach and sang settings that she had made of Goethe's poems.

By the end of the first week of October the family was safely back in Berlin, where Fanny noted how her brother had matured during the summer. 'He had grown a lot taller and stronger; both his features and his expression had developed out of all recognition, and the cutting off of his long curls contributed not a little to the alteration in his appearance. His lovely *child's face* had disappeared, and his figure already showed a manliness very becoming to him. He had changed, but he was just as good-looking as ever.'

In 1822 Felix, who had not played again in public since his debut four years earlier, made two further appearances before Berlin audiences: on 31 March at a concert given by Aloys Schmitt, and on 5 December at one organized by Anna Milder, the Berlin *prima donna* for whom Beethoven had written the name-part of his opera, *Fidelio*. An account of the latter concert appeared in the English *Quarterly Musical Magazine and Review*, which mentioned that 'the young Felix Mendelssohn performed a concerto, composed by himself, on the pianoforte'.[1] The year, too, in spite of the long interruption of the Swiss tour, was remarkably productive of compositions, of which Hensel lists the following:

The 66th Psalm for three female voices
Piano Concerto in A minor
Two songs for male voices
Three songs
Three fugues for the piano
Piano Quartet in C minor (op. 1)
Symphonies for strings
First act of the three-act opera, *The Two Nephews*
'Jube Domine' in C major
Violin Concerto in D minor
Magnificat and Gloria for chorus and orchestra

Several of these have already been mentioned, and others no doubt deserve to be forgotten; but among the remainder should be noted the so-called 'little' violin concerto, written for Felix's friend and teacher Eduard Rietz. The manuscript given to Rietz is now in the possession of Yehudi Menuhin, who first performed it in public and had it published in 1952, and there is a second manuscript which has been since 1878 in the Berlin State Library, West Berlin. Though the work is a remarkable achievement for a boy of thirteen, it seems doubtful whether it will retain a permanent place in the repertoire of violinists.

[1] In A minor; it has been recorded by John Ogdon and the Academy of St Martin-in-the-Fields.

CHAPTER FIVE

1823-1824

During the next two years, Felix never stopped working. Among the major compositions of this time (besides his fourth opera, to be discussed in a moment) were two concertos for two pianos and orchestra, a Piano Sextet in D (op. 110),[1] a Piano Quartet in F minor (op. 2), a Sonata in F minor for violin and piano (op. 4), an andante and a sparkling rondo capriccioso for piano (op. 14) and a number of symphonies for strings. Few of all these are to be heard in the concert hall today; but most have now been recorded, and their resurrection is amply justified. In particular, the Symphony No. 12 in G minor, with its delightful andante – like a gentle stroll through woods in spring – is unusually attractive. The influence of Scarlatti, Bach, Haydn, Mozart, Beethoven, Hummel, Weber and Moscheles is to be found in these youthful works.

Much of what Felix wrote was immediately performed at the Sunday morning concerts at the Mendelssohns', in which all the children took part: Rebecka sang, Paul played the cello, Fanny of course the piano, and Felix not only the piano but also the violin and viola. All musicians of eminence visiting Berlin asked to be allowed to attend, and thus, or through Zelter's wide acquaintance in the musical world, the boy had already met, or was soon to meet, Weber, Moscheles, Hummel, Spohr and Spontini. Another was the famous pianist and teacher, Friedrich Kalkbrenner. 'He heard a good many of Felix's compositions,' wrote Fanny, 'praised with taste, and blamed candidly and amiably. We hear him often and try to learn from him. . . .'

It was not only as a composer and a pianist that Felix was developing; in a remarkable letter addressed to a young lawyer and amateur composer with the splendid name of Wilhelm von Boguslavski, he shows the trouble he is prepared to take on behalf of a friend and the maturity of his musical judgment. Boguslavski, who was twenty at the time, had submitted a symphony to the boy for criticism, and Felix, quite unembarrassed by the difference in their ages, assesses it with no punches pulled. He writes (on 30 September 1823):

Since you really want me to give you my opinion, then I must do so.

In general, let me begin by saying that I like all the themes of the opening movement very much. I thoroughly approve of the adagio movement except for the forte theme in the middle, and the minuet seems pleasant and gay except for the end, which is too protracted. The theme of the last movement, including the first forte and as far as the piano, isn't bad

[1] Posthumously published works carry opus numbers from 73 onwards.

Felix's brother Paul, aged sixteen. Drawing by Wilhelm Hensel

either; but after that I feel it is a bit weak, and I don't at all like the trumpeting at the end.
Now for details: . . .

And he proceeds to a close examination of each movement in turn.

The opening adagio he finds much too long. It is meant to be an introduction but
Boguslavski has really made it a virtually independent movement, elaborating the theme so
extensively that the listener is exhausted before he reaches the allegro. Detailed criticism
follows, such as: 'You ought to conclude in A major (the dominant of D major), but you
close instead in D major and begin again in G major; this makes the modulation very
monotonous.' And so on, at some length. He is, however, gracious enough to repeat that the
symphony as a whole had given him great pleasure.

In August 1823 Abraham was obliged to go to Silesia on business and took his two sons with
him. At Breslau, wrote Felix, 'we all went to the [St Elizabeth] church to hear Berner play.
First he took off his coat and put on a lighter one, then asked me to write down a theme for
him and began to play. He took the low C on the pedal and then attacked the manual
furiously.' Next he played the theme on the pedals also, developing it in a manner that
greatly impressed the boy but apparently exhausted the performer, who soon broke off to
fortify himself with several glasses of wine from a bottle which was brought to him in the
organ-loft. The recital continued with many further intervals for refreshment, and concluded
with variations on 'God save the King' and the finishing of the bottle. Felix adds that while
Berner played he kept a chorister at his side to draw out and push in the stops: these he
indicated by touching them lightly with his finger.

Berner then showed Felix the inside of the organ, which had suffered badly from the
bombardment of the French, and was afterwards carried off by the Mendelssohns to dine
with them. Mellowed no doubt by further alcohol, he entertained his hosts by describing
a number of his 'funny practical jokes' – the details of which we are mercifully spared.

Zelter was a great admirer of Bach, and sometimes at his Friday music-makings, which were
attended by a few select members of the Singakademie, 'We used [wrote Devrient] to sing
what Zelter called the "bristly pieces" of Sebastian Bach, who at that time was generally
considered as an unintelligible musical arithmetician with an astonishing facility for writing
fugues; few of his motets were sung by the Society, and these but seldom.'

Here Felix first heard parts of the *St Matthew Passion* and longed to possess a copy of it.
The story of this copy, as usually told and based on contemporary accounts by Devrient and
others, is as follows. Zelter had obtained his manuscript from 'the estate of a cheesemonger,
by purchasing it as wrapping-paper', and had placed it in the library of the Singakademie.
Approached by Felix, he at first refused to allow a copy to be taken, but eventually yielded.
It was made by Rietz at Bella Salomon's expense and presented by her to her grandson for
Christmas.

But recently a musicologist named Martin Geck has revealed that probably the only true
fact in all this is that Bella Salomon did give Felix a score that Christmas. This manuscript,
marked and used by him, now belongs to Miss Helena Deneke, and was not made from
Zelter's copy. The matter[1] may seem unimportant, but it shows how even apparently reliable

---

[1] Fully discussed in George R. Marek's *Gentle Genius*, Funk & Wagnalls, New York, 1972.

contemporary evidence cannot always be trusted. That Felix was able to study the *St Matthew Passion* was, however, of enormous importance and was, as we shall see, to have far-reaching results.

On 3 February 1824, Felix's fifteenth birthday, the first rehearsal with orchestra of his new opera, *The Two Nephews*, took place, and four days later came the première before a small invited audience. After the rehearsal Zelter gave a little party, at the end of which he took Felix by the hand and said, 'My dear boy, from today you are no longer an apprentice, but a fully fledged member of the brotherhood of musicians. I proclaim you independent in the name of Mozart, of Haydn, and of old father Bach.' Then he embraced and kissed him heartily. It may be remembered that in Wagner's *Die Meistersinger* the end of David's apprenticeship was marked, not by an embrace, but by a box on the ear.

The day after the première Zelter reported on it to Goethe, praising it in terms that he would never have used to the boy himself:

> Yesterday we performed Felix's fourth opera, dialogue and all. There are three acts which include two ballets, and the whole takes about one and a half hours. In my humble opinion, it is truly amazing that a boy of only just fifteen should have advanced so rapidly. Everywhere in it we find novelty, beauty and individuality; wit, fluency, control, euphony, unity and dramatic power. It has 'substance' of a kind that experience alone can produce. The orchestration is interesting: not oppressive, not tedious, not mere accompaniment. . . . The overture is a remarkable piece of work. . . .
>
> I know that I speak like a doting old grandfather; but I do know what I am saying, and I can prove everything I have said.

The real test, he continued, was always the reaction of the singers and the orchestra, and of their enthusiasm there could be no possible doubt.

The score of *The Two Nephews* is now in the Deutsche Staatsbibliothek, East Berlin. Werner, who admits his indebtedness to an article by Professor Schünemann, says that the dramatic part of the music is clearly modelled on Mozart and Weber, though 'the young composer occasionally shows originality and lovely melodic lines'. It was to be Felix's last 'student's essay' in opera – a field in which real success was always to elude him; before the year was out he had begun work on his ill-starred major opera, *Die Hochzeit des Camacho* ('Camacho's Wedding'), whose failure after a single performance in 1827, which will be discussed in its proper place, should have convinced him that opera was not his *métier*.

Another valuable and lifelong friendship was begun in the autumn of 1824.

Ignaz Moscheles, a Bohemian virtuoso pianist, composer and teacher, and a friend of Beethoven's, was, like Mendelssohn, by birth a Jew. Thirty years old and already internationally famous, he set out on a concert tour of Germany which brought him at the end of October to Berlin. Here he inevitably gravitated to the Mendelssohns' hospitable house and was quite overwhelmed by what he found there. In his diary he wrote:

> I have never met such a family. Felix, a boy of fifteen, is a phenomenon. What are all other prodigies compared with him? Mere gifted children. But this Felix is already a mature artist. . . . We settled down at once to a session which lasted for several hours. I had to play a good deal, when all I really wanted was to hear him and look at his compositions.

At last the boy was persuaded to produce his Piano Concerto in C minor, a double concerto and other works – 'all bursting with genius, and at the same time so correct and so thorough'. Then Fanny played some Bach, with which Moscheles was hardly less impressed. Of the parents, he wrote that they were enormously cultured and civilized:

> They are far from overrating their children's talents; in fact, they are worried as to whether Felix is sufficiently gifted to win a real success as a professional musician. Might he not, like so many brilliant children, suddenly go to pieces? I said that I was absolutely convinced that he would become a great master, that I had no doubt whatever that he had genius. But I had to repeat this time and again before they would believe me. These two are not specimens of the genus 'prodigy-parents', from whom I so often have to suffer.

Both Devrient and another close friend of Felix's at that time, the musicologist Adolf Bernhard Marx, joined Moscheles in trying to persuade Abraham to let the boy follow his bent; but Abraham still doubted the wisdom of it, and the advocacy of Marx, whom he both disliked and mistrusted, did nothing to help Felix's cause.

Abraham and Lea begged Moscheles to give Felix a few lessons while he was in Berlin, but at first he refused. 'Felix has no need of lessons,' he said. 'If he likes to take a hint of anything new to him when he hears me play, well and good.' But Lea persisted and at last Moscheles agreed. On 22 November he notes in his diary, 'This afternoon, from 2 to 3 o'clock, I gave Felix his first lesson, never for a moment forgetting that I was sitting beside a master, not a pupil.' Six days later he is still more amazed; Felix is playing Moscheles's *Allegri di Bravura*, his concertos and other works – 'and how! The slightest hint from me, and he understands exactly what I want.'

In his diary Moscheles lists the occasions on which he made music with Felix and Fanny; on almost all other events of his Berlin visit he remains silent:

> 23 November . . . to the Mendelssohns'. The brother and sister played Bach.
> 28 November (Sunday). Music in the morning at the Mendelssohns'. C minor Quartet and D major Symphony by Felix, Concerto by Bach, Duet in D minor for two pianos by Arnold.
> 30 November. At Frau Varnhagen's[1] with Felix. Extremely interesting.
> 3 December, 12 o'clock. Music at Zelter's. Fanny Mendelssohn played the D minor Concerto by S. Bach which I saw in the original manuscript. A Mass in five parts by S. Bach was performed.
> 5 December. At Geheimrat Crelle's Felix accompanied Mozart's Requiem, in commemoration of the day of his death. Zelter and others were present.
> 11 December. A birthday party at the Mendelssohns', at which we were treated to some delightful private theatricals. Felix distinguished himself as an actor quite as much as did Eduard Devrient.
> 12 December (Sunday). Music at the Mendelssohns'. Felix's F minor Quartet. I played with him my Duet in G for two pianos [his *Homage to Handel*]. Young Schilling played Hummel's Trio in G.

But Moscheles's time in Berlin was now up. The following day he gave Felix back his album, in which he had copied out his Impromptu (op. 77); this the boy 'played admirably at sight'.

---

[1] The famous 'Rahel', whose receptions were a rallying-point for Berlin artists, scholars and statesmen.

OPPOSITE *Ignaz Moscheles. Drawing by Wilhelm Hensel, 1832*

Nach einer Photographie gravirt v. A. Weger, Leipzig.

A year or two later Moscheles and his young wife settled in London, where they remained for twenty years and extended much hospitality to Felix during the many visits he paid to England from 1829 onwards. In 1832 Felix gave Moscheles an interesting and valuable eighty-eight-page musical sketch-book in which Beethoven had jotted down his first ideas for his *Missa solemnis*.

Before leaving the subject of Moscheles's visit to Berlin it is impossible to resist introducing the reader to Elise Polko, who describes in her *Reminiscences of Felix Mendelssohn Bartholdy*[1] (a work of charming absurdity curtly dismissed by Hawes as 'almost disfigured by enthusiasm'), one of the musical parties at the Mendelssohns' that autumn.

Frau Polko, though long a worshipper of Mendelssohn from afar, did not actually meet him until 1845, when 'in suitable elfin attire', she sang, under the composer's baton, in a performance at Leipzig of *A Midsummer Night's Dream*. She was at that time a very young girl, and her hero had only two more years to live, but after his death she augmented her stock of personal recollections by first-hand information gleaned from 'the dearest friends of the departed one'.

At the party in question the guests included Moscheles, Zelter, Hummel, Berger and other distinguished local and visiting musicians. After dinner, during which 'dazzling flashes of wit played around the golden wine' and conversation was 'devoid of all restraint', everyone 'repaired at a late, very late hour to the music-room, where at the sight of the pianoforte and music-desks the conversation took a higher flight'.

Then Zelter, 'with his rough bass voice, sang, to the universal delight of all present, his *Sanct-Paulus war ein Medicus*; Ludwig Berger, a player full of soul, attempted, in spite of his crippled arm, a movement from his new F major Sonata; and, lastly, Hummel extemporized on a theme of Mozart's. During all this wondrous variety of performances, the handsome boy [Felix], in a jacket, stood modest and motionless beside the piano, a worthy study for a painter. His delicate features lit up with inspiration, he listened with burning cheeks, while his eyes never quitted the hands of the players.'

There was now a general demand, led by Zelter, for Felix to play; but he stubbornly refused, saying ' "After those two there" (glancing with swimming eyes at Hummel and Moscheles) "I neither can nor ought to play" – and, bursting into a flood of tears, he rushed out of the room.'

[1] 1868; English translation by Lady Wallace, 1869.

Elise Polko. Engraving by A. Weger, after a photograph, c. 1850

CHAPTER SIX

The Judgment of Paris 1825

Felix's sixteenth year was an eventful one. In the spring a visit to Cherubini in Paris finally decided Abraham that the boy should be allowed to make a career of music; in the summer the family moved to a palatial house in the Leipzigerstrasse; and in the autumn Felix composed his Octet for Strings (op. 20), the first work in which he revealed himself as a mature artist.

Abraham had always been a great admirer of the distinguished veteran Italian composer, Cherubini (1760–1842). He had known him personally in his Paris days, and in 1800 had unforgettably attended the première there of his most famous opera, *The Water-carrier*. Being now about to go to Paris to bring back his sister Henriette, released at last by the marriage of her pupil from her duties as a governess, he seized the opportunity to take Felix with him, so that he might get the frank opinion of the man who was at that time the Director of the Conservatoire and the doyen of the Parisian musical world. If Cherubini's verdict proved favourable, then he would raise no more objections.

They arrived in Paris towards the end of March and found rooms at the Hôtel de l'Etoile in the rue Caumartin. Their first call was of course on Tante Jette, and Felix, who had not seen her since he was a child, thought her charming. 'And how cleverly she talks!' he wrote. 'I am delighted that we are bringing her home to you.' Both Moscheles and Hummel happened to be in Paris, and Felix relates how, soon after his arrival, he paid a surprise call on the latter:

> I found Onslow and Boucher with him. For a moment he didn't recognize me, but as soon as he heard my name he went quite crazy, embraced me a hundred times, tore up and down the room, shouted and wept, made an exaggerated and ridiculous speech about me to Onslow and then rushed off with me to see Father. But when we found that Father wasn't in, he made such a shindy in the hotel that everyone came out to see what was the matter. He said goodbye but ran back after me up the stairs, embraced me, etc. Then yesterday morning he came rumbling in with four porters and his wife's grand piano, taking home our bad instrument instead.

This George Onslow was an Anglo-French pianist and composer who was soon afterwards accidentally shot during a wolf-hunt and left permanently very deaf. Boucher, a talented French violinist, sometimes attended the Mendelssohns' musical parties in Berlin, and in 1822 had given Felix a handsome album which he used for the rest of his life. He looked exactly like Napoleon I. 'He used to trade on his Bonaparte profile,' wrote Devrient, 'by putting his fiddle aside during the *tuttis* of the orchestra and exhibiting himself in the well-known imperial attitudes. Sometimes he would play holding his fiddle behind his back; and these tricks, together with his occasional really fine playing, brought him very big audiences. He was an extraordinary mixture of naïveté, craziness, and a French adroitness in turning everything to profit.'

Now came the fateful audition with Cherubini. The composer had been living in Paris for nearly forty years, and by the age of sixty-five had become a crabbed old pedant who detested every deviation from the 'rules' and deplored the experiments and innovations of the young. That stormy young rebel Berlioz, who had just entered the Conservatoire, gives in his *Memoirs* a glorious account of his battles royal with its sour Director. Nobody denied Cherubini's genius, and Beethoven himself had greatly admired his work; yet of 'late' Beethoven, which broke the rules, Cherubini could find no more to say than that it always made him sneeze. Like Zelter he was notorious for his rudeness, of which he seemed quite unconscious (and of which even Napoleon had been subjected to a sample). All stories about the boorishness of musicians are much the same. For example, there was that of the young singer who asked Cherubini for his advice and was told that, talented though he was, with a face like his he should abandon all thoughts of the concert platform; 'I put it *delicately*,' Cherubini explained, 'because I didn't want to hurt his feelings.' Even the twelve-year-old infant prodigy, Liszt, who grovelled at his feet and kissed his hand as he begged to be admitted to the Conservatoire, had met with a flat refusal because it was 'against the rules' to accept a foreigner. The rules could, it seemed, be bent only for a director.

It must have been with considerable trepidation that Felix showed Cherubini his scores and, supported by the fine French violinist Pierre Baillot and two other members of his quartet, performed for him, probably at a musical soirée, the Piano Quartet in B minor (op. 3) that he had just written and dedicated to Goethe. To the amazement of everyone present the old tiger sheathed his claws, listened attentively and, purring like a household cat, pronounced his verdict: 'Ce garçon est riche; il fera bien; il fait déjà bien. Mais il dépense trop de son argent; il met trop d'étoffe dans son habit.'[1] The composer Halévy, Cherubini's favourite pupil yet in his time much snubbed by his master, simply refused to believe the story when it was told to him. Perhaps Cherubini was not wholly unmoved by the Mendelssohn millions and the charm and good looks of this boy of whom Thackeray was later to say (to Richard Doyle), 'His is the most beautiful face I ever saw; I imagine our Saviour's to have been like it.'

Felix's opinion of Cherubini is less flattering. Though he admired his earlier work, he considered him to be now nothing more than 'an extinct volcano, still throwing out occasional sparks and flashes, but quite covered with ashes and stones', and was cheeky enough to write a hurried *Kyrie* (now lost) parodying Cherubini's style. In fact, there are now for the first time signs that the boy, formerly so unspoiled, was getting a bit above himself – as clever boys of sixteen often do. Hiller had noticed it too, though he put it more kindly: 'His opinions on art and artists at that time [he wrote] were full of the vivacity natural to his age, and had in them something – what shall I call it? – over-ripe, almost arrogant, which as he grew older

---

[1] 'This boy is richly endowed; he will do well; he is already doing well. But he squanders his talents; he makes excessive use of his material.' Professor Dika Newlin is surely mistaken in translating this (in Eric Werner's *Mendelssohn*), 'The boy is rich . . . but he spends too much money and is too elegantly dressed.'

not only became balanced but finally vanished. . . . I remember his speaking of Hummel in very much the same condescending sort of way that Zelter, in his letters to Goethe, used to speak of God. . . .'

Werner has unearthed a few amusing but rather pert comments, previously unpublished, on musicians, both young and old, who had some claim to be considered at least as gifted as Felix himself. Of Liszt at fourteen the idol of musical Paris, Felix wrote (and perhaps not without a touch of jealousy) that he 'plays very well; he has many fingers but few brains, and his improvisations are absolutely wretched. . . .' Others fared even worse at his hands: 'Meyerbeer gave an instructive discourse on the nature of the French horn in F; I shan't forget it as long as I live. . . . I laughed so uproariously that I almost fell off my chair.'[1] 'Rossini has an intricate face, a mixture of roguery, boredom and disgust . . . there you have the great Maestro *Windbeutel* [windbag].' Eleven years later, however, on meeting Rossini again in Frankfurt, he admitted that the Italian was at all events marvellous company.

Writing to Fanny he is still more sarcastic at the expense of Auber, the enormously popular composer of innumerable light operas, who had formed a kind of Gilbert-and-Sullivan partnership with the dramatist Scribe. Felix went to hear his once famous *Léocadie* at the Théâtre Feydeau, and after some complimentary remarks about the building and even the orchestral playing he launches out into a vicious attack on both the libretto and the score. Of the former, which was based on Cervantes at his earthiest, he says that he finds it almost impossible to believe that the French, who after all are a sensitive race, could stomach anything so vulgar and improper. As for the music – it had no fire, no substance, no life, no originality (it was just a *réchauffé* of Cherubini and Rossini by turns), no seriousness, and not a spark of passion; and for the most crucial moments the singers were allotted nothing but gurgles and trills and pyrotechnics. The orchestration was lamentable (which, since the publication of the scores of Haydn, Mozart and Beethoven, was inexcusable), while practically every set-piece – and it was nothing but set-pieces – was dominated by the piccolo, which Auber employed impartially to illustrate the brother's fury, the lover's anguish and the peasant girl's joy. 'In short, the whole opera might perfectly well be transcribed for two flutes and a Jew's harp *ad libitum*.'

Some of this criticism was justified, but there were times when he was really rather silly. For example, he told Fanny that he was 'trying to teach Onslow and Reicha to love Beethoven and Sebastian Bach', apparently unaware that Reicha – a distinguished professor of counterpoint at the Conservatoire and, incidentally, a man more than three times his age – was a close personal friend of Beethoven and a keen student of Bach, whom he certainly did not consider 'nothing better than an old-fashioned wig stuffed with learning'. Possibly Onslow was less well informed, for when Felix played the overture to *Fidelio* to him (on a dreadful piano) 'he became quite distracted, scratched his head, added the orchestration mentally, and finally got so excited that he started singing with me; in short he went completely wild.'

Paris may have been, as was generally alleged, the musical centre of Europe at that time, but certainly a great deal of very frivolous stuff was to be heard in the salons. When, at one of them, Felix played at Kalkbrenner's request two organ preludes by Bach, his audience pronounced them 'sweetly pretty', and somebody remarked that the beginning of the A minor

---

[1] Hans von Bülow later wrote, 'Those young wiseacres who turn up their noses at Meyerbeer would do well to stick them in his scores'.

Rossini. Lithograph after a drawing by Ary Scheffer, c. 1835

Prelude was exactly like a favourite duet in an opera by Monsigny. 'It made me feel quite faint.'

Fanny, the recipient of all this acerbity, replied suggesting that her brother might be prejudiced, and was immediately and firmly put in her place:

> Your last letter made me pretty angry. . . . Do stop a moment and think, I beg you! Are *you* in Paris, or am *I*? So I really ought to know better than you! Is it like me to let my musical judgment be influenced by prejudice?
>
> But even supposing it were, is Rode prejudiced when he says to me, '*C'est ici une dégringo-lade musicale*'? Is it prejudice that makes Neukomm say, '*Ce n'est pas ici le pays des orchestres*'? Is Herz prejudiced when he says, 'The public here can only understand and enjoy variations'? And are ten thousand others prejudiced who abuse Paris? It is you, and you only, who are so biased that you really believe in the reality of your lovely day-dream of Paris as an El Dorado, rather than in my entirely impartial account of it. . . .

In short, Felix was quite disillusioned about French music in general and Paris in particular, so that it was with few regrets that, after a two months' stay, he left with his father and his aunt for Berlin.

On the outward journey Felix and his father had looked in on Goethe at Weimar, and the visit was now repeated. 'But it was far too short,' Goethe told Zelter. 'Felix produced his new quartet and astonished us all with it. To have it thus specifically dedicated to me . . . pleased me greatly.' In June the boy sent Goethe a handsomely bound copy of the score, and received in return what Zelter described as 'a beautiful love-letter' expressing his appreciation.

*   *   *

In spite of the recent collapse of a number of important international banking-houses – Goldschmidt in London had failed with many millions, and the instability of the great house of Reichenbach in Leipzig had toppled lesser establishments – Abraham's affairs had gone from strength to strength. Now a very rich man, he decided to move into a larger house, Leipzigerstrasse 3, near the Leipziger Platz (later Potsdamer Platz) which was at that time on the very edge of the city. This was no mere change of address: it was a turning-point in the lives of the Mendelssohn family, for whom, wrote Sebastian Hensel,

> this house was not just a piece of property of a certain value, or mere dead bricks and mortar, but a living individuality, one of themselves, sympathizing with and sharing their happiness, and considered by them and their nearest friends somehow as the representative of the family. In this sense Felix often used the expression 'Leipzigerstrasse 3', and in this sense they all loved it and mourned its loss when, after the deaths of Fanny and Felix, it was sold, and became the Upper Chamber of the Prussian Parliament.

It was a princely house – the former Reck'sche Palais – standing in a seven-acre park that had once been a part of Frederick the Great's hunting preserve (later the Tiergarten). The rooms were big and high. The most spacious of them, which Lea made her drawing-room, overlooked the court and was connected through a triple arch with a further room, the two together constituting an ideal setting for small theatrical performances.

Across the court stood a single-storeyed garden house in which Fanny and her husband were to live after their marriage in 1829. This was delightful in summer, its windows embowered in vines and opening on to a garden beyond full of lilacs and avenues of ancient trees; and, being shielded from the noise of the street by the house itself, it was always beautifully quiet. Its only drawback was the cold and the damp in winter at a time when double-glazing was still almost unknown in Berlin. The principal feature of the garden house was its enormous and sumptuously decorated central hall, flanked on the garden side by a portico that was open in summer and closed by glass doors in winter; it could seat an audience of two or three hundred, and in it the Sunday morning concerts took on a new importance.

The house was not only a long way from the centre of the city, it was also in a very dilapidated state. Friends of the family at first deplored Abraham's decision, taken in February, to buy it; but after the builders had worked on it (at vast expense) for several months its suitability was acknowledged and its inaccessibility forgiven. Everyone who was anyone in Berlin, Jews and Gentiles alike, flocked there, and distinguished visitors clamoured

Rebecka's room, Leipzigerstrasse 3. Pencil drawing by Felix Mendelssohn

to be received: musicians, of course; scientists, too, and writers and philosophers including the much-admired but little-loved poet Heine, the historian Leopold von Ranke, the philosopher Hegel, Jacob Grimm of the *Fairy Tales*, Wilhelm Müller who wrote the poems of Schubert's '*Die schöne Müllerin*', and Ludwig Tieck who edited August von Schlegel's German translation of Shakespeare. To these may be added the brilliant and versatile brothers Wilhelm and Alexander von Humboldt, the latter of whom was given permission to set up in the park, in a hut made of non-magnetic materials, a small observatory in which to study the variations of the magnetic declination. Both Humboldts were totally unmusical, Alexander calling music a 'social calamity'. Finally, Frau Polko assures us, a softer touch was provided by the presence of 'an ever-blooming *Flora* of the most attractive and fascinating fair forms'.

LEFT *Title-page of 'The Very New Garden Times', 19 September 1826.* RIGHT *Two drawings of the Garden House, by contributors to the paper*

There was so much space in the house that Abraham was able to transact his business from an office in one of the wings, while some rooms on the first floor of the main building were rented for use as the Hanoverian Legation. Among the secretaries at the Legation was a young man of twenty-seven named Karl Klingemann, amusing and talented, a skilful poet and competent musician, who soon became almost one of the family. Everyone in the house was devoted to him – and not least Lea, who may well have hoped that he might help Fanny to forget her absent Hensel. It was a sad day when, two years later, Klingemann was transferred to London – though in fact Felix was subsequently to see much of him there.

A part of the garden house was at first occupied by an old lady who had two pretty nieces. These girls also seem to have become more or less assimilated in the household, joining in the various activities, athletic as well as intellectual, of the young Mendelssohns and their friends. With Klingemann and Marx, Felix started an ephemeral called *Gartenzeitung* ('Garden Times') in summer and *Thee und Schneezeitung* ('Tea and Snow Times') in winter; it was written by hand, and jotting-pads were left lying about to encourage visitors to contribute an aphorism or a few lines of verse. Abraham fitted up a small gymnasium for Felix, and in the summer the parallel bars would be pulled out into the garden where the boy was often to be found practising on them, even just before he had to play at a concert.

Karl Klingemann. Pencil drawing by Wilhelm Hensel, 1835

His friend Julius Schubring[1] recalls how on one occasion, after Felix had thus managed to run a splinter into his finger, he sat beside the pianist during a performance of Beethoven's Concerto in E flat major and mopped the blood off the keys as he played.

Felix, wrote Schubring, was a very good all-round athlete. He rode, danced and swam extremely well, and would no doubt have been a proficient skater if he hadn't given up skating because he disliked the cold so much. His favourite way of celebrating his birthday was to have a masked ball. Swimming took place in the Pfülsche Baths, which were a long way from the Leipzigerstrasse, and almost every evening in the summer he and a few of his friends would go out there in a carriage provided by his mother. A swimming club was formed, for whose members he and Klingemann composed swimming songs to be sung in the water. Schubring mentions his irritation that though he was bigger, stronger and three years older than Felix, when they wrestled together in the water the boy always succeeded in ducking him.

After the swim they returned to the Leipzigerstrasse for a light meal which no doubt often included Felix's favourite rice pudding. Then came music. 'I enjoyed it most of all when we were just the two of us,' wrote Schubring. 'He didn't extemporize, as he so often used to later on, but played Beethoven or Bach . . . and he only played something of his own if specially asked.' At nine o'clock the Guard used to march from the Leipzigerstrasse to the War Ministry, right past the house, beating a tattoo. To Felix's fury this always seemed to happen during a soft andante passage, and on one occasion he sprang to his feet and cried, 'This abominable, infantile tomfoolery!'

Inspired perhaps by the happiness of his idyllic life in this delightful house, Felix composed during the summer and early autumn his famous Octet for Strings; it was finished on 17 October and given as a birthday present to his friend and much-loved teacher Eduard Rietz, to whom he had already dedicated his 'little' violin concerto. 'Not even Mozart or Schubert', wrote John Horton in *The Chamber Music of Mendelssohn*, 'accomplished at the age of sixteen anything quite so astonishing as this major work of chamber music.'

Felix's string octet was something quite new, for Spohr's compositions for the same group of instruments were double quartets, for the most part playing antiphonally; twice four does not always make eight. Felix treated his eight players as a little orchestra, writing at the head of his score that the work was to be played 'in symphonic orchestral style', and continuing, 'pianos and fortes must be strictly observed and more strongly emphasized than is usual in pieces of this kind'. By 'pieces of this kind' he must presumably have meant Beethoven's and Hummel's septets, though these, like Schubert's octet, include wind instruments.

There are few moments in nineteenth-century chamber music more exhilarating than the beginning of the first movement of Felix's Octet for Strings, when the first violin climbs, step by step, then suddenly plunges into the abyss; but the whole movement is faultless. A charming andante and a dazzling scherzo follow, and the work concludes with a rushing polyphonic presto – all 'purest, truest Mendelssohn'.

The scherzo is the forerunner of many such fairy-like, gossamer pieces of which the overture to *A Midsummer Night's Dream*, written in the following year, is the most famous.[2]

---

[1] Later ordained, and the compiler of the texts of Mendelssohn's oratorios *St Paul* and *Elijah*.
[2] In the scherzo of his earlier Piano Quartet in B minor Mendelssohn had already given a hint of this characteristic quality.

It was inspired, Felix tells us, by four lines from Goethe's 'Walpurgis Night' in *Faust* – lines which defy adequate translation, though Grove has done his best with them:

> *Floating cloud and trailing mist*
> *Bright'ning o'er us hover;*
> *Airs stir the brake, the rushes shake –*
> *And all their pomp is over.*[1]

Fanny wrote of the scherzo that it was a complete success:

I was the only person he told what he had in mind, which was this. The whole piece is to be played staccato and pianissimo, the tremolandos coming in now and then, the trills vanishing with the speed of lightning. Everything is new and strange, yet at the same time utterly persuasive and enchanting. One feels very near to the world of spirits, lifted into the air, half inclined to snatch up a broomstick and follow the aerial procession. At the end the first violin takes flight, light as a feather – and all is blown away.

Max Bruch wrote in 1900 of the octet and the overture to *A Midsummer Night's Dream*, 'Both works have earned immortality, but to me the octet will always remain the greater miracle.' Felix was to count it his favourite early work, telling Schumann that he often recalled it with affection. In November Zelter reported to Goethe that it had '*Hand und Fuss*' – was complete in every part – and added, 'a few weeks ago Felix also gave his excellent tutor Heyse a delightful birthday present: a metrical translation of Terence's *Andria*, all his own work, which is said (for I haven't yet seen it myself) to contain some admirable lines. He plays the piano like the very devil, and practises stringed instruments as well. Yet with it all he is thoroughly fit and strong, and swims splendidly against the current.'

Even the cautious Abraham was now compelled to admit that he was the father of a genius.

[1] Wolkenzug und Nebelflor
Erhellen sich von oben.
Luft im Laub und Wind im Rohr,
Und alles ist zerstoben.

CHAPTER SEVEN

A Triumph, a Failure and a Holiday 1826-1827

During the exceptionally golden summer of 1826 the life of the young Mendelssohns and their friends revolved round the garden and park of the new house in the Leipzigerstrasse. The hot, scented nights, and also, it seems, a little flirtation with one of the nieces of the old lady who lived in the garden house, had induced in Felix a mood of ecstasy. He was composing frenziedly in the garden, he told Fanny, who was away staying with friends. 'I've finished two piano pieces there – in A major and E minor[1] – and today or tomorrow I'm going to start dreaming *midsummer nights dream* [*sic*, in English] in it; a bit of sheer audacity!' Some years later he confided to the English composer William Sterndale Bennett, 'That night I encountered Shakespeare in the garden.'

The works of two authors at that time dominated the thoughts and the reading of Felix and his companions: Shakespeare, and that one-time hero of the young Romantics – Jean Paul. The Mendelssohns looked upon Shakespeare almost as a member of the family, Abraham's brother-in-law, August Schlegel, having been principally responsible for the brilliant translations of his plays which have remained the standard versions in Germany. It was, and very naturally, *A Midsummer Night's Dream* which exactly matched the present mood of the young composer, and 'in a state of delirium' (he told Marx) he began writing an overture which was to become one of the masterpieces of Romanticism; the incidental music to the play, it should perhaps be mentioned here, was not composed until seventeen years later.

The overture opens with the famous four sustained chords on wind instruments which transport the hearer straight into fairyland. Possibly these magical, evocative sounds came to him as he heard the soughing of a summer breeze in the moonlit garden, for we know that nature made more than one contribution (there is, of course, the braying of the translated Bottom) to the overture. Our informant is Julius Schubring, who one day that summer had gone with Felix into the woods near Berlin: 'As we lay in the grass Felix suddenly whispered "Hush!" He told us later that a large fly had just gone buzzing by, and he wanted to hear the sound it made gradually die away. . . . After the overture was finished he pointed out to me the passage . . . where the cellos modulate from B minor to F minor [bars 264–70] and said, "There – that's the fly that buzzed past us at Schönhausen!"'

As soon as Felix had something on paper he showed it to Adolf Marx, whose opinion he deeply valued. Marx played at this time so important a role in Felix's musical development

[1] Presumably two of the Seven Characteristic Pieces (op. 7).

Adolf Marx. Pencil drawing by Wilhelm Hensel

that it is necessary to interrupt the narrative in order to give some account of this rather stormy petrel.

Marx was the kind of young man whom fathers do not care to see in too close association with their sons. He was fourteen years older than Felix, brilliant and stimulating but arrogant and brash, an uncouth creature with trousers too short and boots so big that somebody was heard to refer to them as 'boats'. Marx, wrote Devrient, 'gained an ascendancy over Felix such as no one else ever exercised. . . . His intellect and his eloquence dominated every conversation; his many new and striking ideas, his adroit flattery so discreetly veiled, made him for a time very popular with the family. . . . Father Mendelssohn alone held aloof from him.' Indeed, the time came when Abraham took Devrient into his confidence and appealed to him for help. 'Do try to detach him from Marx. People like that, who talk so cleverly but can *do* nothing, have a pernicious effect on creative minds.'

Zelter, not a man to hide his dislikes under a bushel, made no secret of the fact that he felt exactly the same, and wrote to Goethe with his customary coarseness of 'a certain Marx or Marcus from Halle, who must have been baptized with soda because his defecations are greenish grey; like flies they stain even the food they enjoy'. Marx, for his part, never let slip a chance of scoring off Zelter – saying, for example, of Felix that 'Zelter saw the fish swim, and imagined he had taught it how to.' But Devrient was not unduly worried at the time, and it was only later that he came to realize that Marx had been aiming at separating Felix from every influence but his own. In 1839 Marx and Felix were to quarrel irreparably when the latter felt that he could not conscientiously accept Marx's oratorio, *Moses*, for performance at Leipzig. Thereafter Marx took his revenge by never missing a chance to speak and write disparagingly of Felix and all his works, and finally by throwing all Felix's letters to him into the lake in the Tiergarten. It would appear that *Moses* was by no means worthless, for Liszt later performed it with great success in Weimar.

Marx tells us in his *Recollections* that in the sketch which Felix now showed him the four opening chords and the dance of the elves were exactly as we know them today:

> Then, alas! came the overture proper – a merry, delightfully vivacious, altogether pleasant and lovely piece, but one which I could not associate with *A Midsummer Night's Dream*. As a true friend I felt that I had to tell the composer exactly what I thought. He was upset, angry, indeed hurt, and ran off without even saying goodbye. I had to put up with this as best I could, and for several days kept away from the house; and all the more so because his mother and Fanny had greeted me, after our quarrel, coldly, almost with hostility.

Then, a few days later, Marx received a pentitent letter from Felix: 'You are absolutely right; now come to my rescue!' So the breach was healed, and, acting on Marx's advice, most of what had been written was abandoned. In fact, so dissatisfied had Felix now become with his score that it was Marx who had to plead for the retention of one or two passages – among them the braying of the ass – which the composer wanted to cut. 'He accepted my suggestions,' wrote Marx, 'and the overture assumed its present form. His mother and sister, when they saw Felix's creative enthusiasm, forgave me, and at the first performance in his house his father went so far as to say that the overture was really *my* work rather than Felix's. This was, of course, quite untrue. . . . The original idea and its execution were his; I only did the duty of a critic. . . .' That Marx was telling the truth is confirmed by Devrient, certainly not a partial witness. There was no doubt, he wrote, that Marx played an important part in the astonishing advance that the overture showed. 'It was he who caused the original draft to be rejected, and who urged a consistently characteristic elaboration of the principal ideas.'

The overture – too well known to need further description – was completed in August, and Moscheles mentions his great delight when, in November, he heard Felix and Fanny play an arrangement of it for piano duet. 'And how grand I thought his Sonata in E major [op. 6],' he continues. 'He also played me his splendid Overture in C [op. 101] with the leading subject for trumpets, and a small caprice which he called "*Absurdité*". This great and still youthful genius has once again made gigantic strides forward. . . .'

A private performance of the orchestrated *A Midsummer Night's Dream* Overture was given at the Mendelssohns' shortly before Christmas, and in a bitterly cold February Felix went to Stettin for its first public performance under Karl Loewe, the famous composer of ballads and *Lieder*.[1] It was a memorable concert, for the programme included, besides Felix's overture and his Concerto in A flat for two pianos (played by Felix and Loewe), the first performance in northern Europe of Beethoven's Ninth Symphony. For the Beethoven Felix joined the first violins in the orchestra and so made his public bow as a string-player.

The overture was warmly acclaimed; indeed, nothing that Felix was to write in the future earned him more unqualified praise from his distinguished musical contemporaries, who were quick to appreciate the novelty and brilliance of the conception and the scoring. True, critics have drawn attention to one or two points of similarity with the overture to Spohr's *Jessonda*, and with Weber's at that time unstaged *Oberon* which Felix had heard at a private concert performance; but these echoes, even if conscious, in no way detract from the basic originality of the work. 'The bloom of youth', said Schumann, 'lies over it. . . . In an inspired moment the mature master took his first and loftiest flight.' As for the English, they were amazed that a German, hardly more than a boy, who spoke their language imperfectly and had never even set foot on their shores, had so exactly understood the genius of their great national poet. What an English musicologist wrote (of the overture and incidental music) is very true: 'With *A Midsummer Night's Dream* we cannot think of Shakespeare without Mendelssohn, or Mendelssohn without Shakespeare.' Not Verdi's *Otello* nor his *Falstaff*, not even Vaughan Williams's *Sir John in Love*, was so completely successful in capturing the spirit of Shakespeare.

*　　　*　　　*

For some time past, Felix's family and his friends had been urging him to follow up the drawing-room success of his four little operettas with a full-scale work for public performance. Devrient, in particular, was at this time still convinced that opera was Felix's *métier*, and to encourage him to set to work he took his 'inexperienced pen' in hand and produced a libretto based on Tasso's *Gerusalemme Liberata*. Felix read it and praised it but said that he did not yet feel competent to tackle so serious a subject; he ought really to have confessed that he had already started work on a libretto written for him by Klingemann. This was *Camacho's Wedding* – a light-hearted piece in which sentiment alternated with comedy, the story being adapted from the then highly popular *Don Quixote* of Cervantes. Felix completed his score in the summer of 1825, and the following year submitted it to Graf Brühl, Director of the Court Opera House and Theatre. The Count seemed to approve of it; but

[1] And singer. As a boy his voice was so high that he could sing the Queen of the Night's arias in Mozart's *Magic Flute*.

LEFT *Gasparo Spontini. Engraving,* c. *1810*   RIGHT *Karl Loewe. After a painting by Most*

where operas were concerned the final decision rested with the Musical Director, Gasparo Luigi Pacifico Spontini.

The son of an Italian cobbler and now a man in his early fifties, Spontini had fought his way to the top of the musical profession, in spite of a very unattractive personality, by great talent and determination. Summoned from Paris in 1820 by King Friedrich Wilhelm III to superintend the music of the Prussian Court, he had immediately fallen foul of almost everyone, and most particularly of Brühl, who is said to have described him as 'grasping, indolent, ill-natured, treacherous and spiteful'. Indolent he was not, but in other respects the cap fitted well enough.

The sensational triumph of Weber's *Der Freischütz* a year after his arrival in Berlin had aroused his jealousy, and thereafter he did all in his power to prevent the staging of any operas which might prove more successful than his own. Nothing, however, was likely to challenge Spontini's supremacy as the composer of gradiose operas sumptuously staged (in one he managed to persuade a live elephant to tread the boards), as a showman (he used to conduct with an ebony rod tipped with two ivory balls and grasped in the middle like a marshal's baton), or as the producer of a hitherto unprecedented volume of noise. The story is told of a doctor who took a patient complaining of deafness to a performance of Spontini's *La Vestale* in the hope that it might unblock his ears. At the end of the first act the patient turned to the doctor and said, 'Now I can hear!' There came no answer: the doctor had become deaf.

Huntsmen's Chorus from Der Freischütz. *Hand-coloured woodcut, c. 1835*

'Spontini', wrote Devrient, 'asked to see the score of *Camacho's Wedding* before coming to a decision. Dignity required that the examination should last some time; it might have lasted still longer had he really read the score, for this was by no means his forte.' At last Felix was summoned and subjected to a withering criticism, after which Spontini led him to the window and, pointing theatrically to the big dome of a nearby church, said patronizingly, 'Mon ami, il vous faut des idées grandes, grandes comme cette coupole.'

However, to Felix's surprise Spontini followed up this grandiloquent gesture by agreeing to the opera being staged; he had no doubt read enough of the score to feel confident that it would fail. There now followed even more than the usual delays and frustrations: other works were found to have precedence; innumerable difficulties were discovered or manufactured. Finally Abraham Mendelssohn, who had known Spontini in Paris and often entertained him in Berlin, provoked an angry scene which resulted in their permanent estrangement.

Rehearsals began early in 1827 and continued 'at the usual snail's-pace that then prevailed in operatic matters'. Devrient had previously read the libretto but had so far heard only a few excerpts on the piano. He considered the plot stale: it was yet another permutation of the hackneyed story of the girl in love with a handsome, penniless student but ordered by her father (sung by Devrient) to marry a rich landowner. He further thought that Klingemann (of whom, it must be remembered, he may have been jealous) had completely failed to develop any dramatic stiuations. And now, as rehearsals proceeded, he became convinced

The Royal Theatre, Berlin. Lithograph, c. 1850

that the music too, though extremely competent, showed no real advance on that of the early operettas. 'In invention the work was poor; in melodies worth preserving I thought it inferior to *The Two Nephews*, because during the entire course of the rehearsals I hadn't grown attached to a single one of them – which I certainly had to several in the previous work.'

It had been decided that the theatre, rather than the opera house, would best suit the character of the little opera, and stage rehearsals were just about to begin there when Blum, who was to sing the part of Don Quixote, went down with jaundice. This meant the postponement of the première until 29 April, the last day on which Blum was available, and also therefore the preclusion of any immediate second performance.

Blum was well enough to appear on 29 April, and that evening the curtain rose on a house packed with the cream of Berlin society together with many family friends and well-wishers. The first act was warmly received, but Felix did not fail to detect that much of the applause stemmed from a personal regard for the composer rather than from admiration of his work. Too late he realized that he had long since outgrown this music, though it had in fact been written in the same year as his immortal octet. The applause at the end of the second act rang still more falsely in his ears and, almost in tears now, he ran headlong from the building and out into the night, leaving Devrient to explain, as best he could, the composer's non-appearance after the fall of the final curtain.

Felix found cold comfort in the well-meaning congratulations of his friends, and was deeply wounded by some spiteful reviews in the press. The opera was 'not really too bad for the work of a rich man's son', said one critic; another spoke of 'half-baked stuff' that ought never to have left the drawing-room, while a third (who wrote anonymously but was easily identifiable as a clever young student often a guest at his father's house) informed his readers that *Camacho's Wedding* 'had in no way enhanced the greatly overrated reputation of Herr Mendelssohn Bartholdy'. As Felix later told Devrient, 'the most brilliant praise of the best newspaper has not so much power to gratify, as the most contemptible abuse of the most obscure rag has to vex'. Any creative artist will confirm the truth of this.

There was to be no second performance of *Camacho's Wedding*.[1] According to Hensel, 'Illnesses and other obstacles, real or pretended, prevented a repetition several times appointed to take place.' It seems probable that Felix decided to cut his losses and to try to forget what he knew in his heart had been a failure. In the past, everything had gone so very right for him, and this made his humiliation the harder to bear. He had never much liked Berlin (except for the little oasis in the Leipzigerstrasse); now he began to hate the city, and with each year that passed he came to hate it more.

With the failure of *Camacho* there began what Jacob calls 'that curious game of hide-and-seek' which Felix was to play for the rest of his life. He was not hunting for the right subject, the perfect libretto, as he gave his friends to believe; 'on the contrary, he was terrified of opera. As soon as a libretto loomed on the horizon, he made himself scarce; and if a libretto was thrust under his nose, he demurred and cavilled until the author and his friends gave up in despair and somebody else set it to music.' There was, for example, the devoted Devrient's libretto of *Hans Heiling*, which after being rejected by Felix was used by Heinrich Marschner for an opera which still has a place in the repertoire of opera houses in Germany. (Incidentally, Devrient, who longed to cooperate with Felix, was much saddened when the latter told him that the libretto did not appeal to him. 'I parted from the glorious youth as my heart's friend,' he wrote, 'the brotherly *du* on my lips and the despised poem in my pocket.')

Among those who clung most tenaciously to the belief that Felix ought to become a second Mozart was Abraham Mendelssohn, and to him, at least, the young man made no secret of his conviction that opera was not his *métier*. An interesting letter from the father to the son, written in 1834, shows how deeply Abraham continued to feel on the subject. 'I must return to the question of a dramatic career for you,' he wrote, 'because I am very concerned about it on your behalf. In my opinion you have not yet had sufficient experience . . . to decide with any certainty whether your distaste for it is due to anything fundamental in your character or your talent.' Beethoven excepted, he could not, he said, think of a single dramatic composer who had not written a number of long-since-forgotten operas before suddenly scoring a success. Felix had made only one public attempt, and even that (he added more kindly then truthfully) had by no means been a complete failure. Since then he had been really too fastidious where a libretto was concerned. Abraham concluded, 'I can't help thinking that if you searched harder and demanded less, you would in the end get what you want.'

But Felix never did. His very last attempt, the *Loreley*, remained at the time of his death

[1] Except, apparently and improbably, a single performance in Boston, Massachusetts, in 1885.

no more than an agreeable fragment, and soon his chorus of Rhine spirits were to be well and truly out-sung and out-swum by Wagner's Olympic trio of Rhine maidens.

Felix could not throw off his depression, and it was no doubt in order to get a change of scene that he accepted at Whitsun an invitation to spend a few days at Sakrow, an estate near Potsdam belonging to the Magnus family. And here, it would seem, he fell in love – though how seriously we do not know; he always had a keen eye for a pretty girl, but rarely if ever did he allow one to interfere with his work or disturb his peace of mind. If a little flutter of the heart provoked a song or a caprice for the piano, then the experience had not been wasted. On this occasion we do not even known the girl's name, but a song, '*Ist es wahr?*' ('Is is true?'), which he also made use of in his String Quartet in A minor, is believed to be a record of his feelings for her.

About the same time he matriculated at the University, submitting his translation of Terence's *Andria* as evidence of his proficiency. Among the lectures he attended were those of Hegel on aesthetics, and Zelter, writing to Goethe, mentions that Felix, who was an excellent mimic, could take off the great philosopher's little idiosyncrasies to perfection.

During the summer vacation Felix went with two young friends, Gustav Magnus (later a well-known doctor) and Albert Heydemann, on a tour through the Harz Mountains, Franconia, Bavaria, Baden and the Rhineland; Eduard Rietz accompanied them as far as Thuringia. Felix's letters home suggest that he had by this time entirely recovered his spirits.

In the Harz, the highest mountains in central Germany, an attempt to ascend the Brocken, the traditional meeting-place of witches on Walpurgis Night, ended in disappointment and pouring rain, their drunken guide ultimately confessing that he had never climbed it before and was completely lost. 'Our anger now knew no bounds, and we rushed at him brandishing our sticks; but as he merely took off his coat, smiled, and said, "Hit me if you like; what do I care?" we contented ourselves with recovering our belongings and getting rid of him.'

They walked a good deal of the way, but they also rode or availed themselves of river-steamers and the post. And sometimes they slept rough – one night on benches in the innkeeper's bedroom, a place of exceptional squalor with a hog's bladder hanging up by the door. At Baden, however, there was a large and comfortable hostelry, the Golden Sun, with a music-room and a pretty young Frenchwoman who monopolized the piano and played it execrably.

Felix had various acquaintances in Baden who in the evening captured the piano for him and made him play. Soon he had an audience of forty or fifty, among them 'a heavenly moustachio'd Frenchman', a complete caricature, who accosted Felix, introduced himself as M. Charpentier, librettist to several French opera composers, and implored him to accept his *Alfred the Great* for immediate composition. Their conversation was interrupted by the stormy entry of the croupier from the roulette tables in a neighbouring room, complaining angrily that Felix had enticed away his clientele and was ruining his business. Next day Felix found that the piano had mysteriously vanished. However, a friend soon some up with the offer of one, and that evening there was great music-making which ended up with supper and a good deal of carousing at the Golden Sun.

*Walpurgis Night on
the Blocksberg.
Woodcut, 1669*

The highlight of the trip was Heidelberg, where there lived a remarkable man named Justus Thibaut – a lawyer by calling but also a distinguished musicologist and the author of a recent and important work, well known to Felix, entitled *On Purity in Musical Art* ('Read it often, as you grow older,' wrote Schumann of it). He was, in particular, a champion of Palestrina and Luis de Victoria (Vittoria). Felix, who was at that moment setting the text '*Tu es Petrus*' to music, was anxious to see the score of another setting of the same words which Thibaut mentioned in his book:

> So, plucking up my courage and putting on my decent coat, I walked straight to the Kaltethal and into his house. He could not give me the piece in question, but had other and better ones and immediately showed me his large musical library which contained music of all countries and all periods, played and sang to me, and explained the pieces. Thus several hours passed, till a visitor arrived and I took my leave; but not without my being invited to come again in the morning. What I liked best was that he never asked who I was; I loved music, and that was enough for him; and as I passed for a student they had ushered me into his study without first sending in my name.

Even on the following day, two hours passed before it occurred to Thibaut to ask the name of his guest – 'and, kind as he had been all along, he now became even more so', lending

Felix a fine score of Lotti's to copy. They parted with mutual regret, Thibaut being obliged to leave Heidelberg next morning. Felix wrote of Thibaut that he was 'worth six ordinary men', but added:

> It is strange: he doesn't really know much about music – even his historical knowledge of it is limited, he generally judges only from instinct, and I understand more of it than he does – and yet I have learned a great deal from him and am deeply grateful to him. For he has shown me the merits of old Italian music and aroused my enthusiasm for it. . . . I have just said goodbye to him, and as I had told him a lot about Sebastian Bach, adding that he did not yet know the fountain-head and what was most important in music, because all that was comprised in Bach, he said as we parted, 'Farewell, and we will build our friendship on Luis de Vittoria and Sebastian Bach, like two lovers who promise each other to look at the moon, and then fancy that they are near each other.'

At Frankfurt, where he stayed with Schelble, Felix ran into Hiller, who for a moment did not recognize this young man 'in a tall shiny hat. . . . He had changed a lot: his figure had filled out; there was a general air of smartness about him, and none of that careless ease which he sometimes adopted in later life. . . . He stayed only a short time in Frankfurt, but it was long enough for me to see that since our last meeting he had grown into a man.'

On reaching Köln, Magnus and Rietz went home, while Felix joined his Uncle Joseph at Horchheim to be present with him at a local wine festival. Finally Felix too returned to Berlin – but by way of Frankfurt, Schelble having begged him to pay this second visit in order to attend a concert of the Cäcilienverein.

View of Frankfurt-am-Main. Drawing by T. T. Siegmund, early nineteenth century

CHAPTER EIGHT

From Dürer to Bach 1828-1829

It is the fate of many great men to be neglected in the century after their deaths. Bach, as we shall see, was one of these, Dürer another. But though Dürer could claim no possible connection with Prussia, his now re-established position as the greatest of all German artists led to the tercentenary of his death, on 18 April 1828, being celebrated all over Germany, and not least in Berlin. A festival was organized by the Berlin Academy of Fine Arts, and for it Felix was invited to compose appropriate music. He was none too eager; yet in the event, and urged onwards by his father, he succeeded in producing in a bare six weeks 'a grand cantata for chorus and orchestra, with airs, recitatives, and so on'. It had originally been his intention to burn the work when it had served its immediate purpose, but the reception it received made him change his mind.

The concert was held in the Singakademie on a perfect spring afternoon. The hall had been superbly decorated by local artists; everyone was in festive mood, and even the female singers (Fanny wrote to Klingemann in London) were, 'contrary to their usual custom, very elegantly and beautifully dressed'. The festival began with Felix's Trumpet Overture in C major. 'Next came a speech by T[ölken] which lasted three-quarters of an hour – an age! Hardly ever have I seen an audience more joyfully moved than when he spoke of Dürer's approaching death. . . . Then followed the cantata, which lasted upwards of an hour and a quarter. . . . Everything went off so successfully, and the reception was so genial, that I do not remember ever passing more agreeable hours.'

After the concert there was a banquet for two hundred of the leading citizens of Berlin, at which Felix was much fêted and made an honorary member of the Artists' Association. Fanny was delighted – and chiefly because Felix seemed to enjoy this sudden popularity, which for a time almost reconciled him to the Berlin he had recently so reviled. In fact, everybody was delighted – except Devrient, who was of the opinion that the cantata 'made no impression' and added that these works dashed off hurriedly for special occasions (there was a further cantata in the autumn for a scientific conversazione given by Alexander von Humboldt) 'did not excite his best powers'.

But the year 1828 did see the birth, after four years of gestation, of one important composition – a sea-piece.

Felix had seen the sea for the first time during a family holiday at Dobberan, on the Baltic, in the summer of 1824 – that unhappy holiday when he and Fanny had been stoned and

tormented by Jew-baiters. The splendour of the ocean, its constantly changing colours, its calms and sudden storms, made a deep impression on him and were to inspire several of his orchestral compositions – in particular, of course, his famous *Hebrides* Overture. At Dobberan, while reading Goethe's twin poems *Meeresstille* ('Calm Sea') and *Glückliche Fahrt* ('Prosperous Voyage'), he had conceived the idea of writing an overture in the form of two separate tableaux.

He was not the first composer to see the musical potentialities of these two noble and contrasting poems. The slow and solemn lines of *Meeresstille* had been majestically set by Schubert in 1815 to a succession of languorous arpeggio'd chords; but Schubert did not make use of the brisk companion piece which describes the sudden stirring of the breeze that carries the ship to port. Beethoven, however, combined the two in a cantata for chorus and orchestra, composed in the same year that Felix was at Dobberan; it had been published in 1824, and Felix was familiar with it – no doubt through the omniscient Marx.

Felix did not at the time commit a single note of his overture to paper, but in February 1828 we find him writing of it to Klingemann in London, 'I have the whole thing already in my head, and the great waves will be represented by double bassoons.' In the summer Fanny told Klingemann that Felix was writing 'a great instrumental piece, *Calm Sea and Prosperous Voyage*, after Goethe's poems; and it will be worthy of him'; worthy, she means, of Goethe. Presumably the overture was finished soon after this; but it was Felix's practice, whenever circumstances permitted, to subject a new work to constant revisions until he was satisfied that he could improve it no further, and the overture was not publicly performed until 1832. It has never attained quite the same popularity as the *Hebrides* Overture, and perhaps the best-known theme in it is that which Elgar quotes in the thirteenth of his *Enigma Variations*. The influence of Beethoven is strong throughout.

As Philip Radcliffe has pointed out, the least successful part of this work is the triumphant arrival of the ship at the quayside, where 'after some pompous official greetings' the overture ends, like that of Wagner's *Flying Dutchman*, in a mood of unanticipated calm. He adds, 'Tovey has described this as "a poetic surprise of a high order"; Ernest Walker, on the other hand, saw in it an unwelcome reminder of the presence of the chaplain among those who had assembled on the shore to welcome the vessel.' Mendelssohn, who disliked the idea of 'programme' music, snubbed Schubring when the latter announced that a passage in this overture suggested to him 'the tones of love entranced at approaching nearer the goal of its desires'; 'To me', he said jokingly, 'it suggests a nice old man sitting in the stern of the vessel and blowing vigorously into the sails to help it along.'

Goethe was delighted that his poems had been a source of inspiration for Felix: 'Sail well in your music', he wrote, 'and may your voyages always be as prosperous as this one.'

The level tenor of life in the Leipzigerstrasse was interrupted that autumn by the return, not of a prodigal, but of a very patient and harshly treated young lover: Wilhelm Hensel.

Jacob (the Bible tells us) served Laban seven years to win Rachel, 'and they seemed unto him but a few days, for the love he had of her'; to Hensel, however, his five years of exile in

Dürer, aged twenty-six. Self-portrait

Rome had seemed interminable. Hard work had been his only solace. It took him the best part of four years to clean and then copy Raphael's great *Transfiguration* in the Vatican,[1] and among his many original works was the big *Christ and the Woman of Samaria* which was later purchased by the King of Prussia. At last, however, came the long-awaited letter from Lea. Packing up his things, he hurried across the Alps in a two-wheeled carriage, and in the middle of October arrived in Berlin, to find that his Fanny was still free. He was now thirty-three, she twenty-two.

There can be no doubt that Lea had at first hoped that absence might not make these two particular hearts grow fonder, and that one fine day she would learn from Hensel that he had given his elsewhere. Or might Fanny, perhaps, grow weary of waiting? Lea's long and

Fanny Hensel. Pencil drawing by her husband

newsy letters to Klingemann in London would seem to suggest that she saw in the young diplomat a far more acceptable husband for her elder daughter. Fanny, too, wrote to him often and affectionately; and it is very suggestive that in a letter to him, written two months after Hensel's return, she dismisses this far from unimportant event in one short sentence. But Klingemann was in no hurry to settle down; only at the age of forty-five did he finally take the plunge and marry the half-sister of one of his best friends. He may, indeed, really have been more devoted to Felix than to Fanny.

Hensel knew exactly what he wanted: he wanted Fanny. But Fanny (her son tells us) was 'at first timid, and bashfully retreated before the man who by so long an absence had grown a stranger to her, into the beloved circle of her parents, sister, brothers and friends. The

[1] Left unfinished at the time of Raphael's death. The lower half of the picture is by Giulio Romano.

parents, fully aware of the approaching decisive moment when they would have to share their child with another, did not perhaps receive the stranger with their wonted kindness.' In other words, everybody behaved extremely badly to the unfortuate young man. Everything possible was done to make him feel out of things: uncomfortable and unwanted. Of course this resulted in his becoming insanely jealous, imagining every young male in the Mendelssohn circle, even Felix, to be a potential rival.

But he was a man of much determination; he had waited five long years for his prize, and no one was going to wrest it from him now. By sheer perseverance he gradually won her affection. In January the engagement was announced, and we are assured by Sebastian Hensel that the letters his mother wrote to her fiancé during the nine months that elapsed before the marriage – letters 'which a kind fate has preserved to her son, but which must be withheld from publicity' – were of 'a truly pathetic and heart-moving beauty'. His letters to her have not survived.

There is every reason to think that the marriage was an extremely happy one. Nor did Abraham and Lea really lose a daughter by it, for the Hensels were allowed to live in the garden house, where they remained until Fanny's death in 1847. From a financial point of view it was no doubt a very convenient arrangement, for even so talented an artist as Hensel had a fight to earn a living; but one cannot help wondering whether there may not have been times when a virtually resident and rather formidable mother-in-law was something of a burden to him.

When writing to Klingemann in December, Fanny mentions that Felix had given her for her birthday 'three presents: a piece for my album – a *Song Without Words*, of which he has recently written some very lovely ones; another piece for the piano . . . and a big work for four choruses . . . which is to be performed by the Akademie.' This is the first reference to those *Songs Without Words* with which Felix's name was to be so closely associated.

There were eventually to be forty-eight of them – published in eight volumes, the last two of which appeared posthumously. Probably no piano music was performed more often, or more painfully, in the drawing-rooms of Victorian England than these charming and slight, but by no means insignificant, miniatures. Queen Alexandra, when Princess of Wales, had a musical box especially made to play them. It is easy enough to mock them today – and certainly they include some that are simply sentimental; but in their time they were strikingly original. Benedict wrote of them:

> At the period [1832], mechanical dexterity, musical claptraps, skips from one part of the piano to another, endless shakes and arpeggios, were the order of the day; everything was sacrificed to display. Passages were written for the sole purpose of puzzling and perplexing the musical dilettanti, causing amazement by the immense quantity of notes compressed into one page. Mendelssohn, who would never sacrifice to the prevailing taste, took, in this new species of composition, quite an independent flight: his aim was to restore the ill-treated, panting pianoforte to its dignity and rank. . . . Long hence, when even the trace of the thundering pianoforte school shall have disappeared, the musician and amateur will recur with delight to these charming fruits of a refined and elevated taste.

Among these 'polite little pieces for the salon' are barcarolles, spinning songs, dirges, folk-songs and hunting songs. Many of them have been given titles (but mostly not by Felix):

for example, 'Sweet Remembrance', 'Spring Song', 'Consolation' and 'The Bee's Wedding'. When asked by one of his wife's relations what he had in mind while writing a wordless song, Felix replied:

> The song, just as it stands. Even if, in one or other of them, I had a particular word or words in mind, I would not want to tell anyone, because the same word means different things to different people. Only the song says the same thing, arouses the same feeling, in everyone – a feeling that can't be expressed in words.

*   *   *

But by far the most important contribution made by Felix at this time in the field of music was not by an original composition but by an act of piety. Even if he had never written a note of music, he would have earned the eternal gratitude of posterity by his resuscitation of Bach's *St Matthew Passion*. His staunch ally in this historic rescue operation was Eduard Devrient, who shared his enthusiasm for the work and longed to sing the part of Jesus in a public performance of it.

After his death in 1750, Bach had been remembered as a great organist; as a composer, however, he was generally thought of, even in Germany, as little more than a learned but arid pedant. During the second half of the eighteenth century only one of his complete works had been published, and such of his music as continued to be performed was for the most part instrumental rather than vocal. But after the year 1800 came signs of an awakening interest. Zelter, as we have already mentioned, introduced one or two of his motets and other lesser works into the repertoire of the Singakademie, where (wrote Devrient) 'they were performed as a curiosity and received as a piece of antiquarianism'. Schelble in Frankfurt also made his contribution; and some organ and clavier compositions, published at this time in England, aroused the enthusiasm of Samuel Wesley, who spoke of his hero as 'Saint Sebastian'. But most of Bach's compositions were hard to come by, and those who possessed manuscripts had to be cajoled into lending them or allowing them to be rented for copying.

Of one of the greatest of all Bach's choral works, the *St Matthew Passion*, there had not been a single public performance since Bach's death. In a sense it was hardly surprising, for this huge oratorio, with its double chorus and double orchestra, made enormous demands. But Felix, as he studied and restudied the score which had been given him by his grandmother in 1823, became more and more convinced that it ought to be heard again in Germany. During the winter of 1827 he assembled a small choir in the Mendelssohn house and rehearsed a few of the numbers from it. His excitement was infectious, and soon the singers were clamouring for more.

Yet the difficulties of a full-scale public performance seemed almost insuperable, and Felix was far from optimistic. Zelter, for all his interest in Bach in general, was a humanist who found the text of the Passions distasteful and was not at all inclined to help. Abraham and Lea both thought that their son might again be courting disaster, and Marx too, though a Bach enthusiast, was very doubtful of the wisdom of such a venture. Finally even Felix himself lost heart, and began to ridicule the whole thing: he would manage without an orchestra – just a rattle and a penny trumpet would do, and so on. But Devrient and one or two of his

OPPOSITE *Chrubini and his Muse. Oil painting by Ingres, 1836–42*

friends were still absolutely determined that the *St Matthew Passion* could, and should, be publicly performed.

One evening in January 1829, after a particularly moving rehearsal of the little choir, Devrient returned home to a sleepless night during which he made up his mind to take drastic action. As soon as it was light he hurried round to the Leipzigerstrasse, where Paul Mendelssohn told him that his brother was still asleep but that it was quite time to wake him. Felix was famous for his alleged deathlike sleep, and Devrient was now able to verify the truth of the legend; for though tugged, shaken and shouted at, several minutes passed before Felix finally opened a bleary eye and said, 'Why, *Ade*-ward!' – he always pronounced Devrient's Christian name with a Berlin drawl – 'Where on earth have you appeared from?'

Over breakfast Devrient explained his plan. The performance must be given at the Singakademie, with Felix conducting; Devrient would make himself responsible for the organization and would sing the part of Jesus; and finally, to silence all cavillers the proceeds would be given to charity. As for Zelter, both he and the Akademie owed Devrient some return for his eight years' cooperation at all their concerts, and this he would now claim. Zelter must be prevailed upon to make the hall of the Akademie available, and to use his influence to persuade the choir to sing for them.

They set off at once to beard Zelter in his den at the Akademie. But at the very door Felix faltered: he owed Zelter so much; he simply could not face a row with him. 'If he gets abusive,' he said, 'I shall go away. I can't quarrel with him.' 'Of course he will be abusive,' replied Devrient; 'but leave that to me.'

We knocked, and a loud, rough voice cried 'Come in!' We found the old giant in a thick cloud of tobacco smoke, a long pipe in his mouth, sitting at his old two-manualled instrument. His quill was in his hand, a sheet of music paper in front of him; he was wearing dun-coloured knee-breeches, thick woollen stockings and embroidered slippers. He raised his head, with its white hair combed back, turned his coarse and plebeian but manly features towards us and, recognizing us through his spectacles, said amiably in his broad accent, 'What's all this? What do two such fine young fellows want with me at this early hour? Here, sit down!'

Devrient began his carefully prepared speech, stressing that it was through Zelter himself that they had first come to know and love Bach. Zelter heard him out, then began to enumerate and enlarge upon difficulties of which they were only too well aware. Growing more and more excited, he now sprang to his feet and began striding up and down the room. Felix, convinced that the battle was already lost, seized Devrient by the sleeve and tried to drag him towards the door.

But Devrient was far from beaten. Ignoring the abuse with which Zelter kept on interrupting him, and the constant attempts of Felix to get him to leave, he patiently repeated his reasons for believing that, with Zelter's support, the project, though daring, was feasible. Zelter was now almost beside himself with rage, shouting that it was a piece of sheer impertinence for 'a couple of snotty-nosed boys [*Rotznasen*]' to imagine that they could succeed where far better men would inevitably fail.

Charles Kemble with the masks of Tragedy and Comedy. Oil painting by H. P. Briggs, 1832

ABOVE *The Singakademie, Berlin. Engraving after a drawing by Klose,* c. *1830*
OPPOSITE *Johann Sebastian Bach. Engraving by R. Bong*

Felix, his hand on the doorknob, looked pale and miserable, but Devrient had not yet finished. The angrier Zelter grew, the more calmly did he ply him with reasoned argument finally seasoned with judicious flattery. Then, quite suddenly, it became apparent that opposition was weakening, and soon the unbelievable had happened: Zelter had capitulated! 'Well, I'll say a good word for you when the time comes,' he said kindly as they left. 'Good luck to you! We'll see how things go.' His bark had always been very much worse than his bite.

In the hall, Felix, almost beside himself with joy, cried, 'Do you know, Eduard, you are a *scoundrel* and an *arch-Jesuit*?'

'Anything you like', replied Devrient, 'for the honour of Sebastian Bach.'

Suddenly every difficulty seemed to vanish. The choir of the Singakademie, which Zelter had predicted would gradually fade away as rehearsals proceeded, grew ever larger and ever more enthusiastic under Felix's inspired direction: they noticed, too, that he knew the work so intimately that he dispensed with a score; his musical memory was extraordinary. He and Devrient had long sessions together at which cuts were discussed and other decisions taken; and Devrient's joy knew no bounds when Felix said, 'What pleases me most about all this is that we are doing it *together*.'

Now came the engagement of the soloists, and the two friends settled to make the round together. 'Felix was child enough to insist on our being dressed exactly alike. We wore blue

coats, white waistcoats, black neckties, black trousers, and the yellow chamois-leather gloves that were then the fashion.' Devrient adds that he now had occasion to appreciate how, even at the age of twenty, Felix was ruled by his mother: 'His pocket-money having run out, I lent him a thaler to buy the gloves. His mother was annoyed with me for doing this, and said, "One oughtn't to encourage young people in their extravagance."'

While walking together they talked about the curious coincidence that a work last performed in 1729[1] should be revived exactly a hundred years later. 'And to think,' said Felix, 'that it should be an actor and a Jew who give back to the world the greatest of Christian works.' It was the only time that Devrient ever heard him refer to his Jewish descent; this was, however, a thing of which he never – unlike his sister Fanny and many German Jews – grew to be ashamed.

Devrient describes in detail the growing excitement in the cultural world of Berlin as the great day, 11 March, approached, for the choirs, three or four hundred strong, had passed the word round that the work was a revelation: that old Bach, that desiccated pedant, was after all capable of drama, passion and melodiousness; that here was 'an architectonic grandeur of structure' undreamed of by those familiar only with his smaller instrumental works. Zelter himself attended the orchestral rehearsals and even on occasion lent a hand, thus giving them the weight of his official approval.

[1] The *St Matthew Passion* had, in fact, been performed on at least three further occasions during Bach's lifetime, but not since his death.

Everything had gone so well that it seemed impossible that, on the day itself, the standard achieved during rehearsals could be surpassed. Yet it was. 'Never', wrote Devrient, 'have I known any performance so consecrated by one united sympathy. Our concert made an extraordinary sensation in the educated circles of Berlin.' More than a thousand people had been unable to get tickets, and two further performances which were called for followed almost immediately; Spontini spitefully tried to get these stopped, but Felix and Devrient outmanœuvred him by appealing direct to the Crown Prince. Incidentally, Spontini was almost the only person to accept the free tickets to which he was entitled, but which most people refused when a performance was given for charity. The last performance, in Holy Week, was conducted by Zelter, Felix having by that time left Berlin to pay his first visit to England.

On the day after the first performance Zelter had written to Goethe:

Our Bach music yesterday was a great success, and Felix showed himself a cool and collected conductor. The King and his whole Court were there, and the hall was completely full. I sat with my score in a corner near the orchestra, from where I could watch both my team and the audience. . . . If only old Bach could have heard our performance! That was what I felt at every place where it went really well; and here I cannot refrain from according the highest praise to my entire choir, the soloists, and the double orchestra. . . .

In Weimar, the eighty-year-old Goethe received the good news with joy: 'It is,' he wrote grandiloquently, 'as if I heard the roaring of the sea from afar.' They had succeeded where success seemed almost unattainable. How lucky Zelter was in his pupil! Of all his own pupils, not more than a handful had rewarded him thus. And later Berlioz was to write of the Bach-worship that soon became a cult in Germany, 'There is but one God – Bach, and Mendelssohn is his prophet.'

OPPOSITE *Mendelssohn sketching. Probably drawn by one of the Misses Taylor*

PART TWO
Travel 1829-1832

CHAPTER NINE

England 1829

At some time during the summer of 1828 Abraham Mendelssohn had come to the decision that in the following spring Felix should go abroad for several years to widen his outlook and to find himself as man and as artist. The young man was eager to go. Not only must he instinctively have felt that he was too closely bound – though with fetters of love – to his strong-minded and domineering parents; he also saw that Berlin was losing faith in him as a composer. The success of the cantata for the Dürer festival had been no more than a flash in the pan, and probably a smaller flash than Fanny had imagined, while Felix's preoccupation at that time with Bach, though it had led to a signal triumph, made many people begin to believe that he was at heart a scholar and antiquarian rather than a truly creative artist.

A poem, written by Felix rather earlier than this but in a mood which now recurred, describes his periodic irritation at the way in which his works were sometimes received by the critics. Sir George Grove's translation of it is neat, though some of the pithiness of the original is inevitably lost:

> If the artist gravely writes,
>   To sleep it will beguile.
> If the artist gaily writes,
>   It is a vulgar style.
>
> If the artist simply writes,
>   A fool he's said to be.
> If an artist deeply writes,
>   He's mad: 'tis plain to see.
>
> If the artist writes at length,
>   How sad his hearer's lot!
> If the artist briefly writes,
>   No man will care one jot.
>
> In whatsoever way he writes,
>   He can't please everyman.
> Therefore let an artist write
>   How he likes and can.

The fortunate preservation of a letter written by Felix on 18 October 1828 to a Berlin conductor named L. A. Ganz is more immediately informative:

... You asked me the other day to let you perform my *Calm Sea and Prosperous Voyage* at your concert, and at the time I was so surprised by this flattering and agreeable proposal that I overlooked all the objections and obstacles involved. ... On thinking it over, however, I saw at once how difficult it would be. ... It is a long time since the public has had any important composition from me (a couple of hastily written cantatas cannot be taken into account), nor have I played the piano or shown myself as a composer; and so I have gradually slipped into oblivion, and want to remain in it until after my great journey.

People are tired of me, and in some respects I can't blame them; so I would rather wait until I come back fresh from abroad before I show myself to them again. At the moment they would only overlook my successes and blame me for my failures. ... Meanwhile the orchestra has, to say the least of it, behaved in such an unfriendly way to me that I daren't come forward again as their leader; and naturally I don't want to entrust my overture to anyone else, for as my latest composition it is very dear to me. I was very upset when I heard that the King's band has refused to let me conduct it in public. ...

This letter – which refers largely to troubles, part real and perhaps part imagined, of which we know nothing – was of course written several months before Zelter had agreed to a performance of the *St Matthew Passion*, and no doubt at a moment when Felix was feeling particularly low; for his was far from the unbroken sunny disposition that his earlier biographers liked to maintain. So the plan for Felix to travel was a very sensible one. Moscheles, consulted by Abraham Mendelssohn as to whether his son should begin his grand tour with Vienna or London, favoured the latter. 'I thought and believed that the young man was a genius, so I advised that he should come to us [in London] at Easter, and promised faithfully to introduce him to the great London world.'

At this point in his volume of recollections of Felix, Devrient pauses to sum up the appearance and character of his friend. What he tells us is of especial value because, devoted though he was to Felix, he was far from blind to his faults. Of his appearance he writes:

His features, of the Oriental type, were handsome: a high, intellectual, and strongly receding forehead; large, expressive dark eyes with drooping lids and a peculiar veiled glance through the lashes which sometimes flashed distrust or anger, sometimes happy dreaminess and expectancy. His nose was arched and of delicate form, still more so the mouth, with its short upper and full under lip, which was slightly protruding and hid his teeth when, with a slight lisp, he pronounced the hissing consonants. An extreme mobility about his mouth betrayed every emotion that passed within.

He had not lost his boyhood habit of gently rocking his head and the upper part of his body from side to side, and of shifting his weight from one foot to the other. He would throw back his head, especially when playing the piano, and one could always tell by the way he nodded and shook it whether or not he liked anything new that he heard others play. He was already outgrowing, and soon entirely lost, his former shyness.

There was something almost 'religious and patriarchal' in his veneration of his father, and he was devoted to his two sisters. With Fanny he had of course most in common, but Rebecka was much the prettier. He once told her, in a letter, that if she ceased to exist he would not write any more music. She was intelligent and had a nice sense of humour. The strange picture of walruses and medieval warriors painted in an album that he gave her seems to illustrate some esoteric joke that cannot be interpreted today. Paul is dismissed by Devrient as being 'still somewhat divided from [Felix] by disparity of age', and of Lea, surprisingly, he makes no further mention. It is possible that he did not approve of the way she dominated Felix.

Of Felix's highly strung nature he says, 'When anything excited him he would become completely overwrought, and nothing but profound, deathlike sleep could restore him to his senses. This never failed. He used to tell me that he had only to find himself alone and unoccupied in a room with a sofa in it, for him immediately to fall asleep.' Devrient attributed his hypersensibility to years of overwork, and 'often doubted whether his nervous system could possibly survive the strain for a normal life-span'. But as the result of his mother's upbringing Felix was incapable of relaxation or idleness, and sometimes gave offence by repeatedly looking at his watch when cornered in an unprofitable conversation.

To his friends, wrote Devrient, he was 'completely devoted and exquisitely tender; it was, indeed, a happiness to be loved by Felix.' But

he loved only in the measure as he was loved. . . . To receive his music with coldness or aversion was to be his enemy, and he was capable of denying genuine merit in anyone who did so. A solecism, an expression that displeased him, could alienate him altogether, and he could then be disagreeable, even absolutely intolerable. For example, he simply could not stand a certain highly talented musician named Bernhard Klein just because, many years back, when sitting next to Klein in a box at the opera on a chair too high for him, Klein had muttered impatiently, 'Can't the child stop dangling his feet!'

Devrient knew Felix well enough to tease him about such things, but it did no good: 'His irritability, his distrustfulness even towards his most intimate friends, were sometimes quite incredible. A casual remark or silly little joke that he would normally have taken from me in good part would sometimes suddenly make him lower his eyelids, look suspiciously at me and ask doubtfully, "What do you mean by that?", "Now I want to know what you wish me to understand by this?" and so on, and it was difficult to restore his good humour.' Those who loved him and knew him well forgave him; but others took offence, and he thus made enemies.

These defects of character were easily outweighed by his many virtues. He would put himself to endless trouble to help a friend or even a chance acquaintance, and, like all his family, he was enormously philanthropic. When a young composer asked for his opinion he would first praise all that was praiseworthy and only then, with infinite tact, offer criticism. Where his own compositions were concerned, he never gave the world anything less than his best; and he was in the fortunate position of never having any temptation to pot-boil. He would delay publication of his works until constant revision had made them as perfect as possible, often being heard to say that he had 'a tremendous reverence for print'. With his good looks, exquisite manners and social gifts it would have been only too easy for him to have become no more than a society pianist, a drawing-room idol; but a fundamental seriousness, and perhaps also the warning of the young Liszt, saved him from such a fate.

Though it was of course principally music that took Felix to London, the presence there of his old friends Klingemann and Moscheles made the prospect doubly agreeable. He also intended to mix pleasure and sightseeing with business, and to include a visit to Scotland with Klingemann when the London season was over. Klingemann, an excellent correspondent, had written constantly to the Mendelssohns describing his experiences. London, he said, was far too large – 'I told them so at once, but they take no notice.' His front teeth ached from trying to pronounce the English 'th', his back teeth from trying to masticate English mutton. He was amazed by the vastness of English whiskers and the smallness of English oysters; by the beauty of the schoolgirls who crocodiled endlessly through Regent's Park under the watchful, disapproving eyes of their 'ayahs'; by the beauty even of the house-maids, one of whom astonished him by her knowledge of the works of Kant. He was fascinated by the stage-coaches 'on which the passengers clung like wasps on a sweet pear', and depressed by the unimaginable gloom of English Sundays and English fogs.

Klingemann went several times to the opera and to concerts and reported his experiences to the family in Berlin. It was quite touching, he said, to see what a stomach the English had for listening to music. (Wagner once wrote that the Philharmonic concerts in London reminded him of the cry of the London bus conductors, 'Full up inside!'). But it was *un-critical* listening, for 'like ostriches they swallow pebbles or sweetmeats, whichever they happen to be offered. And everything is so *long*! I really think Beethoven must have been an Englishman.' He was now screwing up his courage to hear an *English* opera, and this was the recipe for making one:

> About 1790 somebody writes a libretto, and a Mr Storace sets it to music. . . . Now the opera is brought out again, remodelled by a new poet and given a new overture by Mr Cooke. Somebody else – I forget his name – writes airs for it, except those that Braham[1] is to sing; these he composes himself. The *prima donna*, Mme Féron, brings her part from Italy, written by Mercadante or some other Italian, and to this is added a Neapolitan song with variations; the rest of the music is what Storace wrote in the first place. This piece – or rather, piecemeal – was originally called *The Pirate*; it is now having a huge success as *Isodore de Merida, or the Devil's Creek*.

In short, Klingemann simply cannot wait to show his friend this enormous, extraordinary city and its charmingly absurd inhabitants.

Mendelssohn left Berlin on 10 April, his father and Rebecka accompanying him as far as Hamburg. The crossing proved regrettably unlike his *Calm Sea and Prosperous Voyage*; it was very rough and very foggy, and he was extremely sick. Then something went wrong with the ship's engines. But at last, on the morning of 21 April, the *Attwood* finally steamed up the Thames estuary to London. As he was ten hours late there was no one to meet him, so he made his way to the lodgings that Moscheles had booked for him in the house of a German ironmonger in (Great) Portland Street – a stone's throw from Nash's newly erected All Souls' Church, still at that time the butt of many caricaturists.

He wrote at once to Berlin to report his safe arrival, and during the months that followed he kept his family regularly informed of his doings. London, he told them, was alarming: London was crazy! It was 'the grandest and most complicated monster on the face of the earth'; he was echoing Heine, who two years earlier had called it 'the most astounding thing that the world can show the amazed mind of man'. There was Nash's Regent Street – wide, bright, arcaded ('but alas! enveloped today in a thick fog'). There were shops with signboards as big as a man, and stage-coaches that looked ready to burst. There were sandwichmen advertising performing cats; there were beggars, and Negroes, and fat John Bulls with their

---

[1] John Braham (1777–1856), famous tenor and composer.

slender, beautiful daughters on their arms. Oh, those daughters! But his parents need not be apprensive. He was, he admitted, constantly in grave danger – but not from the girls; only from the traffic, which was terrifying.

At that time, says Werner, opera in England was 'almost exclusively, and symphonic music for the most part, the domain of the aristocracy and of the developing *upper* middle classes'; and in spite of Weber and Spohr, opera generally meant Italian composers and Italian guest artists. The lower middle classes preferred oratorio, glee-clubs and church music. Instrumental music was dominated by Germans. Patronage was more important than talent, and pyrotechnics than solid worth.

His very first evening, exhausted though he was, Mendelssohn went to the King's Theatre to hear the great Malibran in Rossini's *Otello* – an opera famous in its day but now rarely if ever staged. He was as overwhelmed by her beauty as by her singing; indeed, Felix's letters home were soon so full of her praise that Abraham became concerned. But the Otello (Donselli) ranted, forced his voice and was always sharp, and among the rest of the cast were the inevitable 'beer-bass' and 'semi-beer-tenor'. An interminable ballet followed the second act. Mendelssohn, though half dead with fatigue and half suffocated by the pomades and perfumes of the ladies in the audience, stuck the opera out to its close, which came at a quarter to one, 'when Malibran was dispatched, gasping and screaming disgustingly', but could not face another ballet, *La Sonnambula*, which was still to come. Certainly Klingemann was right: the English musical appetite was insatiable.

London life suited Mendelssohn admirably, and he thought the town very beautiful. He drove in an open carriage to the City, and with Mme Moscheles, who was kindness itself, in Hyde Park. He attended a debate in Parliament and was much impressed. He visited Dr

OPPOSITE *The dressing-case used by Mendelssohn on his travels*   BELOW *His toothbrush and container*

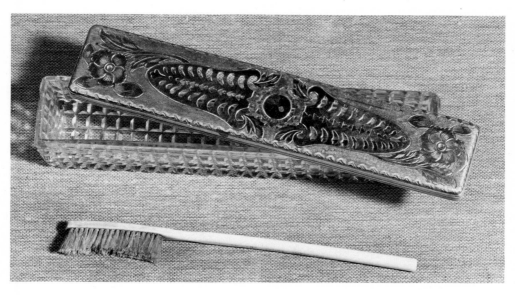

Spurzheim's phrenological cabinet where he was shown sets of plaster casts of heads of famous musicians and famous murderers, placed side by side for comparison, and considered that the musicians came well out of it. Then his own bumps were examined and he was pronounced covetous, methodical, flirtatious, fond of small children and, principally and inevitably, of music.

It was, as we have said, music that had brought Mendelssohn to London, and it is important to remember the status of the professional musician, who was at that time only just beginning to rise from the position of a servant (and usually a very ill-paid one) to that of a guest fit to circulate freely among those he was being paid to entertain. Everyone knows how Mozart was obliged to dine in the servants' hall while his patron the Archbishop of Salzburg dined in state, and that sheer poverty was largely responsible for his early death. Baron Max von Weber in his biography of his father (who visited England in 1826) wrote:

> The artist invited to a house bought a position for himself by his talent, but not in real social circles; the honourable diploma of his God-given genius did not suffice there to make him worthy to tread the same floor with the latest-created baronet. His performance was just one more among others. . . . He performed, was paid, and then had to leave without being regarded as one of the guests of the house. The insolent lackeys served him differently from the 'guests', and would have blushed at the idea of offering him refreshments in the drawing-room. His host greeted him condescendingly and pointed out to him a place, which in many salons was separated by a cord from that of the guests. . . .

Liszt was not exaggerating when he wrote, 'In the aristocratic houses of London, artists of the first rank, such as Moscheles, Rubini, Lafont, Pasta, Malibran, and others are forced to enter by the service stairs'; and the violinist Lafont used to recall how on one occasion the Duke of —— stopped him in full flight with a tap on the shoulder and a 'C'est assez, mon cher!' Liszt himself was among the first to break down these degrading barriers and to attempt to exact common politeness from arrogant audiences; and anyone who has ever had to perform in drawing-rooms will recall with pleasure his famous snub to Tsar Nicholas I, who began to talk while he was playing. Liszt stopped, and the Tsar asked him why he had done so. 'When Nicholas speaks,' replied Liszt, 'Music herself must be silent.'

But Mendelssohn was no common itinerant musician, eager to snatch at any adequately paid engagement that was offered him and ready to swallow such humiliations as might be deemed a part of the contract. The powerful letters of introduction with which he had been provided immediately gave him the entrée into the greatest houses in London. In fact, it might almost be said that he had come to England as a distinguished foreigner who happened to be a musician, rather than as a professional artist: a 'gentleman' rather than a 'player'. He was well educated and well mannered; he was handsome, elegant and witty; he could dance and he could ride; he could even speak tolerable English, and he was rich enough to be forgiven his Jewish blood. Most astonishing of all, when he played in drawing-rooms he refused a fee!

So Mendelssohn joined in the London season and was sought after by the most fashionable hostesses. There was a memorable ball at Devonshire House at which the Duke of Wellington and Sir Robert Peel were present, as well as quantities of dowagers half smothered in diamonds and chaperoning daughters 'of quite celestial beauty'. Titians, Correggios and Van Dycks hung on the walls, and the principal ballroom was lit by hundreds of little lamps attached to a suspended fourteen-foot wreath of red roses; 'there was nothing anywhere that was not in perfect taste'. Then came a ball given by Lord Lansdowne, who received his guests in his sculpture gallery, 'a large vaulted room with a rotunda in which were crimson niches each containing a large grey antique frowning statue'; his latest (and very expensive) purchase, 'Seaport'[1] by Claude, was proudly displayed in an adjoining room.

The arrangements for Mendelssohn's first public appearance in London went by no means as smoothly as Sebastian Hensel would have us believe. Sir George Smart, principal conductor

---

[1] Now in the collection of the Viscountess Mersey, and condemned by Marcel Röthlisberger as an 'old, simplified, small, and rather coarse copy'.

Devonshire House, c. *1800*

of the Philharmonic Society's concerts, had met Mendelssohn in Berlin in 1825, heard him play, and had enjoyed an 'excellent tea and fishy supper' at his parents' house. He had then come to the conclusion that the boy made music 'only for fun'; he therefore now used every kind of delaying tactic to postpone, and hopefully to prevent, his being engaged. Eventually this misunderstanding was cleared up, and on 25 May Mendelssohn made his musical bow to the English public at a concert of the Philharmonic Society in the Argyll Rooms in Regent Street (which a year later were to be burnt to the ground). 'Old' Johann Baptist Cramer, a German musician still in his fifties, led him on to the stage 'as if he had been a young lady' to conduct his C minor Symphony, composed at the age of fifteen, in which he substituted for the minuet an elegantly orchestrated version of the lovely scherzo from his Octet for Strings; 'I added some jolly D-trumpets to it,' he wrote. 'It was very silly, but it sounded very nice.' The work was received with tremendous enthusiasm, and though he refused to encore the adagio he was finally obliged to repeat the scherzo. This triumph 'lifted a stone from his heart', and he dedicated the symphony to the Society, of which he was soon afterwards made an honorary member.

A few days later, dressed (he tells Rebecka, who loved to hear about clothes) 'in *grande toilette*: very long white trousers, brown silk waistcoat, black necktie and blue morning coat', he played by heart (which at that time was most unusual) Weber's very exacting *Conzertstück* at a matinée in the Argyll Rooms, again to great applause and a subsequent flattering review

LEFT *Henriette Sontag. Lithograph by I. Becker, 1828*   RIGHT *Malibran. Lithograph, 1830*

in *The Times* and a remarkably silly one in the *Literary Gazette* (6 June): 'A German gentle-man – with a long Christian name, too long for any Christian to pronounce with impunity . . . performed on the piano a piece termed on the card a "concert-stück". The pianist, however, never once *stuck* in his performance . . .'.[1]

After the concert came a dinner at which Mendelssohn tells us he became intoxicated – 'but only', he hastens to add, 'from the effect of a wonderful pair of brown eyes'. So *exalté* was he, his head so bursting with musical ideas, that he walked home singing at the top of his voice. Presumably he was staying with friends – perhaps with the Moscheles, who spoke of the rural 'solitude' in which they lived – for he mentions that he took 'a lonely path through meadows and met nobody'.

Other concerts followed. On 24 June he conducted his *A Midsummer Night's Dream* Overture and played the solo part in the first performance in England of the Piano Concerto in E flat by Beethoven, who had died two years earlier. On the way home from the concert, Thomas Attwood, a trumpet-playing coal-merchant's son who had sat at Mozart's feet and risen from them to become organist of St Paul's, left the score of the overture in a hackney-cab; it was never recovered, but Mendelssohn was able to rewrite it from memory in time for a charity concert in aid of the flood victims in Silesia and Danzig.

This concert had originally been proposed by the famous Berlin *prima donna* Henriette Sontag, Malibran's rival who was also singing in London at that moment. She had invited

[1] Quoted by Marek.

Mendelssohn, known to her already from Berlin days, to support her; but her plan had come to nothing – allegedly because of the malevolence of Smart, whom Mendelssohn denounced as 'intriguing, deceitful, and a liar'.[1] Mendelssohn now entered the lists on his own, and after some effective string-pulling triumphed. Various distinguished artists, Sontag of course among them, agreed to give their services free.

Though the season was almost over, so great was the demand for tickets that the Argyll Rooms, also offered without charge, were filled to bursting-point and many people had to be turned away. 'Ladies peeped out from behind the double basses when I came on the platform. The Johnston ladies, who had strayed between the bassoons and the French horns, sent to ask me *whether they were likely to hear well*; and one woman sat on the kettle-drum.' In addition to *A Midsummer Night's Dream* Overture the concert, which was of course intolerably long, included Mendelssohn's juvenile Concerto in E for two pianos, played by Moscheles and himself. The charity benefited by nearly three hundred guineas – a remarkable achievement in view of the extent of the poverty at that time in England itself.

Two odd events of this London visit deserve to be recorded. The first was an invitation from the Governor of Ceylon, Sir Alexander Johnston, to compose a festival song to be performed there annually on the anniversary of 'the emancipation of the natives'. 'It really is crazy,' Mendelssohn wrote. 'I haven't stopped laughing for two whole days.' The other was a performance of *Hamlet* with Charles Kemble in the title-role – a production that, as a whole, seemed to him 'quite mad'. Mendelssohn, as we have already seen, knew his Shakespeare well and firmly believed that the English often failed to understand him; he now found support for his theory:

> [Hamlet's] appearing, for instance, with one yellow and one black leg to indicate madness, his falling on his knee before the ghost in order to strike an attitude, his ejaculation at the end of every little phrase in that well-known applause-exacting high tone of his, his behaving altogether like a John Bull Oxford student and not like a Danish Crown Prince – all that might pass. But that he should completely ignore poor Shakespeare's meaning regarding the proposed death of the king, and therefore coolly skip that scene where the king prays and Hamlet comes in and goes out again without having made up his mind to the deed (for me one of the finest passages in the play), and that he constantly behaves like a bravado, treating the king in such a manner that he deserves to be shot down at once [he gives examples] . . . these things are unpardonable.

The English might like their music in large doses; but they seemed to prefer their Shakespeare in more modest quantities, and Mendelssohn thought that another tragedy might really have been made out of what had been recklessly cut or abridged. The climax of bad taste was reached when, after Hamlet's dying words 'the rest is silence', instead of the expected flourish of trumpets and entrance of Fortinbras, Horatio left Hamlet's side and, advancing to the footlights, announced, 'Ladies and gentlemen, tomorrow evening *The Devil's Elixir*.' Really, Mendelssohn reflected as he left the theatre, there was sadly little poetry in England.

Of other extraordinary conditions then prevailing in the English theatres Mendelssohn makes no mention; but the Austrian playwright Grillparzer, who saw Kemble in *Julius Caesar* a few years later, wrote of the indescribable chaos that ensued when the 'half-pricers'

---

[1] From an unpublished part of a letter, quoted by Werner.

were admitted at half past eight. The theatre was then 'literally stormed. Doors of boxes torn off, a cold blast piercing the hot air. No chance of driving the interlopers away. They clambered on to the benches behind the backs of the people who had seats. Prostitutes forced their way through every loop-hole. The chatter never stopped, and there was some fighting.'

Perhaps there were moments when English insensitivity made Mendelssohn feel rather homesick. He spent much time with his German friends, and one evening, as he was walking home with two of them from 'a highly diplomatic dinner-party' at the Prussian Embassy, he came upon 'an irresistibly enticing sausage shop in which "German sausages, twopence each" were displayed for sale. Patriotism overcome us. Each of us bought a long sausage and, turning into Portland Street which was quieter, we there consumed our purchases, Rosen and I laughing so much that we could hardly join in some three-part songs with Mühlenfels singing the bass.' This Rosen was an able and charming young German who had recently been appointed Professor of Oriental Languages at University College, London; always delicate, he died when only thirty-two, and some years later Klingemann married his much younger half-sister.

Rosen, Klingemann and Mendelssohn formed an inseparable trio – like the three leaflets of a clover, someone said; but Mendelssohn found no greater or more loyal friend in London than Moscheles, who wrote in his diary that he had enjoyed 'the greatest happiness' in making music with him:

> It is absolutely delightful when he brings some of his new compositions and after playing them waits with childlike modesty for my opinion of them. Anyone else would long since have realized that I consider him my master . . . but, do what I can, he still insists upon looking on me as his teacher. The brilliant success of his *Midsummer Night's Dream* overture hasn't turned his head a bit . . . and when I praise him he merely answers, 'Do *you* like it? Well, that makes me *really* happy.'

Mendelssohn by J. W. Childe, 1829. The twenty-year-old composer was painted at the time of his first visit to London

CHAPTER TEN

Scotland and Wales 1829

On 23 June Mendelssohn told Zelter, 'Music here is coming to an end; nobody is going to concerts, and the theatres are shut. . . . There is a general exodus from the city.' He was, he wrote, about to leave for Scotland, where 'the bagpipes and the echoes are said to be quite extraordinary' and where he expected to be stimulated to composition. But almost another month was in fact to pass before he and Klingemann set out for Edinburgh and, as we have already seen, his two successful concerts on 24 June and 13 July proved the season to have been far from over.

The two young Germans reached Edinburgh on 28 July, a Sunday, and managed to crowd a good deal into the three days they spent there. Mendelssohn thought the view from Arthur's Seat incomparable, and he was not forgetting Switzerland. 'When God Himself takes to panorama-painting the result is strangely beautiful. . . . Everything here looks so stern and robust, half-enveloped in haze or smoke or fog.' He admired the men 'with their long red beards, tartan plaids, bonnets and plumes, bare knees, and their bagpipes in their hands', as they came out of church, 'exultantly escorting their girls in their Sunday best and proudly gazing round'. He attended a bagpipe competition which, from something he wrote later, it may be assumed he found an excruciating experience.[1] He bathed in the sea. He saw Holyrood 'where Queen Mary lived and loved', and in the ruined chapel where she had been crowned Queen of Scotland found the inspiration for his 'Scottish' Symphony, which was not to be completed until thirteen years later.

And of course he made the almost obligatory pilgrimage to Abbotsford, the home of Sir Walter Scott who with his *Waverley* – described by Goethe as one of the greatest books ever written – had made Scotland the Mecca of the Romantics. This proved a disappointment. Klingemann sent the Mendelssohns in Berlin a facetious and purely fictitious account of their wonderful reception by Scott, to which Mendelssohn appended a factual postscript: 'Klingemann has made all this up. We found Sir Walter just leaving Abbotsford, gaped at him like imbeciles, drove eighty miles and lost a whole day for the sake of nothing more than half-an-hour's trivial conversation. Even Melrose Abbey was not much compensation. . . .'

Their plan was to travel north through Stirling and Perth to Blair Atholl, then westwards

[1] A Scottish friend, to tease him, put bagpipes into a farewell piece in his album.

Durham Cathedral. Watercolour by Mendelssohn after a pencil drawing made by him at Durham in 1829

to the Inner Hebrides and back up the Clyde to Glasgow. Mendelssohn was fascinated by the Scottish landscape: its rocks and waterfalls, its rivers and lovely valleys, its sombre woods and endless stretches of pink heather. Sometimes they drove; sometimes they walked for miles, stopping now and then for Mendelssohn to sketch and Klingemann to compose a poem to accompany his drawing. Then the heavens opened, with 'earth and sky soaked through, and whole regiments of clouds still on the march'. On the evening of 3 August Mendelssohn reported to his family from a Highland inn at the Bridge of Tummel. The storm was still howling and raging, doors banging and shutters bursting open; you couldn't tell how much of the sound of rushing water came from the sky, how much from the mountain torrent. They were sitting by the fireside, Scottish clogs on their feet, in a large bare damp room whose floorboards were so thin that drunken singing and laughter and a flood of unintelligible Gaelic surged up from the ground-floor rooms where the servants were. Tea with honey and potato cakes had been brought them, with whisky to follow, and two beds with crimson curtains awaited them. Like many a traveller in a foreign land Mendelssohn chose to read himself to sleep that night with a favourite book in his own language: Jean Paul's *Flegeljahre*, or 'Salad Days'.

Their principal objective in the Hebrides was Fingal's Cave on the island of Staffa – discovered by Joseph Banks in 1782, named by the islanders after the hero of Gaelic mytho-

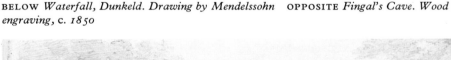

BELOW *Waterfall, Dunkeld. Drawing by Mendelssohn* OPPOSITE *Fingal's Cave. Wood engraving, c. 1850*

logy, and in the nineteenth century so great a tourist attraction that Wordsworth, who visited it in 1833, lamented that though he *saw* it he was able to *feel* nothing because of the swarm of trippers. Everyone went there: Scott of course, Turner, Heine, Queen Victoria and the Prince Consort, and Sir Robert Peel who described it as 'the temple not made with hands'. The cave, according to the way you looked at it, was Gothic architecture as well as classical architecture: 'It was romantic, classical, natural all at once – a cave-cathedral "placed far amid the melancholy main".'

Both Klingemann and Mendelssohn wrote on 7 August 'from the Hebrides', and both again and more fully on their return to Glasgow. Klingemann is our livelier correspondent, describing amusingly the shocking sea journey from Oban during which he proved himself a better sailor than his friend, and a dreadful night on board when they were so tightly packed that the flies he tried to brush from his face turned out to be the grizzly locks of an ancient hirsute Scot sleeping at his side. He was fascinated by an intrepid old woman who was determined to see the cave before she died, and who had to be hoisted in and out of the little rowing-boats in which they were 'lifted by the hissing sea up the pillar stumps to the celebrated Fingal's Cave'. 'A greener roar of waves,' he wrote, 'surely never surged into a stranger cavern, whose many pillars made it look like the inside of an immense organ, black and resonant, utterly without purpose, completely isolated.'

Unlike Wordsworth, Mendelssohn was able to forget the presence of his fellow sightseers. He told his family, 'In order to make you understand how extraordinarily the Hebrides affected me, I send you the following which came into my head there.' This was the sketch of the opening bars of what is generally agreed to be Mendelssohn's finest work: his *Hebrides* Overture, popularly known as *Fingal's Cave*.[1] The first subject, a haunting little two-bar descending tune, a pre-Wagner Wagnerian 'motif' which had come to him so pat as he heard the waves hurl themselves against the rocky Hebridean shore, must be familiar to all but the tone-deaf. The development of it germinated slowly, and it was not until December of the following year that he completed in Rome his first version of the overture. But for a long time to come he was to be far from satisfied with it. Writing more than a year later from Paris he told Fanny that he could not perform the work there because he did not consider it ready: 'The D major middle section is very silly, and the whole so-called development smacks more of counterpoint than of whale-oil and seagulls and cod-liver oil; it ought to be just the other way round.' Not till November 1833 was he certain that 'by *threefold revisions*' he had made it as perfect as he could.

The *Hebrides* Overture is by any standards a magnificent work and in its day revolutionary; for many years to come, few composers of water music could escape its influence (one has only to recall the storm in Wagner's *Flying Dutchman*, or Smetana's *Moldau*), and constant repetition has not staled it. It is as bracing as a weekend by the sea; it brings, wrote Heinrich Jacob, 'the perils of nature straight into the concert hall'. Surging waves pound the shore, breaking further and further up against the rocks; the wind howls and the gulls shriek, and those possessed of ornithological knowledge or the ears of faith can further identify 'the gliding of great albatrosses and the forlorn twittering of a much smaller bird, performed by clarinets and flute'. Then a shaft of sunlight pierces the cloud.

This tone poem is for music what the works of Turner and Constable were for painting: an anticipation of Impressionism. Wagner, who was far from blind to Mendelssohn's weaknesses, called him 'a first-class landscape-painter', adding that this was his masterpiece: 'The passage where the oboes rise alone, wailing through the other instruments like the wind above the waves of the sea, is of an extraordinary beauty.' Brahms went still further: 'I would gladly,' he said, 'give all I have written, to have composed something like the *Hebrides* Overture.'

When it was first heard in London the overture was an instant success; indeed this tribute paid by a German to the beauty and splendour of Scottish scenery was such as to make him seem almost a British composer. Shakespeare (thought the Germans) was a spiritual German; Mendelssohn (thought the English) had, like Handel, become one of themselves. Had his name chanced, like *Händel*'s, to carry an *umlaut*, the English would undoubtedly have paid him their highest compliment by depriving him of it; they did the next best thing by pronouncing it 'Mendleson'.

From Glasgow the two travellers made an expedition to Loch Lomond, on which their boat nearly capsized and in whose only inn they endured unspeakable squalor; then on 19 August they turned their faces to the south. 'We flew away from Glasgow at ten miles an hour on the top of the mail,' wrote Mendelssohn, 'past steaming meadows and smoking chimneys to the

[1] The opening bars were in fact jotted down shortly *before* he reached the cave.

Cumberland Lakes, to Keswick and Kendal and the prettiest towns and villages. The whole countryside is like a drawing-room, the rocky walls papered with bushes, moss and firs and the trees neatly wrapped up in ivy.' At Liverpool they parted company, Klingemann, whose leave was up, returning to London. Mendelssohn, after a trip at the 'crazy speed' of fifteen miles per hour in a truck on the new and as yet unopened Liverpool to Manchester Railway, headed for Wales with the intention of paying a brief visit to Ireland before going to stay with friends near Holywell. But wind and rain, with the prospect of a very nasty crossing, made him decide to give Ireland a miss.

He did not much care for his first view of the Welsh, and still less for their music. Though Zelter had urged him to collect folk-songs, Scotland had soured his taste for homespun music, and from his inn at Llangollen he wrote:

> Ten thousand devils take all national music! Here I am in Wales, and, heaven help us! a harper sits in the hall of every reputable tavern incessantly playing so-called folk melodies – that is to say, dreadful, vulgar, out-of-tune trash with a hurdy-gurdy going at *the same time*! It has given me toothache already. Scotch bagpipes, Swiss cow-horns, Welsh harps – all playing the Huntsmen's Chorus with hideously improvised variations. . . . It's unspeakable. Anyone who, like myself, can't stand Beethoven's national songs ought to come to Wales and hear them bellowed by rough nasal voices to the crudest accompaniment – and then try to keep his temper. As I write, a fellow in the hall is playing this [here follows a silly little tune]. . . . It's making me so angry that I can't go on.

But next day he made a double discovery: that there was a piano in the house, and that the innkeeper had three very pretty daughters who played on it. After an evening of music-making with them he began to feel much more sympathetic towards the Welsh.

The climax of Mendelssohn's first visit to Britain was the week that he spent with the Taylors at Coed Du, near Holywell. He had met John Taylor, a rich mine-owner, in London, and the glimpse he had then had of his three young daughters – Susan, Honoria and Anne –

Telford's suspension bridge at Conway. Pencil drawing by Mendelssohn, 26 August 1829

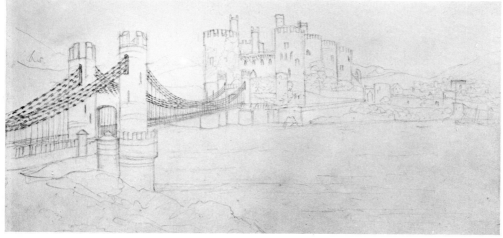

Coed Du, near Mold, Flintshire. Probably drawn by one of the Taylor family

had made him only too eager to accept an invitation to break his journey from Scotland at their house in Wales.

Mendelssohn's letters paint an idyllic scene of happy family life in a country house in one of the most beautiful parts of Wales. There was a small house-party, and the presence among the guests of 'three long, withered, ugly, spiteful cousins from Ireland – ancient spinsters dressed in short green skirts and incessantly whispering together', merely provided an additional source of entertainment for the young. There were picnics, sketching-parties, riding, romping, dancing, the descent into a lead-mine, plenty of music-making, and also a tour of several days, made with a young cousin of the house, through north Wales as far as Carnarvon and Snowdonia. Susan, who could draw figures nicely, added little Highlanders to enliven Mendelssohn's Scottish landscapes, and she and her sisters ('with whom I do nothing but flirt – and that in English!') plied him with bunches of flowers, begging him to 'set them to music'. 'I owe three of my best piano pieces to them', he wrote.

These were three fantasies (op. 16): Andante and Allegro in A minor, Capriccio in E minor, and Andante in E major ('The Rivulet'). The first, inspired by a handful of carnations and a rose, had arpeggios intended to suggest 'the rising scent of the flowers'. The capriccio he owed to the youngest daughter, who came to him with sprays of 'little yellow bell-like flowers in her hair, assuring me that they were trumpets'. He drew the plant in the margin of his composition, and it appears to be a species of *Eccremocarpus*, a very recent introduction from western South America; John Taylor must have been a very keen horticulturist to have acquired it within four or five years of its reaching England.

Many years later Anne recalled Mendelssohn's visit and her gradual discovery (for news of his recent successes in London had not reached the wilds of Coed Du) that she and her sisters had been entertaining an angel – a musical genius – unawares. She mentions that his English vocabulary was charmingly individual, that he spoke with a slight lisp, and that when nodding his head in approval of something his long dark hair flopped down over his forehead. As for Mendelssohn, he treasured 'the flowery memory' of those happy innocent days for the rest of his life, and never failed to look the Taylors up if they happened to be in London when he came to England.

In the middle of September, just as he was about to leave London for Berlin to attend his sister Fanny's wedding on 3 October, Mendelssohn had a carriage accident in which his leg was badly injured. He was in bed for nearly two months, devotedly tended by Klingemann and visited and quite spoiled by his innumerable English friends. There followed a fortnight's recuperation with the Attwoods at Norwood, where he found among other musical treasures a full score of Weber's *Euryanthe*. 'It's lovely music,' he wrote; 'and isn't it odd that I should be studying Weber's favourite work here in England, where nobody knows it or can know it, where they treated him so badly, and where he died [in 1826].'

Incidentally, in writing that Weber was treated so badly in England, Mendelssohn was not being quite fair; he was treated no worse than any other distinguished visiting artist at that time except Mendelssohn himself. Weber, a very sick man, had come against medical advice to London because he had signed a highly profitable contract with Kemble for his new opera, *Oberon*. Though living almost cost-free as the guest of Sir George Smart (who must have been far less black than Mendelssohn imagined), on the rare occasions when he had to pay for his dinner he grumbled fiercely at the high prices of London restaurants, telling his

Capriccio in E minor composed by Mendelssohn for Anne Taylor and decorated with 'little yellow bell-like flowers'

wife that the only thing cheaper in England than in Germany was having one's hair cut –
which, Ernest Newman suggests, may perhaps account for the traditional long hair of the
German musician then and later.

By the end of November Mendelssohn was well enough to return home. The many kind-
nesses he had received in England had made a deep impression on him, and from Calais he
wrote: 'So England lies behind me and my visit is at an end. It is a beautiful and beloved
country, and when its white cliffs disappeared and the black French coast came into view
I felt as if I had taken leave of a friend.'

It is interesting to compare Mendelssohn's account of his visit to England and Scotland with
that made in 1848 by his exact contemporary, Chopin, who was also given preferential
treatment. The circumstances were of course very different; for Mendelssohn was young
and eager, the thirty-eight-year-old Chopin a dying man.

It was not only the circumstances that were different, but the men themselves. Mozart
might perhaps have written the following letter (addressed by Chopin to his friend Julian
Fontana in Paris); Mendelssohn never:

> I will tell you later . . . the impression made on my nose by this sooty *Italian* sky: it can
> scarcely support such columns of grey air. . . . I will only say now that I am having a
> *respectable* time. You can tell Johnny[1] that one can have a good time here, if one takes care
> and doesn't stay too long. There are such tremendous things! Huge urinals, but all the same
> nowhere to have a proper p——! As for the English women, the horses, the palaces, the
> carriages, the wealth, the splendour, the space, the trees – everything from soap to razors –
> it's all extraordinary, all uniform, all very proper, all well-washed BUT as black as a gentle-
> man's bottom! Let me give you a kiss – on the face. . . .[2]

During the spring and early summer Chopin was lionized and exploited and patronized
almost to death by London society hostesses, then carried off to Scotland by two doting,
pious, well-connected middle-aged Scots sisters who dragged him from relation to relation,
from castle to castle, making their tame lion roar until he was ready to drop. He thought the
Scots crazy and quite uncivilized (his letters from Scotland make glorious reading), the
English kind enough but eccentric, boring, mercenary, and with no genuine interest in
music: 'they love art only because it is a *luxury*'; they were 'so different from the French, to
whom I have become attached as if they were my own countrymen'.

It was Chopin's only visit to our shores, and within a year he was dead. But further
acquaintance with England would merely have strengthened his Francophile leanings; for
Mendelssohn, on the other hand, England had immediately become, and was all his life to
remain, his second home: he even thought well of English cooking.

[1] A Polish friend who was a doctor.
[2] *Selected Correspondence*, translated and edited by Arthur Hedley (New York, 1963).

OPPOSITE *Berlioz. Oil painting by Emile Signol, 1832 (though dated 1830)* OVERLEAF *The
Caffè Greco, Rome. Watercolour by the Viennese artist Ludwig Passini, 1842. In 1953 the
Ministry of Public Education designated the Caffè Greco 'a building of public and
national interest'*

CHAPTER ELEVEN

The Return of the Native 1829-1830

Felix arrived home on 8 December; he was still very lame, and dependent on a stick.

During his convalescence in England he had busied himself with two projects that were for the present to be kept secret from his parents. The first was that the whole family should join him at Easter in Rome, where he hoped to go for some months in February. His plan was to wait for a propitious moment and then spring the suggestion on his father and mother. But because of Lea's selfishness the journey was never realized. She opposed it on the grounds of expense; the real reason, however, was her dislike of travel and her obsessive love of her house and garden. The young Mendelssohns, who had taken her acquiescence for granted, were bitterly disappointed.

The second was a gala performance in honour of Abraham and Lea's silver wedding on 26 December, for which Felix had composed, to a libretto by Klingemann, a little operetta entitled *Die Heimkehr aus der Fremde* (literally, 'The Return Home from Abroad', but known in England as *Son and Stranger*). This secret could not be kept for long, for everyone was soon conspicuously busy with scene-painting and rehearsals. The plot was slight, the characters suited to the talent available. Naturally Devrient was allotted the principal role, but a part was specially devised for the totally unmusical Hensel; it was entirely on one note – but a note which, on the day, no amount of prompting could enable him to find.

On the eve of the performance, disaster struck: Devrient found himself summoned without warning by the Crown Prince to take part on the following evening in a concert at Court. Felix, to whom at that moment his operetta was the most important thing in the world, was completely shattered and suddenly 'began to babble incoherently, and in English, to the alarm of everyone. The stern voice of his father at last checked the wild torrent of words; they carried him to bed, where a profound sleep of twelve hours completely restored him.'

A royal command could not be disobeyed (though Felix implored Devrient to refuse to appear); but through the good offices of an influential Court official it was agreed that the

The Pifferari. Oil painting by Sir David Wilkie, 1827. In one of his letters Mendelssohn said of these strolling musicians : 'Regularly at six in the morning the pifferari *rouse me from my slumbers. Theirs is the most horrid music ever produced by human lungs and goat's hide. . . .' Berlioz, on the other hand, found it extraordinarily exciting, and recalled it when writing the third movement of his* Harold in Italy. *The* piffero *is a kind of oboe ; the other instrument shown is a* zampogra *(bagpipes)*

singer should be released just in time to take part in the operetta. The evening was an out-standing success, and Lea begged Felix to give a public performance of *Son and Stranger*; but he very sensibly felt, as did Devrient also, that this tribute to his parents was too slight and too intimate for general release. After his death, however, it was staged (in 1851) in Leipzig, and in London at the Haymarket Theatre and at Covent Garden (1860/61). The overture, which the young Richard Strauss called a masterpiece, is still sometimes heard.

The winter of 1829/30 was exceptionally severe, and the cold in the garden house, where both the Hensels and the Devrients were now living, must have been almost unbearable; but the young people were busy and happy with music, reading, chess and drawing. Hensel drew, chiefly in pencil, portrait after portrait; by the time of his death there were to be more than a thousand of them, mounted in forty-seven volumes, and his subjects ranged from the family circle to celebrities such as Weber, Zelter, Paganini, Gounod, Clara Schumann, Ingres, Heine, Goethe, and Horace Vernet.[1] Felix was working on what was finally to be called his 'Reformation' Symphony, a work intended for the tercentenary of the Augsburg Confession; after its rejection by the Paris Conservatoire[2] – he always considered it one of his failures, but later generations were to judge it less harshly. Fanny, too, was endlessly busy with concerts and choir rehearsals and private pupils, till in July these activities were interrupted by the premature birth of a very delicate child, Sebastian, who lived to write the history of his mother's family.

There was also that winter a good deal of political talk, especially about the tension in Paris which was soon to culminate in the July Revolution and the overthrow of Charles x. Felix, a liberal, did not share Abraham's political views and was heard to say, 'It's terrible to see one's father such a conservative!'; it was the first time that Devrient had known him to criticize his father. It so happened that Abraham was in Paris on business when the Revolution broke; but though much concerned with its outcome he found time to write about ladies' fashions, the Louvre ('in the sculpture rooms I saw nothing new except a Venus de Milo, who has lost both her arms; I know nothing more about her'), and the musical world where he met Berlioz, 'whom I thought agreeable and interesting, and a great deal more sensible than his music'.

In February, just as Felix was about to leave for Italy, his sister Rebecka caught measles. He was advised to postpone his journey, and in due course both he and Fanny caught them too. It was not until the beginning of May that he was finally considered well enough to travel. Then came the leave-takings from family and from friends. Devrient and Felix had grown very close to one another during the winter, and both felt the parting – 'though Felix, with his affectionate nature, felt it even more than did I. . . . I shook his hand (I never liked the idea of men kissing each other), but after I had gone a few yards he called me back and said with the most loving and appealing expression, "I think you might have embraced me!" So I did – with all my heart, and thus parted from the charming youth.'

[1] Now in the New National Gallery, West Berlin.
[2] See page 147.

Fanny Hensel and her son, Sebastian. Oil painting by her husband – in the Italian manner

CHAPTER TWELVE

A Winter in Rome 1830-1831

Mendelssohn left Berlin on 8 May 1830, and more than two years were to pass before he saw his home and family again.

His journey was a leisurely one. Travelling by way of Munich, Vienna, Venice and Florence, he reached Rome at the beginning of November and spent the winter there. In April and May 1831 he was in Naples, then made his way up Italy and through Switzerland to Munich again, and finally to Paris, where he arrived shortly before Christmas. In the following April he went for a couple of months to London, returning to Berlin at the end of June 1832. The whole journey is fully reported in a series of admirable letters to his family and his friends; a selection of them was published in Leipzig in 1862, and a year later in an English version (which I have made use of but not always followed) made by the indefatigable Lady (Grace) Wallace – translator, harpist, and friend of Sir Walter Scott.

Of course Mendelssohn broke his journey to Munich at Weimar to visit Goethe. The 'drowsy old lion', now over eighty, was overjoyed to see him again and almost by force prevented his guest from leaving; usually, said Ottilie, he begged people to go rather than to stay. Much music was made, Mendelssohn's playing being acclaimed by Goethe with his latest catch-phrase, 'ganz stupend!' (terrific!); then after the old man had gone up to bed there was dancing and romping until midnight. In the mornings Mendelssohn, at Goethe's request, gave him a series of what would today be called 'lecture recitals', beginning with Bach and dealing with his successors in chronological order, while Goethe 'sat in a dark corner, like a Jupiter tonans, his old eyes flashing at me'. At last Beethoven was reached, and Goethe wanted none of him:

> But I said that I could not let him off, and played the beginning of his [Fifth] Symphony in C minor. It had an extraordinary effect on him. At first he said, 'This arouses no emotion, nothing but astonishment; it is *grandiose*.' He went on grumbling like this, and then after a long pause began again, 'It is very grand, very wild; it makes one afraid that the house is about to fall down; and what must it be like when played by a number of men together!'[1]

When Mendelssohn was finally allowed to leave, Goethe gave him a manuscript sheet of his *Faust* on which he had written, 'To my dear young friend F.M.B., mighty yet delicate master of the piano, in friendly remembrance of happy May days in 1830. J. W. von Goethe.' Goethe died two years later, and Mendelssohn never saw him again.

[1] Cf. Tennyson, on hearing Joachim play a Beethoven violin sonata: 'I wish I could understand it. I could perceive a rushing as of a torrent, and flashes of light.'

In Munich, where he spent some weeks, Mendelssohn heard *Fidelio* and put the finishing touches to his ill-starred 'Reformation' Symphony. He was much in society and, according to Marx who was also in Munich at the time, 'the darling of every house, the centre of every circle'. Mendelssohn mentions a soirée where 'Excellencies and Counts were as thick on the ground as fowls in a poultry-yard.' Artists were also present, and in particular a sixteen-year-old pianist named Delphine von Schauroth 'who is adored here – and deservedly'. He followed her about 'like a pet lamb', persuaded her to play Hummel's sonata for four hands with him, and came to her rescue by striking and holding for her an A flat 'because her tiny hand could not reach it'. 'We flirted dreadfully,' he told Fanny (in a letter omitted from Paul's published selection); 'but there isn't any danger because I'm already in love with a young Scotch girl whose name I don't know.'

Delphine inspired him to compose a piano concerto (in G minor) which he dedicated to her, and which he finally committed to paper, in the short space of three days, on his way back to Munich the following year. The work soon became enormously popular – so popular, indeed, that Berlioz, who had a nice taste in fantasy, used to tell the story of an Erard piano at the Conservatoire in Paris which, after having been used for twenty-nine consecutive performances of it at a competition, began to play it of its own accord. Erard, hastily summoned, sprinkled the piano with holy water, but to no avail; nor was dismantling it or even chopping it up any more successful, and only by consigning it to the flames was it silenced for ever.

While in Munich Mendelssohn did all he could to promote the study of the keyboard works of Bach, Mozart, and Haydn, which seemed regrettably little known there. In Vienna he found things even worse: 'not one of the best pianists, male or female, ever plays a note of Beethoven, and when I hinted that he and Mozart were not to be despised, they said "Oh, so you admire *classical* music?"' While in Vienna he was given by a friend, Franz Hauser, a volume of Luther's sacred poems, which he immediately began to set to music.

From Vienna he visited Pressburg (Bratislava) to be present at the coronation of King Ferdinand v of Hungary, and the dazzling festivities and processions associated with it. He describes it all: The dashing horsemen, dark-eyed and moustachio'd; the superb richly caparisoned horses; 'mad' Count Sandor – 'a mass of diamonds, real aigrettes and velvet embroidery . . . an ivory sceptre in his hand, with which he prodded his horse'; the oxen roasted whole, and the fountains flowing with red and white Hungarian wines. . . . 'Never can I forget the effect of all this brilliant and almost fabulous magnificence.'

Then came his first sight of Italy, though of a part that was at that time under Austrian rule: 'The pale olive faces of the men, the innumerable beggars who besieged the carriage, the various small chapels brightly and carefully painted on every side with flowers, nuns, monks, and so on. . . .' In Venice (Austrian also) he fell in love with Titian and Giorgione but found the music deplorable. How, he asked, could an organist sit beside Titian's *Martydom of St Peter*[1] (in the Church of SS. Giovanni e Paolo) and play such rubbish as this (a musical quote follows)? While in Venice he composed the *Song Without Words* known as the 'Gondola Song' (op. 19, No. 6).

Mendelssohn spent only a week in Florence. 'The air is warm and the sky cloudless;

[1] This famous picture was destroyed by fire in 1867.

everything is lovely and glorious', he wrote home on 23 October. Everything except the local inhabitants, who cheated him abominably. He stayed at 'Schneider's famous hotel', visited the galleries (returning again and again to the *Venus de' Medici*, 'on whose charms one cannot expatiate before the ladies, but whose beauty is truly divine'), and when 'satiated with art' wandered out among the vineyards. He passed through Siena ('which I gather is worth seeing') in the middle of the night, and on the morning of 1 November entered at last the Eternal City. He was just reading, for the first time, Goethe's *Italian Journey*, and observed with pleasure that 'it was on the very same day' that Goethe had arrived there.[1]

Mendelssohn found an apartment on the first floor of a house in the Piazza di Spagna – a south-facing room overlooking the square and provided with a good Viennese grand piano. He was feeling well, happy, and tremendously excited at having at last reached his goal.

But hardly had he arrived when rather disturbing news came from home: his father was being 'impossibly difficult'. Lea wrote, 'Your father ruins, for him and for us, our good and pleasant life. . . . He goes about like a man weighed down by grief, gloomy and dispirited. O God, how happy he could be, and how much happiness he could radiate! Yet he, the perfect father and husband, is perpetually in doubt, deep down in his heart, about something; and I don't know what it is.'

Mendelssohn's brother and sisters must also have written in the same vein, though we only have his reply in which he implores them to humour the old man. He recalled how in his time he had been abused, and even sent out of the room, for exalting Beethoven, till he had learned the wisdom of avoiding controversial topics. 'My father considers himself both much older and more irritable than, thank God, he really is; but however much we may be in the right, it is our place to yield to him as he has often done to us. So try to praise what he likes, and don't attack his firmly held convictions. . . .' Few sons today would recommend turning the other cheek to a father who had become impossibly domineering and dictatorial.

What was the cause of Abraham's gloom and irritability? Werner attributes it to his regret at having renounced Judaism; Marek inclines to believe that it arose from 'the struggle of the banker versus the artist. . . . He longed to be a creative artist. Yet he could not create.' But need depression always have a rational cause? Today Abraham's condition would perhaps have been cured, or at all events alleviated, by drugs or even by shock treatment.

In any case Felix could do no more to help, and he must have tried to put the matter out of his mind. For Rome called him. As soon as he had settled in he began to plan his time-table of work and relaxation. 'After breakfast', he wrote, 'I play, sing and compose until about noon. Then Rome in all her splendour awaits me. . . . I go to work methodically, selecting a particular object of interest. One day it will be the ruins of the ancient city, another the Borghese Gallery, the Capitol, St Peter's, or the Vatican. Thus each day is made memorable, and since I take my time I remember what I have seen. When noon comes I hate stopping work, but I say to myself that I must see the Vatican; yet once there I equally hate leaving. . . .' Then came social calls, and almost every evening he would find himself in the company of musicians or artists, or attending one of the innumerable balls for which Roman hostesses were famous.

---

[1] In fact, the poet reached Rome on 29 October 1786, but the first entry in his journal is dated 1 November.

The Spanish Steps, Rome. Bartholdy's house is shown on the extreme right. The drawing, made by Mendelssohn in February 1831, is one of his best topographical studies

An Italian musician who had eagerly awaited his arrival was the Abbate Fortunato Santini, a man deeply interested in early German music who was preparing a performance in Naples of a Passion cantata, *The Death of Jesus*, by Karl Graun (1703–59), the text admirably translated by himself. The Abbate, a zealous collector, had an extensive library of early Italian music, and of a morning would bring round the score, neatly wrapped in a blue pocket handkerchief, of any work that had seemed to interest Mendelssohn during their music-making on the previous evening. Mendelssohn repaid Santini's generosity by escorting him home after musical parties at which they had both been present, because, absurdly, 'for a priest to be seen alone in the streets at night would ruin his reputation'. Santini may also have been afraid of cut-throats, who were a real menace at that time.

Mendelssohn had provided himself with innumerable letters of introduction and was soon to be seen in some of the best houses in Rome. But once or twice he was snubbed – for example by Cardinal Albani, an amateur musician, who immediately announced that he despised German music but declined to produce his own compositions. Very probably he also despised German Jews. He concluded his rather frigid reception of his guest by inviting him to take his friends to see his villa in the country, omitting, however, to mention that it was in any case open to the public.

One of those who received Mendelssohn often and with particular kindness was Christian von Bunsen, Prussian Envoy to the Vatican and a distinguished scholar, in whose house there was music every Monday evening. Here Mendelssohn heard the Papal Choir sing Palestrina and in return played Bach for them. 'They are growing old,' he wrote. 'Almost all of them are unmusical and do not sing even the most routine pieces in tune. The whole choir consists of thirty-two singers, but that number are rarely together.' One day after he had improvised on a given theme, the 'black-frocked Abbati . . . clapped their hands like mad' and called him *l'insuperabile professorone* (the unsurpassable great professor). It was one of these Abbati who told Mendelssohn that he had heard mention of 'a young man of great promise called Mozart'.

Of the general state of music in Rome, Mendelssohn wrote that it was such as to render the performance there of any of his works quite out of the question:

> The orchestras are worse than anyone could possibly imagine. . . . Such violinists as there are play just as they like and come in whenever they please. The wind instruments are tuned either too high or too low, and execute flourishes that sound like farmyard noises. . . . Nobody seems to care, so there is no hope whatever of any improvement. . . . I heard a flute solo in which the flute was more than a quarter of a tone sharp. It set my teeth on edge, but no one appeared to notice it; and as there was a trill at the end they automatically applauded. If only the singing were even a shade better! But all the best singers have left the country. . . .

At Bunsen's house Mendelssohn met many interesting people including the Danish sculptor Thorvaldsen (1768–1844), a leader of the Classical Revival and very famous in his time, who was then working on a statue of Byron. One of his best-known sculptures was the colossal lion at Lucerne; and indeed, wrote Mendelssohn, 'he looks like a lion, and the very sight of his face is invigorating. You feel immediately that he must be a fine artist.' He had an excellent piano on which Mendelssohn would sometimes play for him while he sculptured, proud in the knowledge that he was in the presence of 'the creator of works that will endure for ever'. Yet of the two men it is the composer who is better remembered today.

Then there was the painter Horace Vernet (1789–1863), Director of the French Academy in Rome – 'a little thin Frenchman with stiff grey hair and the ribbon of the *Légion d'Honneur*', who was later to earn even greater fame by his vast battle-pieces of the Franco-Algerian War. He had his studio in a small house in the grounds of the Villa Medici:

> As you approach it you invariably hear some kind of noise – shouting, wrangling, trumpet-playing, or dogs barking. . . . The most picturesque disorder prevails everywhere: guns, a hunting horn, a monkey, a brace of dead hares or rabbits. The walls are covered with finished and unfinished pictures: 'The investiture of the National Cockade' (an eccentric picture which I don't care for), portraits recently begun of Thorvaldsen, Eynard and Latour-Mauborg, some horses, a sketch of a Judith and studies for it; the portrait of the

LEFT *Horace Vernet in Arab dress. Pencil drawing by Hensel. Below it Vernet has written 'Far too handsome'*   RIGHT *Bertel Thorvaldsen. Engraving after a portrait by Horace Vernet*

Pope, a couple of Moorish heads, bagpipes, Papal soldiers, my unworthy self, Cain and Abel, and last of all a drawing of the interior of the studio.

Mendelssohn tells how his portrait came to be painted. Finding himself one day at a small party at which Vernet was also present, and having been told that *Don Giovanni* was his favourite music, he changed his intended programme and improvised on themes from the Mozart opera. Vernet was in ecstasies. 'Afterwards he suddenly came up to me and whispered that we must make an exchange, for he also was an *improvisatore*; and when I was naturally curious to know what he meant, he said it was his secret. But he is just like a child, and could not keep it for more than a quarter of an hour.' He then produced a canvas and asked if Mendelssohn would sit for his portrait, which he was to accept in gratitude for his *Don Giovanni*. 'I was only too delighted to give my consent, and I can't tell you how happy I was that my playing obviously pleased him so much.'

Berlioz was also at this time at the Villa Medici, having at his fourth attempt won the long-coveted *Prix de Rome*; he was now twenty-seven, and with his tremendous mop of hair looked the complete Bohemian or, as Théophile Gautier put it, like an 'exasperated eagle'. He conceived an enormous admiration for Mendelssohn both as a man and as a musician, and refers to him again and again in his letters:

> He is a wonderful boy, as talented a performer as he is a musical genius – and that is saying much. I was delighted with all I heard of him; I firmly believe him to be one of the greatest musicians of his day. . . . His talent is enormous, extraordinary, superb, prodigious; and we have formed no mutual admiration society because he has told me frankly that he cannot make head or tail of my music. . . . He is one of those pure souls one so rarely comes across; he believes firmly in his Lutheran religion, and I sometimes shock him badly by joking about the Bible. I owe to him the only tolerable hours I have had in Rome. . . . He is rather stand-offish, but although he doesn't realize it I like him a lot. . . .

In a letter written many years later to his friend the composer Stephen Heller, Berlioz gives an entertaining and informative account of his relationship with Mendelssohn, which began, he says, 'in a somewhat curious fashion':

> At our first meeting he mentioned my *Sardanapalus* Cantata, which had won the Institute prize, and parts of which my fellow laureate Montfort had played to him. On my revealing a positive dislike for the opening allegro, he exclaimed delightedly, 'Thank heavens for that! I congratulate you . . . on your taste. I was afraid you might be pleased with it. Frankly, it's pretty awful.'
>
> We nearly quarrelled the following day. When I spoke with enthusiasm of Gluck, he replied in a tone of quizzical surprise, 'So you like Gluck, do you?' The implication seemed to be, 'How can your kind of musician possibly have sufficient intellectual understanding and feeling for grandeur of style and truth of expression to like Gluck?'[1]

But Berlioz was soon able to take his revenge:

> I had brought with me, from Paris, Asteria's aria from Gluck's Italian opera *Telemaco* – a fine but little-known piece – and I placed a manuscript copy, without the composer's name on it, on Montfort's piano one day when we were expecting a visit from Mendelssohn. He came, noticed the music, and at once sat down and began playing it. He had reached the last four bars, where . . . the music becomes truly sublime, and was parodying it extravagantly in imitation of Rubini, when I stopped him and said, with an air of blank astonishment, 'Oh, don't you like Gluck?'
>
> 'Gluck?'
>
> 'Alas, my dear friend: this piece is by Gluck, and not by Bellini as you thought. You see, I know him better than you do. . . .

In fact, Berlioz could never resist pulling Mendelssohn's leg. One day the subject of metronomes cropped up in the conversation, whereupon Mendelssohn declared that they were perfectly useless and that 'any musician who can't guess the tempo of a piece by just looking at it, is a duffer'. Some time later Berlioz showed Mendelssohn the score of his *King Lear* Overture:

> Mendelssohn read it through slowly and carefully, and was about to begin playing it on the piano (which he did, with incomparable skill) when he stopped and said, 'Give me the right tempo.'

[1] This quotation and the three that follow are taken from *The Memoirs of Hector Berlioz*, translated by David Cairns, 1969. The chapters dealing with Berlioz's stay in Rome vividly portray student life in the city at that time.

'What on earth for? I thought you said that any musician who couldn't guess the tempo was a duffer?

'He would not admit it, but these ripostes, or rather unexpected thrusts, annoyed him intensely.'

Berlioz never mentioned Sebastian Bach to Mendelssohn without adding teasingly, 'Your pupil':

[Mendelssohn] was as prickly as a porcupine whenever the talk was of music; you never knew where to take hold of him without getting your fingers hurt. But being fundamentally good-tempered and blessed with a naturally sweet and charming disposition, he never minded being contradicted on any other point, and I on my side used to abuse his forbearance during the heady discussions on philosophical and religious arguments that we sometimes engaged in.

One evening we were exploring the Baths of Caracalla together, while debating the question of merit or demerit in human behaviour and its reward in this life. As I was propounding some outrageous thesis or other in answer to the strictly orthodox and pious views put forward by him, his foot slipped and the next moment he was lying in a bruised condition at the bottom of a steep ruined staircase.

'Look at that for an example of divine justice,' I said, helping him on to his feet. 'I blaspheme, you fall.'

This irreverence, accompanied by roars of laughter, apparently went too far, and thenceforth all religious argument was banned. . . .

People who get teased usually invite it, and for the prim young German, spoilt at home by two adoring sisters, this treatment was very salutary.

And what was Mendelssohn's opinion of Berlioz? In public he was tactful, but in a letter to his mother he wrote, 'He hasn't a spark of talent . . . writes the most dreadful stuff . . . appallingly conceited'; and several years later, after hearing his overture, *Les Francs Juges*, 'Berlioz's instrumentation is so disgustingly filthy . . . that one needs a wash after merely handling one of his scores.' After studying the score of the *Symphonie Fantastique* and playing it through on the piano with Berlioz, he wrote that the instruments 'vomited music as though they had a hangover'. Berlioz would pour abuse on Haydn and Mozart till Mendelssohn 'felt like murdering him', but then suddenly save the situation by loudly singing the praises of Gluck. In short, 'If he weren't French – and one can always get on with the French because they always have something interesting to talk about – he would be quite intolerable.' Nowhere does Mendelssohn show his limitations more clearly than in his total inability to appreciate the genius of Berlioz. As Marek wisely observes, 'Would that there had been a little of Berlioz in Mendelssohn, and a little of Mendelssohn in Berlioz!'

Mendelssohn gave as much time as he could spare to looking at pictures. The modern Italian, he said sadly, seemed quite indifferent to his great artistic heritage. People scribbled on the Raphaels in the Loggie; the view of Michelangelo's *Last Judgment* had been obstructed by a large altar, and the splendid saloons of the Villa Madama, decorated by Giulio Romano, were being used as a cattle byre. 'The fact is that the people are mentally enervated and apathetic. They have a religion in which they do not believe, a Pope and Government which they ridicule, a brilliant and heroic past which they disregard. So it is no wonder that they don't enjoy art, for they aren't interested in anything serious.' But at least they couldn't spoil the countryside; couldn't, as he said, scribble their names on the Alban hills or deface the Campagna, where he loved to walk for hours on end or sit and sketch the brow of a hillside or the fragment of an ancient building.

But where art was concerned, Mendelssohn felt that he had even less cause to admire some of his own countrymen in Rome: the so-called 'Nazarenes' – a group of German painters, inspired by religious ideals and the works of the young Raphael, who had been established there since 1810. Mendelssohn was not the only visitor to form a very low opinion of them, for Byron had written to John Murray in 1817 that if only, instead of trying to *look* like Raphael, they would 'cut their hair, convert it into brushes, and *paint* like him', it would be much more to the point. The remark has a very modern ring.

These Germans frequented the still extant Caffè Greco in the Via Condotti:

> I scarcely ever go there [wrote Mendelssohn], for I dread both them and their favourite place of resort. It is a small dark room, about twenty-five feet wide, where you may smoke on one side but not on the other. They sit round it on benches, with sombreros on their heads and huge mastiffs beside them; their throats and cheeks and their entire faces sprout hair, and they puff fearful clouds of smoke (on one side of the room only) and hurl abuse at one another, while the mastiffs provide for a due distribution of vermin. A tie or a coat would be quite an innovation here. Spectacles conceal any part of the face left visible by the beard. And so they drink their coffee and talk of Titian and Pordenone just as if they were sitting next them and wearing beards and sou'westers like theirs. Moreover they paint such sickly Madonnas, such feeble saints, and such milksop heroes that I long to have a go at them. . . .

This vicious attack was directed primarily against the loafing hangers-on of the movement, who had more hair than talent; for we find him visiting the studios of several of the more distinguished Nazarenes such as Cornelius, Koch and Overbeck, and also the house of his late Uncle Bartholdy to see the frescoes painted there in 1815 by four or five leading members of the fraternity.[1] Even the Bohemian Berlioz found the Caffè Greco, with its cigar-smoking idlers, 'the most odious place imaginable'.

'The Pope [Pius VIII] is dying, or possibly dead by now,' wrote Mendelssohn on 30 November; he had in fact died the day before. The Italians, he said, were quite unmoved, merely anticipating with pleasure all the pomp that would accompany his funeral and the enthronement of his successor, while blessing his tact in not lingering on until February to disrupt the Carnival. On 11 December he went to St Peter's for the 'absolutions' which continued until the cardinals began their Conclave. St Peter's, Mendelssohn wrote,

> appears to me like a great work of nature – a forest, for example, or a mass of rocks. I can never realize that it is man-made. The ceiling is as remote and inscrutable as is the vault of heaven. You can lose your way in St Peter's; you can take a walk in it, wander about until you are quite worn out. A service is going on, but you are completely unaware of it until you get quite close. The angels in the Baptistry are monstrous giants, the doves colossal birds of prey. You lose all idea of scale and proportion. And yet, who does not feel a sense of elation as he stands beneath the dome and looks upwards?

The coffin of the Pope had been placed under a catafalque in the nave – a hideous erection more than a hundred feet high and strung with lights, yet extraordinarily effective. Near it

[1] This was the former Palazzo Zuccari, now the Biblioteca Herziana. The frescoes were removed to Berlin in 1887; they escaped damage during the Second World War.

a choir was singing from a gigantic tome illuminated by a gigantic torch; their voices 'echoed and floated in the vast space, so that the most strange and vague harmonies reached the ear'. Everywhere sat cardinals in deepest mourning, each attended by servants holding torches. Then there was the *Baldacchino*, 'as high as the palace in Berlin', and above it 'the dusky cupola filled with a blue haze; all this is quite impossible to describe'.

One morning in early February Mendelssohn was with Santini when the sound of a cannon was heard: the new Pope had at last been elected. They rushed together to the Quirinal where they learned that he was Cardinal Cappellari (Gregory XVI). 'All the Cardinals now crowded on to the balcony . . . laughing and talking. It was the first breath of fresh air they had had for fifty days, so no wonder they looked pleased.' The new Pope then appeared and blessed the crowd for the first time.

> Next morning [3 February] I followed the crowd down the long street to the Piazza of St Peter's. . . . It was swarming with carriages: the Cardinals in their red coaches, driving in state to the sacristy, with servants in embroidered liveries, and people innumerable of every nation, rank and condition; and high above them the dome of the church seeming to float in a blue vapour. . . . I thought that Cappellari would probably appropriate all this to himself when he saw it; but I knew better: it was all done to celebrate my birthday!

The festivities that followed merged with those of the Carnival. Mendelssohn attended a ball at the French Embassy, another at the Duke of Torlonia's, and a grand entertainment given by the Spanish Ambassador. Day after day the sun shone; night after night was given over to pleasure; work was quite out of question until Lent brought all this gaiety to an end.

When Holy Week came, Mendelssohn attended every possible service in the Sistine Chapel, and later sent Zelter a twenty-page letter packed full of musical quotes – one might almost term it a treatise – describing them in detail. He found the singing of the works of Palestrina and Victoria deeply moving, but complained of the harsh and mechanical chanting of the Psalms which sounded like men quarrelling. He was amused when all the cardinals 'scraped their feet vigorously on the floor' to suggest (his guide-book explained) 'the tumult made by the Jews in seizing Christ', but thought it more like the uproar in a theatre pit when the play was late starting or failed to please.

In spite of all his social activities and his energetic sightseeing, while in Italy Mendelssohn found time to compose various motets and other vocal and piano music, to complete his *Hebrides* Overture, and to begin his 'Scottish' Symphony which, however, was soon laid aside because (he said) Rome was no place in which to recapture its 'misty mood'. His two most substantial works of this period were his 'Italian' Symphony and his setting of Goethe's ballad, *Die erste Walpurgisnacht*.

The Symphony in A, which Mendelssohn himself called the 'Italian', began to occupy his thoughts almost immediately after his arrival in Rome, and by the following February he was able to report 'rapid progress; it will be the jolliest piece I have so far written, especially the last movement. I have not yet decided on the adagio and think I shall wait till I get to Naples.' When, in November 1832, the London Philharmonic Society commissioned three compositions including a symphony, Mendelssohn chose this, and after working on it took it to London for performance in the following May. It was published posthumously as op. 90.

The 'Italian' is probably the most generally popular of Mendelssohn's five symphonies for full orchestra, but Berlioz is exceptional among musicians in preferring it to the 'Scottish'. Though it was composed in part during the Roman winter, the fire of youthful blood and the gaiety of the Roman saltarello make the first and last movements among the sunniest and most exhilarating music he ever wrote. The throbbing allegro of the opening movement, heady as champagne, is followed by an elegiac andante representing (it is said) a leisurely procession of pilgrims, sauntering in D minor to some distant shrine. Werner, unlike most critics, considers the third movement the weakest: 'a real bourgeois minuet'; but if so, all thought of it is soon swept away by the breathless onrush of the saltarello which brings the symphony to a triumphant conclusion.

It is strange that Mendelssohn, who could not recapture his Scottish mood in Italy, should have found no difficulty in setting Goethe's very Germanic poem to music there. Strange, too, that he chose so blatantly pagan a text; but then, was not Goethe a god? In a letter to Zelter Goethe describes the historical background of his 'dramatic ballad' (as he termed it, which he had written in 1799 and called *The First Walpurgis Night* to distinguish it from the Walpurgis scenes in his *Faust*. The German heathen priests, driven from their sacred groves by the Christians, had taken refuge in the wild and inaccessible Harz Mountains where they practised each spring their ancient rites, protecting themselves from the spying intrusion of armed missionaries by disguising their sentries as devils. Zelter had attempted to set the ballad to music, but sensibly came to realize that it was a task beyond his powers. Mendelssohn thought in terms of a secular cantata with soli, chorus and orchestra, and the idea had been in his head ever since the previous summer. Most of the cantata was committed to paper in Italy, the overture, which he composed last, being completed in Paris a year later.

The First Walpurgis Night has been justly described by Werner as 'indisputably the finest secular oratorio of the nineteenth century'. The close of the overture, when the storms of winter yield to the radiance of spring, anticipates the first act of Wagner's *Die Walküre* and is supremely beautiful. Mendelssohn, when writing to Goethe for his birthday (28 August 1831), thanked him for 'the heavenly words'; the poet, of course, never heard the work, and it may well be doubted whether he would have understood or enjoyed it. After revision it was published in 1843 as op. 60, and Mendelssohn mentions a performance the following year in London which was received 'with tumultuous applause'.

CHAPTER THIRTEEN

A Walking Tour in Switzerland 1831

In the middle of April Mendelssohn left Rome for Naples with three German artists – not, presumably, of the long-haired variety, but pupils of Wilhelm von Schadow named Eduard Bendemann, Carl Sohn and Theodor Hildebrandt. Though he was later to say that he far preferred Rome, he was intoxicated by the sun and the sea, by the beauty of the landscape and the lushness of the flora. From his balcony he would gaze for hours at the blue bay and 'that knave Vesuvius' which declined to oblige with even the mildest eruption, thus proving Goethe to have been over-optimistic in writing to Zelter the previous December, 'The boy [Felix] was born under a lucky star. In Hungary he saw a coronation, in Rome he finds a conclave, and no doubt Vesuvius will put on a show for him.'

Sometimes Mendelssohn walked for miles through the countryside, often alone. With his friends he went to Pompeii, Paestum, Cumae and Ischia, travelling light ('little in my *rucksack* beyond Goethe's poems and three shirts'). To Capri too, where he raved about the Blue Grotto, 'the most dazzling blue I ever saw, without shadow or cloud, like a pane of brightest opalescent glass', yet in the next sentence thought of London, where his brother had just

Carl Sohn sleeping. Pencil drawing by E. Bendemann, c. 1830

Eduard Bendemann.
Watercolour by Hensel

gone: 'That smoky place is fated to be now and ever my favourite residence; my heart glows whenever I think of it.'

But when the sirocco blew he felt as lazy as did everyone else; indeed the climate of Naples seemed to be designed to suit 'the grand gentleman who rises late, never needs to walk, never thinks (because that makes him hot), takes a postprandial siesta, then eats an ice and at night goes to the theatre where again he finds nothing to provoke thought'. He recalled Goethe saying jokingly that 'the misfortune of the North is that people always want to be doing something . . . and that an Italian was right who advised him not to think so much because it would only give him a headache.' But the climate also suited the poor, who could sleep on the pavement by day or by night, live on a fish or two which they could catch themselves, and dress in a few rags. Much povery there certainly was, and Mendelssohn shrank from the hordes of beggars whose obtrusive misery the beauties of nature seemed to mock.

Julius Benedict was in Naples, and Mendelssohn called on him. Since their first meeting in Berlin there had apparently been some unpleasantness between the two men, but this was now forgiven and forgotten. One evening they went with Donizetti to a musical party given by Madame Fodor, a singer who, though well past her prime, was described by Mendelssohn as 'the only genuine artist, male or female, I have so far come across in Italy'. Towards the end of the evening Mendelssohn was asked to play, and Benedict was completely dazzled when, 'without a moment's hesitation, he introduced first one theme of the pieces just

OPPOSITE TOP *The Théâtre-Italien, Paris. Watercolour by J. V. Nicolle* OPPOSITE BOTTOM
St Peter's, Rome. Oil painting by Louis Haghe, 1867 OVERLEAF *Liszt at the piano. Oil painting by Josef Danhauser, 1840. From left to right : Dumas the Elder, Victor Hugo, George Sand, Paganini, Rossini, Liszt and Marie d'Agoult. On the wall is a portrait of Byron, and on the piano a bust of Beethoven*

performed, then another, added a third and a fourth, and worked them simultaneously in the most brilliant way. . . .' Mendelssohn also met in Naples the famous German poet, dramatist and homosexual, Count August von Platen – 'a little shrivelled, wheezing old man with gold spectacles, yet not more than five-and-thirty! He quite startled me.' Platen, who had fallen foul of his native land, 'abuses the Germans terribly, forgetting however that he does so in German'.

Goethe had spent some weeks in Sicily on his Italian journey, and Mendelssohn was naturally eager to follow in his footsteps. But from his father in Berlin came a letter forbidding him to act on this 'whim'. Both Zelter and Goethe were indignant when they heard of Abraham's veto and Felix's dutiful acceptance of it. 'His Papa was very wrong not to send him to Sicily,' wrote Goethe to Zelter; and the latter, never one to be afraid of speaking his mind, told Abraham exactly what he thought of him. It must, however, be remembered that Abraham was paying the piper and therefore entitled to call the tune.

So at the end of May the obedient young man reluctantly turned his face to the north, and after putting his affairs in order in Rome travelled by way of Perugia to Florence. One episode of this journey deserves mention, for it shows how Mendelssohn could on occasion lose his temper. At Incisa, near Florence, when his landlady (who was also in charge of the post) tried to swindle him outrageously over the hire of a carriage, he 'grabbed her and pushed her into the room (for we were standing in the passage)', then ran in search of the Mayor. It turned out that the Mayor of Incisa lived four miles away; but the local inhabitants, not a little impressed by Mendelssohn's show of force, soon found him an admirable vehicle at a reasonable price, and gave him a hearty send-off when he threw his small change to a beggar as he drove away.

From Florence Mendelssohn wrote his sisters a long letter on the wonders of the Uffizi. One paragraph of it may be familiar to many readers who have never handled a copy of Mendelssohn's *Letters from Italy and Switzerland*, because it is quoted and held up to ridicule by Samuel Butler in his *The Way of all Flesh*. Mendelssohn wrote:

> I then went to the Tribune. This room is so delightfully small that you can traverse it in fifteen paces, and yet it contains a world of art. I again sought out my favourite armchair, which stands under the statue of the 'Slave whetting his knife' (*L'Arrotino*), and taking possession of it I enjoyed myself for a couple of hours; for here, at one glance, I had the 'Madonna del Cardellino', 'Pope Julius II, a female portrait by Raphael, and above it a fine picture of Saints by Perugino; and so close to me that I could have touched the statue with my hand, the Venus de' Medici. . . .

And so on. Mendelssohn concludes, 'This is a spot where a man feels his own insignificance, and may well learn to be humble.'

Butler's cynical comment on it is very witty, very cruel and very unfair – because though Mendelssohn's letter is rather priggish, his interest in art was deep and genuine:

> The Tribune is a slippery place for people like Mendelssohn to study humility in. They generally take two steps away from it for one they take towards it. I wonder how often he told himself that he was quite as big a gun, if the truth were known, as any of the men

Chopin. Oil painting by Delacroix, 1838

whose works he saw before him, how often he wondered whether any of the visitors were recognizing him and admiring him for sitting such a long time in the same chair, and how often he was vexed at seeing them pass him by and take no notice of him. But perhaps if the truth were known his two hours was not quite two hours.

In Milan, where he arrived in the first week of July, Mendelssohn learned that Baron and Baroness Ertmann, friends and devoted admirers of Beethoven, were living there, and though unprovided with an introduction he boldly called on them. The old lady, to whom Beethoven had dedicated his Sonata in A major (op.101), could still play admirably, and there followed some delightful evenings of music-making at the house of this charming couple. 'In the intervals of our music the General [Baron Ertmann] told me some very amusing stories about Beethoven, such as when Baronin Ertmann was playing to him in the evening he often used the snuffers as a tooth-pick!' Karl Mozart, the composer's elder son, was also in Milan – 'an official there, but heart and soul a musician'. Mendelssohn felt immediately attracted to him, and Karl was, he wrote, the first person to hear, and with enormous pleasure, as much as was so far written of the *Walpurgisnacht*.[1]

It would seem that while in Milan Mendelssohn paused to take stock of his position. A letter from his friend Devrient, taunting him – very unjustly, one must feel – with a line from Schiller's *Don Carlos*, 'Two-and-twenty, and nothing done for immortality', may well have provoked this self-examination. So long as he does not actually starve, Mendelssohn replies, he intends to continue writing what his heart dictates. As for opera, to which Devrient once more urges him to devote himself, he repeats yet again that he is only waiting for a libretto that inspires him. Karl Immermann in Düsseldorf might be the right man, and Munich has in fact offered to commission an opera. From Milan he also writes to his father, saying that he would much like to discuss his future with him. Where is he to make his career? In London, Paris, Munich or Berlin? Is there anywhere that they could meet to talk things over? But no meeting took place.

He now continued his leisurely journey northwards – and very leisurely it was to be, for nearly two months were to pass before he reached Munich. A detour took him first to Como, with a letter of introduction from Karl Mozart to friends of his there who much amused him by begging him never to read a frightfully silly play by Shakespeare called *A Midsummer Night's Dream*. Then Lake Maggiore for the Isola Bella, which in pouring rain seemed rather the Isola Brutta, and the Isola Madre where he found himself sharing a boat with 'a fiercely moustachio'd German who examined all the lovely scenery as if he wanted to buy it but found it too expensive'. After two nights made sleepless by fleas and thunder-claps he left the lake and, taking his place in the diligence 'rather sulkily' because of the pouring rain, set out for the Simplon.

The letters written by Mendelssohn during the six weeks he spent in Switzerland are described by Werner as 'literary masterpieces that will probably live as long as men still go wandering on foot to admire Nature.' The doting Frau Polko went even further: anyone, she said, who could put down the letters of 'this *loving human soul*' without '*sincere and heartfelt gratification*' was 'as much to be pitied as the blind, who can see no spring, or the deaf, who

---

[1] He cannot really have been the first. Benedict certainly heard some of the cantata in Naples, and probably Berlioz also did in Rome. But Moscheles must have been mistaken in writing (on 30 April 1832) that he had heard it 'in former days in Berlin' .

can hear no nightingale's note'. They are good letters – but not so good as all that; and here, for lack of space, they must unfortunately be dealt with very summarily.

The route Mendelssohn followed was the Rhône Valley as far as Martigny, from where he visited Chamonix; then from the Lake of Geneva he cut north-east across the heart of Switzerland to the Lake of Constance. Much of his journey he made on foot with his luggage sent on ahead, and in the worst summer weather within living memory. He also climbed the two Scheideggs, the Faulhorn and the Rigi; but these ascents were nothing more than long, wet, rough, uphill walks made in the company of a professional guide or an obliging local inhabitant, and Werner is surely again exaggerating when he writes that 'only a thoroughly experienced mountaineer would lightly undertake such a journey today'.

Nothing – not even the weather – could damp Mendelssohn's enthusiasm for his beloved Switzerland, and he was quite at a loss to understand how such wonderful scenery could have

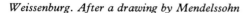

Weissenburg. After a drawing by Mendelssohn

Unterseen. After one of Mendelssohn's drawings

inspired Goethe to no more than 'a few feeble poems and still feebler letters'. For the first time he saw at close range those 'most marvellous monsters in the world', the Swiss glaciers. He revelled in the wild flowers, though they can hardly have been at their best in a sopping August. When the weather allowed – and he did strike a few gloriously fine days – he sketched; when held up by landslides or by roads and bridges washed away, he kept his spirits up by humming a Beethoven adagio,[1] by learning to yodel, or by writing a waltz[2] for the nearest pretty girl. He revisited the Devil's Bridge, and thought the new granite structure far less romantic than the old wooden one he had crossed in 1822. Naturally, too, he explored the Tell country, re-reading Schiller's drama and searching out the places mentioned in it.

One or two brief extracts from his letters may help to give the flavour of them. At Boltigen he passed a very unpleasant night:

Owing to a fair, there was no room in the inn, so I had to stay in a nearby house where there were swarms of vermin quite as bad as Italy, a creaking house-clock which struck hoarsely every hour, and a baby that cried the whole night long. For a time I really couldn't help listening to it, for it screamed in every possible key, expressive of every possible

[1] The one from the Quartet in E flat, op. 127.
[2] It is strange that Mendelssohn, a passionate dancer, composed only one other waltz – the *Song Without Words*, op. 67, No. 6.

Engelberg. From a drawing by Mendelssohn

emotion: first angry, then furious, then whining; and when it could cry no longer it grunted in a deep bass. Let no one tell me now that we ought to want to return to the days of our childhood because children are so happy. . . .

At an inn near the Furka he encountered the less attractive kind of English tourists:

There are two Englishmen and an English lady here, sitting at this moment beside me by the stove; they are more wooden than sticks. We have travelled the same road for a couple of days, and I declare that they have never uttered a syllable except of abuse. They complained that there were no fireplaces, either here or at the Grimsel Hospice; but that there are *mountains* here is a fact to which they never allude. They spend their entire time scolding their guide (who laughs at them), quarrelling with the innkeepers, and yawning in each other's faces. They find everywhere commonplace because they themselves are commonplace. . . .[1]

At Engelberg, where there is a fine Benedictine Abbey, Mendelssohn played the organ at one of the services, taking his place 'in the midst of the monks – a very Saul among the prophets':

[1] Cf. George Sand: 'For an Englishwoman the real aim in life is to manage to cross the loftiest and stormiest regions without disarranging a single hair of her coiffure. . . . For an Englishman, to circle the world and return home without having dirtied his gloves or gone through his shoes.'

An impatient Benedictine at my side played the double bass and others the fiddles, one of the dignatories being the first violin. The *pater praeceptor* stood in front of me, sang a solo, and conducted with a long stick as thick as my arm. The convent scholars in their black cowls formed the choir; a decayed old rustic played on a decayed old oboe, and at a little distance two more were puffing away composedly at two huge trumpets with green tassels; and yet for all this the result was gratifying. One couldn't help liking these people, for they were in earnest and did their best.

We had a Mass by Emmerich, every note of which betrayed its 'powder and pigtail'. I rendered the figured bass, adding wind instruments from time to time when I got bored, made the responses, extemporized on a given theme, and finally, at the request of the Prelate and in spite of my dislike of doing so on the organ, played a march. . . .

One other letter written from Switzerland deserves mention though it has nothing to do with Mendelssohn's journey. While in Milan he had received a batch of songs from a twenty-year-old German quite unknown to him, Wilhelm Taubert. From Lucerne Mendelssohn replied in the kindest and most helpful way and at considerable length, praising his serious approach to composition, asking to see more of his work and inviting criticism of his own. This encouragement must have meant much to young Taubert, who became in due course a distinguished musician and the composer of *Lieder* still to be heard in Germany today.

The letter is of further interest because in it Mendelssohn discusses the state of music and literature in Germany, referring to certain 'little' men of the new generation who delighted in depreciating the great. Does Taubert, he asks, find this arrogance, this repulsive cyncism, as odious as he does? Does he agree that the first qualification for an artist is that he should feel respect for greatness, be humble in its presence and not try to blow out great flames so that his own feeble rushlight may seem to shine a little brighter? In Taubert he recognizes, he says, a kindred spirit: one who will work alongside him to keep true art alive until better times come again.

But for all this, Germany, after Italy, was a land of music. Mendelssohn now realized that he was a northerner at heart, and was delighted when he found himself again on German soil. He arrived in Munich in early September, and remained in the Bavarian capital for seven or eight weeks.

And what eventful weeks they were! For now, and perhaps for the first time, he found himself in serious danger of *really* falling in love. The girl was, of course, the same Delphine von Schauroth with whom he had flirted during his visit to Munich the year before, and to whom he had dedicated his piano concerto. One of the two published letters which Mendelssohn wrote home from Munich has been discreetly cut, and two others are known to be missing – perhaps destroyed later by his wife, who burned much of the intimate correspondence which passed between herself and her husband. But Werner has recovered the suppressed passage which tells how the King himself, Ludwig I, urged Mendelssohn to make 'this excellent match' (for the girl came from a very good family) and asked him why he held back. Mendelssohn found the royal curiosity impertinent; but before he could answer, the King had changed the subject.

It would seem that Delphine's parents favoured the marriage, but that Mendelssohn felt that he was not yet ready or willing to take so irrevocable a step, for some years later he told Schumann that Delphine 'could have become dangerous to him'. Whereas flirtation stimulated composition, the married state might impede it. Or perhaps he was not yet certain that he had found the right girl; was there not also in Munich the sixteen-year-old Josefine Lang – 'one of the sweetest creatures I ever saw' – to whom he gave lessons 'every day at noon'? As Abraham Mendelssohn had once said to Devrient when his son was being hypercritical of a proposed libretto, 'I fear that Felix's fastidiousness will prevent his getting a wife as well as a libretto.' Not long afterwards Delphine married a man named Hill Handley, of whom Mendelssohn wrote that beside her he must look 'like roast beef next to a vanilla ice'. She remained a devoted admirer of Mendelssohn's works, and nearly forty years later gave a memorable performance of their piano concerto at a Mendelssohn Festival at Leipzig.

After being starved of music for so long, Mendelssohn was now able to enjoy a surfeit of it. He mentions in particular a soirée in his apartment – a ground-floor room overlooking the street – where the audience overflowed into the hall, on to the stairs and even into the road, and which drew to a close in an alcoholic haze at half past one in the morning. Another day he played to the Court, when the Queen declared herself 'quite carried away' by his improvisations – 'whereupon,' says Mendelssohn, 'I begged her pardon – for carrying her away.'

Finally came a big charity concert in the recently erected Odeon, a building which remained Munich's finest concert hall until the bombing of the night of 24/25 April 1944 reduced it to ashes. The programme included Mendelssohn's Symphony No. 1 in C minor (again with the scherzo from his Octet for Strings), his overture to *A Midsummer Night's Dream*, and his brilliant new piano concerto. It was a triumphant success, the King himself leading the applause and insisting upon Mendelssohn improvising, by way of an encore, on the theme of Figaro's aria, '*Non più andrai*'. 'I have rarely felt such an ass as I did when I took my place at the piano to present my fantasy to the audience,' wrote the poor pianist, who had at last come to realize that extemporizing in public, however wildly acclaimed, was nothing more nor less than a prostitution of his talent.

After receiving a definite contract for an opera from Baron von Poissl, the Intendant of the Royal Theatre, and very sensibly relaxing at that annual orgy still so dear to the hearts and the stomachs of the people of Munich, the *Oktoberfest*, Mendelssohn left for Stuttgart. At Frankfurt he was received with great kindness by Schelble, who commissioned for his Cäcilienverein an oratorio (the *St Paul*) which was written several years later; at Düsseldorf he met Immermann who agreed to make a libretto for him from Shakespeare's *The Tempest*; and by the beginning of December he was in Paris.

CHAPTER FOURTEEN

Paris and London 1831-1832

Much had happened in Paris since Mendelssohn's visit there with his father in 1825. The July Revolution of 1830 had driven the reactionary Charles X into exile, and Louis-Philippe, the Citizen King, now controlled the destinies of France. In all the arts, as well as in the sciences, we find immense creative activity. In painting, to mention but three names, there were Ingres, Delacroix and Daumier; the almost endless list of writers includes Balzac, Victor Hugo and George Sand, and 1831 saw the publication of Stendhal's *Le Rouge et le Noir*. Of the state of music, young Ferdinand Hiller, who was in Paris at this time and saw much of Mendelssohn, wrote that it could hardly have been more flourishing:

> The so-called Conservatoire concerts, under Habeneck,[1] were in all their freshness, and Beethoven's symphonies were played there with a perfection, and received with an enthusiasm, that I have rarely witnessed since. Cherubini was writing his Masses for the Chapel in the Tuileries; at the Grand Opera Meyerbeer was beginning his series of triumphs with *Robert le Diable*; Rossini was writing *William Tell*;[2] Scribe and Auber were at the height of their activity, and all the best singers were collected at the Italian Opera. . . .
>
> Baillot, though growing old [he was sixty], still played with all the fire and poetry of youth; Paganini had given a series of twelve concerts at the Grand Opera; Kalkbrenner, with his brilliant execution, represented the Clementi school; Chopin had established himself in Paris a few months before Mendelssohn's arrival; and Liszt, still inspired by the tremendous impetus he had received from Paganini, though seldom heard in public, performed the most extraordinary feats. German chamber music was not so popular as it afterwards became, but Baillot's quartet still had its fanatical supporters. . . .

Mendelssohn, it will be remembered, had cared little for Paris at the time of his first visit; but soon after his arrival he wrote to Immermann that he was now thoroughly enjoying himself there:

> I have cast myself headlong into the vortex and do nothing all day but see new objects – the Chambers of Peers and Deputies, pictures and theatres, dio-, neo-, cosmo- and panoramas,

[1] Described by Berlioz as 'able, but limited and unreliable'.
[2] The première was in fact in 1829.

A few of Mendelssohn's sketchbooks and albums. The upper of the two open albums, the gift of Felix to his sister Rebecka, shows a curious scene 'drawn by M. and F.M.B.' of a hermit, a rider, and walruses on the seashore. The Greek quotation is from the fourth book of Homer's Odyssey, *and no explanation can be offered of what is probably an esoteric joke shared by brother and sister*

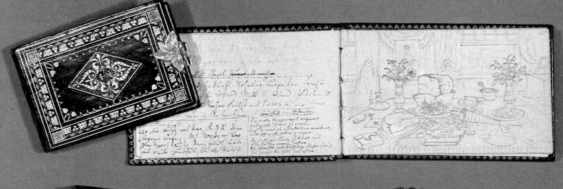

endless parties, etc. Moreover, the musicians here are as numerous as the sands on the sea-shore, all hating each other; so each has to be visited individually, and one has to be highly diplomatic because they are all gossips.

But though what he now found only confirmed him in his opinion that it was in Germany, and not in France, that he must make his career, he could not help being in general more favourably impressed by the musical life of the city. The 'quite admirable' Conservatoire Orchestra performed his *Midsummer Night's Dream* Overture several times, and Mendelssohn also appeared with them in his favourite Beethoven piano concerto (in G major), which was loudly applauded. But alas! his connection with Habeneck and his orchestra, which began so auspiciously, was to end in tears. It had been agreed, to Mendelssohn's great delight, that his 'Reformation' Symphony should be given its première at one of the Conservatoire concerts. At the first rehearsal, however, the orchestra, much though they liked Mendelssohn personally – 'Ce bon Mendelssohn', they used to say; 'quel talent, quelle tête, quelle organisation!' – made it clear that they did not at all like his symphony, and its performance was cancelled. Mendelssohn was too hurt to discuss the matter even with Hiller; but a member of the orchestra told the latter, who had not been present, that they found the work much too dry: 'too much counterpoint and not enough tunes'.

Fortunately, in his less formal music-making Mendelssohn continued to please, and was soon kept endlessly busy. In one of his letters he writes that, in addition to the many hours he has devoted to composition and to making arrangements of works already written, he hardly ever has even an evening to himself:

> Tonight Bohrer's; tomorrow a fête, with all the violin *gamins* of the Conservatoire; the day after, Rothschild; Tuesday, the Société des Beaux-Arts; Wednesday my octet at the Abbé Bardin's; Thursday my octet at Madame Kiéné's; Friday a concert at Erard's; Sunday a concert at Léo's; and lastly, on Monday – and you may laugh if you like – my octet is to be performed in a church at a funeral Mass in commemoration of Beethoven! . . . I can hardly imagine anything more ridiculous than a priest at the altar and my scherzo going on. . . . Finally, Baillot is to give a grand concert on 7 April, and so I have promised to stay here till then and to play a Mozart concerto for him and something else as well.

Yet time had still to be made for relaxation. Mendelssohn would talk for hours with Hiller, with whom he was in agreement on all major musical issues though Hiller adopted a more sympathetic attitude than Mendelssohn did towards French and Italian composers. Sometimes Mendelssohn did not spare even the masters he most revered, and on one occasion observed shrewdly of Handel that one could imagine that he had his different musical drawers for his choruses – 'one labelled "warlike", another "heathen", a third "religious", and so on'. He also played a great deal of chess with a Dr Franck, whom he almost always beat. Franck would never admit that Mendelssohn was the better player, and after each victory the latter would relentlessly repeat, 'We play equally well – *exactly equally* – only I play *just a little bit better.*'

Then there was the theatre. The Gymnase Dramatique, where nothing but small *vaude-villes* were given, was his favourite, but he deplored the fact that politics and sex were dragged into every piece. 'I see plenty of wit and talent,' he wrote 'but a degree of immorality that

St Paul's from Ludgate Hill. Hand-coloured lithograph by T. Shotter Boys, 1843

LEFT *Ferdinand Hiller. Engraving, c. 1855*   RIGHT *Liszt. Drawing by Achille Devéria, 1832*

almost passes belief.' Both he and Hiller were, however, captivated by the charms of a young actress, Léontine Fay, who took the parts of 'young wives in embarrassing situations', and by the dancing of the great Taglioni in *La Sylphide*.

If the theatre was immoral, the opera, Mendelssohn thought, was almost worse. He writes like a frustrated spinster on the subject of Meyerbeer's *Robert le Diable*, in which 'the nuns come on, one after the other, trying to seduce the hero, until finally the Abbess succeeds. . . . In another opera [by Auber] a young girl undresses while singing that this time tomorrow she will be married. It made a sensation; but I haven't any music for such vulgarities, and if *that* is what people want nowadays, then I shall stick to church music.' Where Meyerbeer was concerned, a part of the trouble stemmed from the fact that, although Meyerbeer treated him with great courtesy and genuinely admired his music, Mendelssohn couldn't stand the man. It was unlucky that since both were Jews, and both wore their hair the same way, they looked extremely alike. Hiller and his friends used to tease Mendelssohn about it, and this made him so angry that one day he went out and had his hair completely cropped. 'The affair caused a lot of amusement in our set,' wrote Hiller, 'especially when Meyerbeer heard of it; but he took it with his usual invincible good nature and in the nicest possible way.'

Mendelssohn saw something of Liszt, and was obliged to revise the opinion he had formed of him in 1825. Hiller mentions that one day Mendelssohn rushed into the room announcing that he had just witnessed 'a miracle – a *real* miracle': he had shown Liszt the almost illegible manuscript of his piano concerto, and Liszt had 'played it at sight absolutely perfectly, better than anyone else could possible play it – quite marvellously'. Hiller was not surprised. He knew from experience that Liszt played most things best the first time through, because what

LEFT *Thalberg. Engraving, c. 1840* RIGHT *Paganini. Drawing by Wilhelm Hensel, 1828*

was on the paper gave him enough to keep him occupied; the second time through he could never resist adding his own pyrotechnics.

This was, of course, the great age of the virtuoso: of Paganini on the violin, of Liszt and his great rival, Thalberg, on the piano. 'The attraction of the virtuoso for the public', wrote Debussy, 'is very like that of the circus for the crowd – there is always the hope that something dangerous may happen: that x may play the violin with y on his shoulders, or z conclude his piece by lifting the piano with his teeth.' It was asserted that Thalberg, known as 'Old Arpeggio', had three hands, because he developed a type of composition in which a melody in the middle part of the piano was shared between the hands, while the hand that happened to be free flew up or down the instrument, as the case might be. 'Thalberg plays famously,' Chopin once said. 'But he isn't my man. . . . He takes tenths as easily as I do octaves, and wears diamond shirt-studs.' A few years after Mendelssohn's visit, Liszt (whom Gregorovius called 'the centaur pianist' because he and his instrument seemed to be inseparable), enraged by Thalberg's growing popularity, challenged him to a contest of virtuosity and triumphed with a knock-out. Bunsen, a shrewd critic, considered the virtuoso 'the composer's most dangerous enemy'.

There is an amusing letter from Mendelssohn on the subject, written later that year to Moscheles who had reproached him for not going to hear the famous but notoriously plain pianist Anna de Belleville play in Berlin:

Do you imagine that I didn't go to hear the Belleville because she isn't a 'Bellevue', or because she wears such voluminous sleeves? That wasn't the reason, although there *are* certain faces that can't ever belong to artists – faces from which emanate such icy blasts that I freeze at the mere sight of them. But why on earth should I be forced to listen for the thirtieth time to all sorts of variations by Herz? They give me less pleasure than rope-dancers or acrobats, for with these there is at least the wicked thrill of always fearing that they may break their necks, and of seeing that after all they don't. But piano-acrobats [*Clavierspringer*] don't even endanger their lives, merely our ears. . . .

Further, she played at the theatre between the two plays – and that I can't stand. The curtain rises and before me I see India with her pariahs and palms and cacti, with murder and sudden death – and I'm expected to weep a lot. Then up goes the curtain again, and there is Mademoiselle Belleville with her piano and a concerto in something or other minor – and I'm expected to applaud a lot. Finally comes a farce, 'Half an hour at the Potsdam Gate', and I'm expected to laugh. No, I just can't bear that sort of thing, and that's why I don't deserve your censure. I stayed at home because I prefer to be in my own room, with my own family, or in my garden – which is lovely this year. . . .

Another brilliant virtuoso pianist and teacher at that time in Paris was Kalkbrenner, a German in his early forties whose criticism Fanny and her brother had valued in Berlin in earlier days though subsequently they had had cause to doubt his musical integrity.[1] Kalkbrenner had befriended Chopin on his recent arrival in Paris, but had patronizingly suggested that the young Pole should improve his technique by attending his master classes. This infuriated Mendelssohn, who, though he had made no mention of it in his letters, had already heard Chopin play that autumn in Munich and had been deeply impressed. That 'Chopinetto' (as Mendelssohn called him) admired and respected Kalkbrenner is implied by the dedication to him of his Concerto in E minor. Felix was present and applauded loudly at Chopin's debut in the Salle Pleyel in February. Though financially a failure, the concert was in other respects a triumph, and no more was heard of Chopin's lack of technique.

Hiller wrote:

The relations between Kalkbrenner and Mendelssohn were always somewhat insecure, but Kalkbrenner's advances were such that Mendelssohn could not altogether reject them. We dined with him together once or twice and everything went quite smoothly, though no entreaties could ever persuade Felix to touch the keys of Kalkbrenner's piano. Indeed, we were none of us very grateful for Kalkbrenner's civilities, and took a wicked pleasure in teasing him. I remember that one day Mendelssohn, Chopin, Liszt and I were sitting outside a café on the boulevard des Italiens . . . when we suddenly saw Kalkbrenner coming. It was his great ambition always to be the perfect gentleman, and, knowing how much he would dislike meeting such a rowdy party, we surrounded him in the friendliest manner and assailed him with such a volley of talk that he was nearly driven mad – which of course delighted us. Youth has no mercy.

On 3 February, his twenty-third birthday, Mendelssohn arrived in Hiller's room in tears: he had just heard that his beloved violin teacher, Eduard Rietz, had died of consumption; he was only thirty. 'At first', said Hiller, 'he couldn't find words to tell me . . . and he could hardly keep control of himself'; and to his family Mendelssohn wrote, 'The knowledge that there was a man like him in the world – a man with whom I could talk without constraint, who loved me and whose aspirations and aims were the same as my own – that is now gone for ever. It is the cruellest blow I have yet suffered.' He was never able in later life to make friendships that replaced those of his youth.

This blow was soon followed by another, for at the end of March came the news of Goethe's

[1] See Ferdinand Hiller's *Mendelssohn, Letters and Recollections*, (London, 1874), p. 24.

death. This too touched him deeply; but at eighty-two Goethe had finished his life's work, and Mendelssohn knew that it was old Zelter who would feel the loss most. 'You will see,' he told Hiller, 'that he will not survive it for long.' Nor did he. 'Your Excellency naturally has precedence,' said Zelter, bowing before the bust of his old friend; within weeks he too was dead. Mendelssohn may well (as Kaufman suggests) have recalled the lines of Goethe:

Sie hören nicht die folgenden Gesänge,
Die Seelen, denen ich die erste sang.[1]

In January 1832 the great Asiatic cholera epidemic, which had been ravaging northern and central Europe, reached London and shortly afterwards crossed the Channel to invade France, Spain and Italy. Paris suffered severely and early in April, just as he was about to leave for England, Mendelssohn caught the disease. Or so he liked to believe; but if cholera it really was, and not just colic, it must have been a very mild attack, for it kept him in bed for only about ten days. On 16 April he wrote to a friend in Munich that all the winter he had felt 'as peevish as a guinea-pig' and 'as miserable as a fish on dry land':

There was always something the matter with me, and latterly I've been really ill; had to stay in bed, have my belly massaged by an old crone, cover myself up with masses of bed-clothes, sweat a lot, eat nothing, endure lots of visits and lots of sympathy, swallow enormous pills, get thoroughly bored – and so sweat out my anger and my belly-ache and the cholera that I was supposed to be getting.

Now I've sweated it out, and for the first time for months I feel well and cheerful. . . .

Three days later Mendelssohn left for London; he never saw France again.

★   ★   ★

It was bliss to be back in London, where Klingemann, Rosen and the Moscheles warmly welcomed him. 'I can't describe to you the happiness of my first weeks here,' he wrote to his family on 11 May, for in Paris he had 'never felt quite at home'. Nowhere, he said, could one find such friendly people or such pretty girls as in London. Soon after his arrival he had gone to a rehearsal of a concert of the Philharmonic Society at which none of his works was being given; but the moment he entered the body of the hall one of the orchestra had called out, 'There's Mendelssohn!' whereupon 'they all began shouting and clapping so wildly that for a time I really didn't know what to do. Then somebody else shouted "Welcome!" and I had to cross the hall and clamber up into the orchestra to thank them. I shall never forget it; it meant more to me than any distinction, because it showed that the *musicians* loved me. . . .' No wonder his heart warmed to the English!

There followed several concerts at which some of his own works were played, including the new Capriccio Brilliant in B minor for piano and orchestra (op. 22) especially written for London. What he called his 'Munich' Piano Concerto, which was performed twice, 'sent the audience crazy', as did the *Hebrides* Overture 'though it sounded very strange in the middle of lots of Rossini'.[2] The critics were equally enthusiastic, one (in the *Harmonicon*) begging for a further hearing of the *Hebrides* Overture before the end of the season because 'works like this are like "angels' visits", and should be made the most of'. The overture to *A*

---

[1] Those to whom I first sang will never hear my later singing.
[2] Moscheles mentions, however, that a performance of the (unrevised) *Hebrides* Overture earlier in the year had puzzled the audience and been 'coldly received'.

Midsummer Night's Dream was heard again, and with Moscheles (whom Mendelssohn describes as that rarity, an artist devoid of envy, jealousy and miserable egotism) Mendelssohn played Mozart's Double Concerto for which he had specially composed two long new cadenzas. One day he played the great organ in St Paul's Cathedral and astonished his audience by the brilliance of his improvisations; apparently it was only the piano that he considered an unsuitable instrument for such *tours de force*.

Mendelssohn was reported to be able to do everything on the organ – except one thing: play the congregation out of church. 'The more he attempted it, the less they were inclined to go; the more gracefully insinuating his musical hints, the more delightedly patient they became to remain. It is said that once, when he was playing at St Paul's, the vergers, wearied with endeavouring to persuade the people to retire, resorted at length to the more convincing argument of beating them over the head, and at last cleared the Cathedral.'

Besides public music-making there were many delightful informal evenings at the Moscheles'. Felix Moscheles, son of Ignaz and godson of Mendelssohn, gives a charming account[1] of one such evening at a later date, when the two pianists improvised together, tossing musical ideas to and fro like a shuttlecock and uttering little cries of triumph when a point was scored. There was music, too, with new friends, Dr William Horsley and his family, of whom Mendelssohn was to see a great deal on subsequent visits to London. Horsley, organist and composer, had been one of the founders (in 1813) of the Philharmonic Society. His young son Charles, who later became a pupil of Mendelssohn's in Leipzig, stood as the prototype for Charles Auchester in the novel of that name by the sixteen-year-old Elizabeth Sheppard. Mendelssohn figures in the book as the Chevalier Seraphael, Zelter as Aronach, Berlioz as Anastase and Jenny Lind as Clara. Of *Charles Auchester*, which caused quite a stir when it was published anonymously in 1853,[2] Disraeli wrote, 'No greater book will ever be written upon music, and one day it will be recognized as the imaginative classic of that divine art', while a critic in the *Atlantic Monthly* described its pages as literally 'drenched with beauty'. The modern reader will probably find them drenched with sentiment, and pretty heavy going.

The news of Zelter's death reached Mendelssohn towards the end of May, and the shock made him ill. It was with Sir Thomas Attwood at Norwood that he had convalesced after his carriage accident in 1829, and it was to him again that he now turned, as to a father, for solace. He found nothing changed: his room there untouched, the household as kind and considerate as ever:

> The three years have passed over them and their house as peacefully as if half the world had not been uprooted during that period. . . . The only difference is that now it is spring, with apple-blossom and the lilacs in flower. . . . But how much is now gone for ever, that we then still had! This gives me much food for thought.

Mendelssohn arrived home on 25 June. What he called his 'great journey' lay behind him. He had seen what England, France and Italy had to offer, and much though he loved England he now recognized clearly that he was 'a German, and must remain so'.

[1] Preface to *Letters of Felix Mendelssohn to Ignaz and Charlotte Moscheles*, edited by Felix Moscheles.
[2] Reprinted in Dent's 'Everyman's Library', n.d.

OPPOSITE *Mendelssohn. Drawing by Carl Müller, 1842*

PART THREE

Maturity 1833-1847

CHAPTER FIFTEEN

A Prophet Not Without Honour 1833

After the great success of the *St Matthew Passion* Mendelssohn had been approached about the directorship of the Singakademie in succession to Zelter, who had turned seventy and was increasingly obliged to leave his duties in the hands of his assistant, Karl Rungenhage. Mendelssohn had expressed himself willing; but on his return to Berlin in December 1829 he had heard nothing further of the matter. Then came the years of travel in Italy and France. As soon, however, as Zelter's death had been announced, Abraham had written to his son in London 'ordering' him – the word is hardly too strong – to come home as soon as possible so that he might enter his name as a candidate.

While abroad Felix had corresponded with his father on the subject of his future, making it clear that he wanted on his return to be free, to stand on his own feet, to have time to compose and to accept invitations as a guest conductor. He had come to realize that he was really too young and too lacking in authority to take on a directorship. But as he had already agreed in principle to accept the Singakademie if it were offered him, he said that he would still do so; he was not, however, prepared to send in an application. His father was bitterly disappointed; he was not accustomed to opposition.

The wretched business of the appointment of Zelter's successor dragged on for many months. Rungenhagen, competent and hard-working but mediocre, felt that as Zelter's assistant for many years he had a right to succeed him, and there were others who thought the same. A suggestion was made that he and Mendelssohn might hold the position jointly, but Rungenhagen refused to consider this. Finally and much against his better judgment, Mendelssohn unhappily allowed himself to be talked by Devrient and his father into sending in an application. A ballot was held on 22 January 1833 and Rungenhagen elected by one hundred and forty-eight votes to eighty-eight; Mendelssohn's youth and his Jewish origin had told too strongly against him. Thus, says Devrient, the Akademie was condemned for many years to mediocrity. Moreover, Abraham, formerly a most generous benefactor of the Akadamie, now seceded with all his family.

The whole autumn had been poisoned for Mendelssohn by wrangling and intrigue. In September he had written to Klingemann saying that he was unutterably depressed and suffering from earaches and headaches; his thoughts were black, and Berlin, 'that stagnant dump', had become odious to him. Yet he forced himself to work and gave four very success-ful concerts, at one of which his *Walpurgis Night* was performed publicly for the first time. Fortunately, before the final blow fell he had received the flattering invitation from the

London Philharmonic Society to write for them a symphony (it was to be his still unfinished 'Italian' Symphony) and two other works for a very substantial honorarium. Thanks to this, the fog, he told Klingemann, was 'beginning to lift'; and soon after Rungenhagen's appointment came a still more important invitation to conduct the Lower Rhine Festival, to be held at Düsseldorf at the end of May. It is hardly too much to say that these two commissions, which showed him that it was only in his own country – in Berlin – that the prophet was without honour, saved Mendelssohn from a breakdown.

On 25 April, after a brief visit to Düsseldorf to check that all was under way for the coming festival, Mendelssohn arrived in London, where he was welcomed by the Moscheles and shown their newly born son and heir, Felix, to whom he acted as godfather.

A week later, at a concert organized by Moscheles, the two pianists played, to great applause, a very flamboyant set of variations, on the 'Gypsy March' from Weber's *Preciosa*, which they had hastily, and jointly, written *ad hoc*. Then on 13 May came the Philharmonic concert at which Mendelssohn's 'Italian' Symphony received its first performance; he was also the soloist in Mozart's Piano Concerto in D minor. Critics and public alike were enthusiastic over the symphony; and from an unpublished letter mentioned by Werner we learn that Paganini, who was present, immediately invited the young composer to play Beethoven sonatas with him. Nothing, however, came of this because the great virtuoso fell ill; but apparently Mendelssohn and Moscheles had already come to the conclusion that Paganini 'no longer exercised the old charm over us. That eternal mawkishness', Moscheles had written a year before, 'becomes at last too much of a good thing.'

'Düsseldorf', said Heine of his birthplace, 'is a town on the Rhine where sixteen thousand people live and many hundreds of thousands are buried.' It was a very civilized little place, famous principally for its Academy of Painting, then under the direction of the Berlin artist Wilhelm von Schadow – an old friend of the Mendelssohns and a son of the sculptor J. G. von Schadow. Theatrical and literary life revolved round Karl Immermann, whose unsatisfactory libretto based on Shakespeare's *Tempest* Mendelssohn had received in the previous autumn and had recently so tactfully rejected that its notoriously touchy author apparently bore him no grudge. The Lower Rhine Festival, founded in 1817 and held annually in one of the Rhineland towns, was still in its infancy; among its later conductors were to be Liszt, Brahms, Schumann and Richard Strauss, and Mendelssohn on six subsequent occasions.

Mendelssohn arrived at Düsseldorf in the middle of May, and was soon joined by Abraham Mendelssohn, who had decided to come to see for himself how his son would handle this new and important assignment. Abraham, though only fifty-seven, was now a tired old man with failing sight and only two more years to live; but fortunately he had recovered from his earlier depression and was in a sunny mood. Felix's outstanding success was to make him yet sunnier, and in a series of letters to Lea in Berlin he proudly reported every detail of their son's triumphal progress.

It was, as always, to be a two-day festival, preceded by a number of rehearsals to which ticket-holders for the festival itself were admitted for a nominal charge. In the first concert came Mendelssohn's trumpet overture of 1825 and Handel's *Israel in Egypt*; Mendelssohn had been lucky enough to acquire in England a copy of the original score of the Handel work, which had not been heard before in Germany. The second combined Beethoven's 'Pastoral' Symphony and *Leonore* Overture No. 3 with two recent choral works which (says Werner) 'barely attained the status of mediocrity': a cantata by E. W. Wolf and an oratorio by Peter von Winter; these were not of Mendelssohn's choice, but they had already been rehearsed and he was obliged to include them. Abraham was to find the Wolf 'dreadfully boring', but the Winter even worse in that it was positively unpleasant.

Abraham had asked Felix to book a room for him; but there was none to be had and he found himself the guest of the local Governor (*Regierungspräsident*), the seventy-four-year-old Herr Otto von Woringen, whose 'incredible kindness and truly old-world hospitality, shown me *pour les beaux yeux de mon fils*', he could not find words adequately to describe. Of Felix, Abraham wrote: 'Since a musical festival has a director, I suppose I must say something about this year's – Herr Felix (he is hardly called anything else here). My dear, this young man brings us much happiness, and I often say to myself, Long live Marten's Mill!' This was the Mendelssohn's house on the outskirts of Hamburg, where Felix had been conceived and born.

Abraham had only one regret (other than that he had struck a heat-wave): that he had not persuaded Lea to come with him. 'A musical festival on the Rhine is a singularly beautiful thing,' he told her. The little town was seething with excitement and almost bursting at the seams. 'Since Friday, steamboats, diligences of every description, *Extraposten*, coaches and private carriages convey whole families from all parts of the country as far as twenty miles around and even further (from Breslau, for instance) to this festive town of Düsseldorf.' And how refreshing it was to be in a town where there was 'no court, no meddling interference from above, no *Generalmusikdirektor*, no royal this or that'. And the old Republican adds, 'It's a real *folk* festival.'

The concert hall, which stood about a mile from the town in a large and shady garden belonging to a restaurateur, was an austere building capable of seating an audience of twelve or thirteen hundred. In the intervals 'everyone rushes out into the garden, where there are masses of sandwiches and lots of *Maitrank*.[1] . . . It's all rather like a kermesse.' The audience was recalled by a loud fanfare from the orchestra, followed a couple of minutes later by a second fanfare to gather in 'the lazy and the thirsty – and Israel cries once more to the Lord.'

Rehearsals went on almost uninterruptedly each day from dawn to dusk, and Abraham did not miss a single one. The proud father could not take his eyes off his son. 'I have never seen a face like his,' he wrote,

> nor have I ever seen anyone so petted and courted as he is here. He himself cannot sufficiently praise the zeal of all the performers and their perfect confidence in him, and as always his playing and his memory astonish everyone. That wonderful memory of his has stood him in good stead, because it enabled them to remove from the programme a Beethoven symphony which had been played here several times and replace it by the 'Pastoral'. (It makes me melt to think that I shall have to hear it the day after tomorrow in this dreadful heat!) When it was mentioned, he not only instantly played it from memory but, at a small trial on the eve of the rehearsal, when there was no score at hand, conducted it by heart *and* sang the part of a missing instrument.

It seemed to him 'an absolute miracle that four hundred people of all sexes, classes and

---

[1] A 'cup' made from Hock and Moselle flavoured with woodruff, etc. Felix was renowned for his skill in concocting it.

ages, blown together like snow before the wind, should let themselves be conducted and governed like children by one of the youngest of them all . . . one with no title or office whatever'; he had only one criticism: a slight (Jewish) lisp still disfigured the young man's speech. The orchestra ate out of his hand, and Felix was even able to put an end to two abuses where no other conductor had succeeded. The first was what Abraham calls 'that disgusting practice of "warming up"', the second the interminable chatter in the orchestra between old friends who had not seen one another recently. 'Now, as soon as he knocks and is about to speak, a general "pst!" is heard, and there is dead silence.'

Nothing could go wrong for Felix during that golden fortnight. The rehearsals were a triumph, the performances even more successful, and at the end of the second concert Felix found himself smothered with flowers which 'the young ladies, and I believe also the matrons of the chorus', had brought in and hidden under their seats. Finally the eldest Fräulein von Woringen, who had concealed a laurel wreath beneath her scarf, ran forward to crown him. 'They say,' said Abraham, whose dim eyes could see nothing of what was happening from the back of the hall, 'that he bent nearly double to escape this homage. But a big strong man from the chorus seized him and held him up, and on the fourth attempt succeeded in placing the wreath on his head. . . . People say it suited him very well.'

After the concert came a party at the Schadows. Abraham, quite worn out, tried to make his escape; but Schadow would not hear of his missing the fun and carried him along almost by force. To the sound of 'See the conquering hero comes!' Felix entered the room and was made to put on his wreath. He was then forced to play, but soon surrendered the piano to someone else and joined in the dancing, where he amazed everyone by his proficiency. At supper, where Aleatico and Vino Santo flowed like water, Abraham, in accordance with a vow he had made, did not touch a drop – 'nor did Felix'; was the son, who enjoyed his wine, obeying even in this the order of the father? But, apparently the other guests drank heartily, for afterwards 'everyone started singing in chorus, and very loudly too. We all had to join in and it was two o'clock before we got home.'

Such had been the success of the festival that it was decided to do something quite without precedent: to give a third concert. Some of the pieces previously performed were repeated at it; but a scene from *Der Freischütz* and an aria from *Fidelio* were added, and Felix played Weber's brilliant *Conzertstück*. More festivities followed upon this concert, but Abraham was 'so completely knocked up' that he went straight home to bed and slept for twenty-four hours; he wanted to husband his strength for the farewell banquet the following evening.

If further evidence were needed of Felix's personal triumph, it came now: he was invited by the Düsseldorf Music and Theatre Society, a municipal body, to take charge of the town's music for a term of three years, starting at the beginning of October. The salary was reasonable, and he was to be allowed three months' leave of absence annually. After consulting his father he accepted, for it seemed to provide the perfect solution to his problems: it took him away from the Berlin that he had come to hate, and it gave him his chance to show his worth in a less important post than the one he had failed to get there. Most important of all, it restored his self-confidence. To Lea, Abraham wrote, 'I couldn't wish for anything more suitable for him, or for his future. . . . The days that have fallen to my lot were beautiful and unforgettable.'

Felix was going direct to London after the festival, not to give any public concerts (for the

season was almost at an end) but to see his friends and to relax. Abraham had intended to return to Berlin, but at the eleventh hour he changed his mind and accompanied his son to England. They arrived in London about 5 June and went straight to Felix's old lodgings in Portland Street.

*   *   *

Abraham was much impressed by London, especially of course by Nash's London, but he told Lea that he still preferred Paris:

> I passed Oxford Street, Regent Street, Portland Place and Regent's Park, and must confess that in the splendour and taste of the buildings, elegance and cleanliness of the streets, good pavements, etc. – in short, in everything that impresses your senses without producing an effect on your mind, I have not seen anything to be compared to the wonders of that one hour's walk. But when I think of the grand aspect of the Tuileries, the place Louis xv, the Champs-Elysées, the boulevards and *quais* that encircle it all . . . I can only say, London is the richest town and Paris the greatest town I ever saw.

Although it was June, it amused him to pretend that the weather was detestable:

> This morning at fourteen minutes past nine the sun was just powerful enough to give a yellow tinge to the mist, and the air was just like the smoke of a great fire. 'A very fine morning!' said my barber (here called hairdresser). 'Is it?' I asked. 'Yes, a *very* fine morning!' And so I learnt what a fine summer morning here is like. . . . I have to move my table close

to the window in order to see, not what I am writing, but *that* I am writing at all. Felix has
gone to St Paul's to play the organ . . . and when he comes home I am sure he will say that
nowhere are there such glorious summer days as in London.

He felt that the English Sunday was 'as indispensable to the Londoners as fallow-time is
to the fields', the weekday pandemonium being such that 'if they lived one year without it
they would all go mad'. Since his English was limited to 'How do you do, Sir?', 'Waiter, a
mutton chop', and 'other similarly profound phrases', he felt rather cut off; but in any case
'strangers in London are ignored. They are not considered to exist: there are only the English.'
'I speak Italian with Horsley,' he wrote, 'for he speaks neither German nor French, and at
least *both* of us don't speak Italian.' He was horrified by the high cost of living. 'Guineas run
out of one's pocket here. . . . For what I have spent on carriage hire I could purchase all the
public carriages in Berlin.' After Berlin he found the rich very rich and the poor very poor.

There is plenty of evidence that Abraham had a nice, dry sense of humour. While in
London he learned that his younger daughter, Rebecka, who was now married to a distinguished professor of mathematics named Dirichlet, had given birth to a son. He was,
however, rather indignant that the father, a notoriously bad correspondent, had not troubled
to drop him a line. 'He might at least', he observed, 'have written $2+1=3$!'

A visit to the Royal Academy persuaded him that modern English art was 'a load of
rubbish'. He could not even agree with Felix that Wilkie's picture of a young Capuchin at

LEFT *3 Chester Place, the
home of Moscheles.
Drawing by Mendelssohn,
1835* RIGHT *Fanny and
Sophie Horsley. Drawings
by Wilhelm Hensel,
August 1843*

confession[1] had much if anything to commend it; the young monk looked, he thought, 'as
if he had taken an emetic for the occasion and was just about to bring up his confession'. He
went to Greenwich where he admired the shipping but wondered why the English 'did not
have, and had never had, at least a marine artist'; at that same Royal Academy exhibition,
it may be mentioned, Turner was showing several seascapes.

At a private party at the Horsleys, Abraham heard Malibran sing, and was completely
captivated. In Berlin she had made hardly any impression on him, but now he said he could
not find words to describe (yet did, at some length) 'with what flowing, glowing and efferves-
cing power and expression, what caprice of boldness, passion and *esprit*, with what assurance
and consciousness of her means, this woman, whom I now *do* appreciate, . . . sang in French,
English, Spanish and Italian'. Felix, reluctant to follow the great singer, attempted to hide,
but was dragged to the piano where he excelled in the extemporizations that he so much
hated to perform. Everyone adored the Malibran, and Moscheles has left a charming account
of the kindness she showed to his children. Sadly, in the spring of 1836 she received serious
head injuries in a fall from her horse, and five months later, soon after collapsing at a concert
in Manchester while singing a shake on a top C, she died there of brain fever; she was only
twenty-eight.

But the liveliest account of the Mendelssohns' visit to England is, rather surprisingly, to be
found in the letters of two schoolgirls to their aunt. These girls were Frances (Fanny) and

[1] *Spanish Monks, a scene witnessed in a Capuchin Convent at Toledo* (No. 134).

Sophia (Sophy), aged eighteen and fourteen respectively, two of the five children of Dr William Horsley; Sophy was a very talented pianist. The eldest daughter, Mary, known locally as 'the Duchess of Kensington', was twenty and later married the famous engineer Isambard Brunel. There were two boys: John (aged sixteen) who became a Royal Academician and the already mentioned Charles (aged twelve). The aunt, Lucy Callcott, was only a year older than Fanny, and therefore treated by the Horsley children as a kind of non-resident sister – hence the correspondence.

The Horsleys, whose 'three charming daughters glided like the Graces through the elegant rooms' (Frau Polko, of course), lived at 1 High Row, Kensington Gravel Pits, a large late Georgian house not far from the present Notting Hill Gate underground station, their friends the Moscheles at 3 Chester Place in Regent's Park. Felix, Rosen and Klingemann were constant guests at these houses, and especially at the Horsleys', where the girls never ceased to be amused by the heel-clicking and low bows of the three young Germans. Fanny was more than a little bit in love with Rosen, to whom Felix was also deeply devoted:

Mendelssohn talked to me the other night about Dr Rosen in such affectionate terms that he was quite touching. The tears came quite into his eyes as he said that he was not only great but good, and that though still so young no one knew him without revering and respecting him. It was difficult to know which most to admire, the praised or the praiser. Mendelssohn is a generous high-minded creature, but, to descend from these heights, he was dressed very badly, and looked in sad want of the piece of soap and the nail brush which I have so often threatened to offer him.[1]

[1] Quotations from the letters of Fanny and Sophy Horsley are taken from *Mendelssohn and his Friends in Kensington*, edited by Rosamund Brunel Gotch (Oxford University Press, London, 1934).

He had, however, grown his hair long again – she had last seen him after the 'Spanish crop' he had undergone in Paris – and she thought the new coiffure 'so very becoming'.

Felix's moodiness is mentioned by both Fanny and Sophy. Fanny found him one day 'looking very cross. He sat in deep glumps and sighs all the time till he went, and then went on apologizing in a mumbling tone for nearly ten minutes when he took his leave.' On another occasion Sophy and Mary were at the Moscheles' when Felix appeared 'very cross and sulky and sat at the drawing-room table looking over the score of [Neukomm's] oratorio taking no notice of anyone, not even of his little godchild . . . who was seated on Mary's lap' and now (thought Sophy) no longer resembled 'a pickled walnut'. 'At last Mrs M[oscheles] said "I do not think you care a bit about your god-child" upon which he turned round and made a horrid noise at it, partaking both of the nose as well as the throat, which frightened the poor little thing. . . .' It was perhaps hardly surprising that Mrs Horsley and Mary decided that Felix would never marry; but Fanny thought he would – 'that is if he does not plague his mistress to death before the day arrives. Mr Klingemann told us that he (Mend.) had been much struck with Delphine, she however, being another's, is quite out of the question.' But if Delphine was out of the question, there were other fish in the sea. Werner, drawing his information from an unpublished letter from Rosen to Felix, tells us that the latter was by no means as strait-laced as were his father and his grandfather, and that he 'did not go out of his way to avoid adventures. . . . There was a young girl-friend of Rosen, gifted in painting, whose temperament, aggressive in the erotic sense, charmed Felix. He seems to have had success with her, too.' It is hardly necessary to add that not a hint of such goings-on is to be found in the published letters.

The young Horsleys had been rather alarmed at the prospect of meeting what Sophy calls 'the old gentleman' and Fanny 'the son of Moses' – in other words, Abraham Mendelssohn; but the day he was due to dine with them he was, according to Sophy, 'seized with histerics [sic]'. However, he came a few days later, was pronounced 'delightful', and thereafter was a regular and a welcome visitor. One afternoon Fanny entertained him while the rest of the young played 'Ghost'. She observed that Felix ran the quickest, but Rosen the most gracefully:

> They all looked very droll. Mary's hair came down and they tore about in fine style. Mendelssohn and Sophy at my desire played the beautiful lovely Ottetto; and the bass, though perhaps you don't believe it, was just as good as the treble. . . . Mendelssohn engaged me before tea. He was very droll, in the highest spirits I ever saw, laughing at his own jokes, whirling round in pirouettes and all sorts of 'folies'. . . .

Unhappily, just as the Mendelssohns were about to return to Berlin, Abraham hurt his shin and, like his son four years earlier, was laid up for several weeks. Fanny went to see him, and reported:

> The sufferer was a very odd spectacle. . . . His poor little legs were just like sticks laid flat on the sofa, and precisely the same all the way down, his flannel elastic drawers bound round his diminutive calves with red tape. He looked poorly but he talked a great deal and seemed very glad to see Papa. . . . Felix was very lachrimose and rushed four times in and

William Sterndale Bennett, at the age of sixteen, in the uniform of the Royal College of Music. Watercolour by J. W. Childe, 1832

out of the room in a very phrenzied manner. I gazed at him for some time in such deep amaze that I am sure at last he perceived it. What an odd tempered creature he is. But most geniuses are the same they say, and at any rate he is always delightful for he is always original.

Early in August there were signs that the wound might mortify. Poor Felix became 'quite frantic' and stayed with his father night and day; but Abraham turned the corner. During his illness he was overwhelmed by the endless kindness of friends and acquaintances, who showered him with puddings, pies, grapes (these from his landlady), pots of jam and marmalade, cakes, port ('*without brandy*') and claret. But 'next to God, and even more than to my doctor', he told Lea, 'I owe my recovery to one whom, apart from you, I like best being indebted to – and that is Felix. I can never tell you what he has done for me, what treasures of love, patience, grave kindness and tenderest care he has lavished on me. . . .'

Once Abraham was on the mend, Felix too made a lightning recovery from his neurotic state. Sophy called one day to inquire after the father and reported of the son, 'I have seen him look handsome, but never, never, did I see such a blaze of light as when he stood at the passage door; he appeared so perfectly happy. . . .' He had been composing a capriccio (op. 33, No. 3) and was full of plans for future compositions, though it was Fanny's opinion that 'he had better at the same time compose himself, for his mind wants a little settling in my opinion'.

By the end of August Abraham was pronounced fit to travel. Indeed, he felt in such high spirits that he indulged in a rather ponderous little joke, pretending to Lea that Felix was obliged to remain for a time in England and that he was returning instead with a charming young Frenchman, a M. Lovie – who proved, of course, to be Felix.

Then came the farewells. Fanny Horsley and her mother had walked with Felix and Klingemann as far as Apsley House:

> Actually when we got there Felix wanted to walk with us all the way back again . . . but the diplomatist stood firm. . . . So we shook hands with Felix and wished him happy and then came back. He turned quite as pale as death, though he had been looking as fresh as a great damask rose all the walk, and his eyes filled with tears. 'God bless you' said Mama for the last time, and he walked off alone. . . . And so we have seen the last of him for two years at least and who can say what may happen in that time? His last words almost were 'Oh pray, Mrs Horsley, pray let me find no changes, let all be the same as ever' – but that is not in our own controul.

TOP *Frankfurt from the river. Hand-coloured lithograph by an unknown artist, c. 1815.*
BOTTOM *The Unter den Linden, Berlin. Oil painting by Wilhelm Brücke. The building on the right is the Arsenal*

CHAPTER SIXTEEN

Düsseldorf 1833-1835

The newly appointed Director of Music arrived in Düsseldorf on 25 September 1833. He came in high spirits to a town which had clearly demonstrated that it wanted him; little did he then guess the troubles that lay ahead.

His duties were to direct the rehearsals and concerts of the Music and Theatre Society and to keep a watchful eye on the music of the local churches, most of which were Roman Catholic. The Düsseldorf Society was only one of the contributors to the Lower Rhine Festival, and in spite of his signal success that summer Mendelssohn found that he had not been invited to take charge of the 1834 festival at Aachen. The invitation had been extended to, and accepted by, Ferdinand Ries, a distinguished Beethoven pupil, who had previously conducted the festival in 1832. Mendelssohn must have been disappointed, and to silence rumours soon current that there was unpleasantness between himself and Ries he arranged a concert at which they were both to appear.

Soon after his arrival he was approached by the Mayor's Chaplain. It seemed that the new Mayor, a man rather full of his own importance, demanded that 'music of a better class' should be played during the Church processions, since he intended to take part in them. 'A very crabbed old musician in a threadbare coat was summoned. . . . When they attacked him he declared that he neither could nor would have better music, and that if improvement was required they must get another man. He knew perfectly well what vast pretensions some people made nowadays, that everything was expected to sound so beautiful; this hadn't been the case in his day and he still played just as well as he always had.' Mendelssohn couldn't help thinking how *he* would feel if in fifty years time he were 'summoned and spoken to like this, and a young greenhorn snubbed me, and my coat were seedy, and I hadn't the remotest idea why the music should be better; and I felt rather uncomfortable'.

There being 'not even one tolerable solemn Mass' discoverable in Düsseldorf, Mendelssohn decided to scour what he called his 'domains' in search of suitable scores:

> I got into a carriage and drove off to Elberfeld, where I hunted out Palestrina's *Improperia* and the *Misereres* of Allegri and Bai, and also the score and vocal parts of Handel's *Alexander's Feast*, which I carried off and then went on to Bonn. There I rummaged through the whole library . . . and found some splendid things. I took away with me six Masses of Palestrina, one of Lotti and one of Pergolesi, Psalms by Leo and Lotti, etc., etc. At last, in Köln, I succeeded in finding the best old Italian pieces I yet know, particularly two motets by Orlando Lasso.[1] . . . One of these, *Populus meus*, we are going to sing in church next Friday.

[1] Lasso (1532–1594) was in fact Flemish.

Then Mendelssohn hurried back to Düsseldorf for the visit of the Prussian Crown Prince (afterwards Friedrich Wilhelm IV). Triumphal arches had been erected; bells were incessantly pealed (and Mendelssohn hated church bells), cannons fired, and a gala dinner given at which Mendelssohn was summoned by the Prince, addressed as 'My dear Mendelssohn' and jocularly reprimanded for deserting Berlin. There followed a fête, minutely described by Mendelssohn in a letter to Rebecka, at which Handel's *Israel in Egypt* was repeated to the accompaniment of *tableaux vivants* and magic-lantern projections of pictures by Dürer, Raphael and other artists.

No doubt Immermann and Mendelssohn had worked together in the production of this entertainment, and the former now proposed that they should collaborate further in a number of 'model' performances of operas. Immermann had long been campaigning to establish a National Theatre in Düsseldorf, financed by shareholders, and this was due to open in a year's time; presumably these special productions were intended to establish an

Aachen. Engraving, c. *1840*

*Ferdinand Ries. Engraving
by Carl Mayer, c. 1825*

appropriate standard of excellence for it. Unhappily the choice of the word 'model' (*Muster*) was considered arrogant by some of the public; but what gave far more cause for complaint was the raising of the price of seats that such performances necessitated.

The season was to open with Mozart's *Don Giovanni*, and after twenty rehearsals the first performance took place shortly before Christmas. A riotous element in the audience, which Mendelssohn mistakenly identified as 'mainly beer-house proprietors and waiters (for in fact, by 4 p.m. half Düsseldorf is drunk)', decided to barrack it. One duet was 'completely drowned by whistling, shouting and howling', and 'after a newspaper had been flung to the stage-manager on the stage, for him to read aloud – whereupon he went off in a violent huff and the curtain was lowered for the fourth time – I wanted to lay down my baton (or preferably to throw it at the heads of some of these louts), when the uproar suddenly subsided'. The remainder of the opera passed off without incident and at the fall of the final curtain there was much applause and calls for the cast – who, not surprisingly, refused to appear.

Immermann and Mendelssohn consulted together below stage 'among the black demons and in a shower of fiery rain and gunpowder smoke'. Mendelssohn declared that unless an apology were made to himself and to the company, he would not conduct a second performance, and the orchestra refused to play under any other conductor. The theatre manager, who had already taken advance bookings for every seat in the house, was in despair, and Immermann, whom rage and disappointment had made quite ill, did not improve matters by 'snubbing everybody all round'. But who was going to apologize? Most surprisingly, the instigator of the riot now came forward, 'justified himself, declared that in spite of everything he had enormously enjoyed his evening, and was most grateful to me and to the company. . . . As he was a government clerk, the President [Mendelssohn's old friend Woringen] summoned him and blew him up tremendously, then sent him to the Director who also blew him up tremendously. The soldiers who had taken part in the riot were treated similarly by their officers.'

So the model performances were resumed, and with considerable success. But there were times when Mendelssohn's temper was frayed, and at a rehearsal of Goethe's *Egmont* with Beethoven's music he flew into a rage and tore the full score in two – no small feat of strength! However, he continued to work hard, giving, as stipulated in his contract, six concerts in Düsseldorf (Handel, Beethoven, Weber, Gluck and Cherubini) and further concerts for charity in Köln and Elberfeld. Of the Düsseldorf Orchestra, many of whom were usually far from sober of an evening, he later wrote scathingly to Hiller:

> I assure you that at the beat they all come in separately, not one with any decision, and in the pianos the flute is always sharp, and not a single Düsseldorfer can play a triplet clearly, but all play a quaver and two semi-quavers instead, and every allegro leaves off twice as fast as it began, and the oboe plays E natural in C minor, and they carry their fiddles under their coats when it rains, and when it is fine they don't cover them at all – and if you once heard me conduct this orchestra wild horses couldn't drag you there a second time. . . .[1]

*   *   *

In May 1834 came the Lower Rhine Festival under Ries at Aachen. Mendelssohn, who was not involved, went there with the two Woringens, arriving 'bored and cross' after an eleven-hour journey by the post. Ferdinand Hiller had translated and arranged Handel's *Deborah* for one of the concerts, and to Mendelssohn's great joy he found that both he and Chopin had come from Paris to hear it, Chopin having at the last moment sold a waltz to Pleyel to pay the fare:

> Next morning [Mendelssohn told his mother] we were of course all at the piano, and I enjoyed myself enormously. Both of them have still further improved their techniques, and as a pianist Chopin is now one of the very best – quite a second Paganini, and doing miraculous things which no one would have believed possible. Hiller too is an excellent performer – vigorous and pleasing. They both suffer a bit from the Parisian love of effect and excess of passion, often losing sight of time and calm and real musical feeling; perhaps I err in the other direction, so we make up for each other's deficiencies and I think all learn from each other. . . .

> After the festival we travelled together to Düsseldorf and spent a very pleasant day together, talking and playing.

Hiller tells us that Mendelssohn had 'a couple of nice rooms on the ground floor of Schadow's house, was working on his *St Paul*, associated a great deal with the young painters,

---

[1] Mendelssohn once wrote, 'In the next world . . . there'll be no bad pianos like Geyer's, no silly puffing flutes, no dragging trombones; no breakdowns or wavering or hurrying: of that, I'm certain.'

Mendelssohn. Oil painting by Wilhelm von Schadow, 1835

kept a horse, and was altogether very flourishing'. (Incidentally, Mendelssohn had not dared to buy this horse without getting his father's permission!) In the afternoon came a walk with Schadow and a band of his disciples, 'many of them extremely good-looking', who hung on the great artist's every word. 'Chopin was a stranger to them all, and, shy as always, kept close to me during the walk, watching everything but talking only to me, and almost in a whisper.' Then came coffee with Schadow and a game of bowls, coupled with an invitation to return in the evening. Hiller continues:

> We found some of the most talented young painters there, and the conversation soon became very lively; the only trouble was that poor Chopin sat silent and ignored. However, Mendelssohn and I knew that he would have his revenge, and were secretly delighted at the prospect. At last the piano was opened. I began, Mendelssohn followed, and then we asked Chopin to play. The company looked rather dubiously at him and at us; but hardly had he played a few bars when everybody present, and Schadow in particular, became spell-bound: they had never heard anything like it, and excitedly clamoured for more and more.

Next day Mendelssohn accompanied Hiller and Chopin to Köln. After visiting the Church of the Apostles they reached the bridge where, wrote Hiller, 'we parted in a rather comic way. I was staring down at the river, making some extravagant remark or other, when Mendelssohn suddenly cried, "Hiller getting sentimental; heaven help us! Adieu, farewell!" – and was gone.'

Of Mendelssohn's minor activities that summer we know something from his letters. He tells us that he took lessons in watercolour painting on Sunday mornings from a good local artist, Schirmer, and that he was often driven half crazy by the girl next door, who practised the piano excruciatingly for hours on end. He rode a great deal, and went on a number of very enjoyable picnics. Then came a heat-wave and much boating and bathing in the Rhine, interrupted on one occasion when he and some of his friends were surprised stark naked by the Queen of Bavaria, who suddenly rounded a bend of the river in her steamboat: 'We sprang just *a tempo* into the water as she approached.' Finally, Werner has ferreted out a little affair with 'a widowed aristocratic lady' which was passionate for a time but which, when passion cooled, died for want of any common intellectual bond. News of the liaison came, probably through the Woringens, to the ears of Lea, and a year later Rebecka actually met the widow – and formed a very poor opinion of her.

There now came the engagement of singers for the new theatre. Devrient, in Berlin, had been asked to look for promising material, including 'an efficient young soprano with enthusiasm and a voice (she need have nothing else)'; at the end of August, therefore, Mendelssohn went there to vet his friend's discoveries and arrange contracts – a job that he found far more disagreeable than he had expected. Then he returned to Düsseldorf to prepare for the opening of the season on 28 October with Kleist's *Prince Friedrich of Homburg*; the operas to be given included Weber's *Oberon* and *Der Freischütz*, Auber's *Fra Diavolo*, and Mozart's *Magic Flute* and *Seraglio*.

Mendelssohn and Immermann immediately began to quarrel. Three letters from Mendelssohn – to his mother on 4 November, to his sister Rebecka on 23 November, and to Devrient in 26 November – give his side of the story. The 'Statute' ordained that the theatre should be under the joint control of a theatrical and a musical Intendant – in the event,

Immermann and Mendelssohn. Though Immermann was a highly respected man of letters and thirteen years older than Mendelssohn, the question immediately arose as to which of them should take precedence. 'And this led to a row. I simply wanted to conduct and take charge of the musical side of the production, but that didn't satisfy Immermann. We exchanged very rude letters, then came to an understanding, but immediately quarrelled again when he ordered me to go to Aachen to hear and engage a singer there – which I refused to do.'

The trouble allegedly arose over the administration, which was something for which Mendelssohn had no talent. He had disliked haggling over the contracts of one or two principals in Berlin; he found the task of arranging them for the whole orchestra intolerable. To Rebecka he wrote:

> Then I had to engage an orchestra – that is to say, prepare two contracts for each member, having first fought to the death over a thaler more or less of their monthly salaries. Then they went off; then they came back and signed all the same; then they all objected to sitting at the second music desk. Then there arrived the aunt of a perfectly hopeless performer whom I couldn't engage, and the wife and two small children of another perfectly hopeless performer, to intercede on their behalfs. Then I accepted three fellows on approval, and they all played so abominably that I simply couldn't take any of them. Then they looked very humble and withdrew silently, very wretched, having lost their daily bread. Then the wife reappeared and wept. Out of thirty applicants there was only one who said, 'I am satisfied'; all the others bargained and haggled for an hour. These four days were the wretchedest I have ever passed.

Finally the chorus turned up for a rehearsal completely drunk, and the *prima donna* lost her voice. 'So, three weeks after the reopening of the theatre I decided to resign. . . . And now I feel like a fish thrown back into the water. The mornings are once more my own, and in the evenings I can sit at home and read. My oratorio [*St Paul*] gives me increasing pleasure, and I have also written some new songs. The Choral Society flourishes and we hope soon to do [Haydn's] *Seasons* with full orchestra. I intend to publish six preludes and fugues, two of which you know already. This is the sort of life that suits me, *not* that of an Intendant.'

It was the opinion of most of those best qualified to judge, that Mendelssohn behaved very badly. Devrient, who took the trouble to learn all the facts, declared, 'Felix was entirely in the wrong.' Immerman, had he been approached tactfully, would probably have arranged for him to be relieved of at least some of the burden of administration; but if resignation was inevitable – and Klingemann, who happened to be in Düsseldorf at the time, believed that it was – then it should have taken place without acrimony. 'The breach was not brought about by the theatrical worries, as he represents,' said Devrient, 'but by a personal quarrel with Immermann in which Felix showed a hasty and snappish temper that one would hardly have suspected in him.'

Abraham, who had received a factual account from Woringen, could not remain silent. He reproached his son for his inability to master 'a tendency to surliness and irascibility, to grab things hastily and as hastily drop them', thus creating all sorts of practical difficulties for himself. He did not object to Felix choosing to retire from the administrative side of the theatre (he had been rash in ever agreeing to take it on), but he strongly disapproved of the way he had done it. Instead of trying to discuss the situation calmly, he had simply lost his temper and stormed out. 'Thus you indubitably exposed yourself to the charge of fickleness and unreliability, and made a firm enemy of a man whom at all events policy should have taught you not to offend. . . . If I am wrong about this, then give me a better explanation.' And in an unpublished letter (quoted by Werner) Abraham spoke yet more sharply: 'Through your own calamitous stubbornness you have done yourself more harm than you yet know. But – and this is more important – you could have brought misfortune on a whole institution which you yourself encouraged and now have thoughtlessly deserted.'

In the event, the theatre suffered surprisingly little from Mendelssohn's defection. Shortly before he had walked out he had appointed Julius Rietz, the twenty-two-year-old younger brother of his friend Eduard Rietz, as his assistant. Rietz now stepped into the breach and proved himself not only highly competent musically, but also to be possessed of those very qualities the lack of which in Mendelssohn had been responsible for all the trouble.

On 9 February 1835 Mendelssohn wrote to Immermann, 'In my opinion, only one answer to my letter would have been a proper one. Your answer I cannot accept, and therefore our relationship is at an end. We shall not meet again.' They never did.

In October, just as the trouble with Immermann was beginning, Mendelssohn had received a tentative inquiry from Leipzig as to whether he would consider taking over the directorship of the famous Gewandhaus Orchestra in that city. He gave the matter careful thought and, as always, consulted his father – but no one else. Abraham very strongly approved; he would not, however, even consider his son's plea that he might preferably have several years of complete freedom in order to devote himself entirely to composition.

Leipzig had many obvious advantages. It was an important town with an old university, a long musical tradition, and a population that was mainly Protestant. It was much nearer Berlin and his family. He would have a better orchestra, more scope, no theatrical involvements – and, above all, no Immermann; and a large part of the administration was to be taken off his hands. Last but not least, the shade of old Johann Sebastian Bach would be there to watch over him. Having clarified one or two points – in particular, he satisfied himself that the present Director was retiring through ill health and was not being driven out – he agreed to accept the post if it were offered him; fortunately there was a clause in his three-year contract with Düsseldorf that allowed him to break it at the end of two years. Negotiations were protracted, and during the winter Mendelssohn received the much more lucrative offer of the directorship of the Munich Opera; but both he and his father agreed that his experiences at Düsseldorf had shown him that this was not his *métier*. In April 1835 the contract with Leipzig was signed, Mendelssohn agreeing to take up his new duties in the autumn.

In June 1835 Mendelssohn again conducted the Lower Rhine Festival, which this year was held in Köln; in spite of all his troubles with Immermann the Rhinelanders continued over the years to remain loyal to him. He had assembled an enormous orchestra and choir – nearly five hundred singers and over two hundred players – and the principal works to be given were Handel's *Solomon* (in a translation by Klingemann, who disappointed many people by not coming over from London to hear it) and Beethoven's Eighth Symphony and *Consecration of the House* Overture.

Benedict, who was present at one of the rehearsals of the Beethoven symphony, relates that when the allegretto did not go as Mendelssohn wanted it, 'he remarked, smilingly that "he knew every one of the gentlemen engaged was capable of performing and even composing a scherzo of his own; but that *just now* he wanted to hear Beethoven's, which he thought had some merits".' This kind of pedagogic sarcasm, so resented by schoolboys, is, strangely enough, often relished by musicians or, at the worst, meekly accepted by them as an occupational hazard. At the end of the festival which was a great success, Mendelssohn was promised by the Committee Arnold's collected edition of Handel's works as a token of their gratitude; he modestly rejected their invitation to sit for a portrait 'on the grand scale', but a head-and-shoulders portrait by his friend Wilhelm von Schadow dates from this year.

Abraham and Lea, together with Fanny and Rebecka and their husbands, had attended the festival, and afterwards returned with Felix to Düsseldorf. Here Lea scared the whole family by suddenly collapsing with what was probably a slight stroke. A young doctor, a friend of Felix's, was hastily summoned, and within a couple of days she was declared out of danger. Felix, who had never left her side and was worn out, was surprised sound asleep by the doctor and his wife when they called to see the convalescent. What then ensued is described in her own inimitable style by Frau Polko, who appears to have received her information direct from the doctor's wife:

> Beside her [Lea], exhausted by the fatigue and excitement of the previous days, lay Felix asleep, his slender hand clasped in that of his mother, and his head resting on the corner of the sofa. The mother pointed to Felix with a beseeching glance, while holding out her other hand to greet her visitors. Her son was so sound asleep that he heard none of the little preliminaries attendant on a first introduction. There he lay, his noble forehead bent down, his dark eyelashes resting on his cheeks, his well-cut lips gently closed, pale, and breathing softly – a most charming picture.
>
> Rebecka, a lovely young girl, in a paroxysm of overflowing spirits, so easily excited by the sense of danger escaped, could not withstand the temptation of sewing the skirts of the sleeper's coat to the sofa. Gently the mother, with eyes and lips, protested against this mischievous prank – but in vain. . . . 'Never can I forget,' relates his friend, 'the embarrassed yet laughing face of Felix when he awoke, and, on attempting to rise to welcome us, found that he was held fast!'

By the beginning of August Lea was well enough to return to Berlin, and Felix went too. Rioting had broken out in the capital, during which a number of innocent people were killed by the indiscriminate firing of the troops. Felix, who described the events in a letter to Klingemann, considered that the soldiers had been drunk, and sided with the mob. This uneasy situation, together with some continued anxiety about his mother's health, caused him to put off an intended journey and to remain in what he calls that 'absolutely revolting hole' until the end of the month, when he set out for Leipzig to take up his new duties.

Probably the best known of Mendelssohn's compositions of his Düsseldorf days is his overture, *The Fair Melusine*. He wrote it, he told Fanny, for an opera by Conradin Kreutzer which he had heard a year before. The story, by Ludwig Tieck, told of a mermaid who fell in love with a mortal – needless to say, a handsome young knight – and agreed to marry him on his promising to leave her alone on certain nights of the year: a promise which he broke. Mendelssohn had greatly disliked Kreutzer's overture – 'but *not* Fräulein Hähnel, who took the part of Melusine and was very charming, especially in a scene where she was combing her hair; and this inspired me to write an overture which, though it might not get an encore, would be of more real worth. . . .'

The Fair Melusine was first performed under Moscheles at a Philharmonic concert in London in April 1834. Klingemann, who was of course present, found it 'heavenly, charming and passionate', but 'far too good for that kind of an audience', whom it failed to please; a too-slow tempo was, he thought, in part responsible. To Frau Moscheles, who also told Mendelssohn of its chilly reception, the latter replied: 'So the people at the Philharmonic didn't like my Melusine? Well – that won't kill me! However, I was sorry when I read your letter, and immediately played my overture straight through to see whether I too now disliked it; but it still gives me pleasure. . . .' It was to remain one of his favourite compositions.

After hearing the work in Leipzig in December 1835, Schumann (who, incidentally, thought the tempo on that occasion too fast) wrote, 'Nothing worries people more than the inability to decide which of Mendelssohn's overtures is the loveliest. . . . To choose among the first three was already hard enough – and now comes a fourth!' He calls the Midsummer Night's Dreamers the strongest party, the Fingallians 'not the weakest, especially among the fair sex'; of the Melusinians it was still too soon to form an opinion. Presumably the unspecified party was the Calm Seamen and Prosperous Voyagers, but Mendelssohn had of course also written a trumpet overture.

To understand the *Melusine* Overture there was no need, Schumann added, to read Tieck's 'long but very romantic' tale. For him its exquisite, limpid music conjured up a vision of 'marine abysses full of darting fish with golden scales, of pearls in open shells, of buried treasures robbed from men by the sea, of emerald castles towering one above the other, and so on'. Mendelssohn rejected this 'programme' interpretation, and to someone who asked him what his overture was really about he replied, 'Hm – a *mésalliance*!' What Schumann called its 'magical watery motif' was adopted by Wagner for his *Rheingold*.

Mendelssohn had also been working since March 1834 on his oratorio, *St Paul*. A year later he spoke of finishing it in a month's time; in fact it took him another year. His father, to whom he had played some of it in Berlin in the summer of 1834, showed great interest in its progress, and in a most remarkable letter (10 March 1835), far too long to discuss in detail here, he discoursed brilliantly on the subject of Bach, Handel and Haydn, the place of oratorio at the present time, and the construction of *St Paul*. To this letter Felix replied, 'Often I am at a loss to understand how you, who have had no technical training in music, can have such acute musical judgment. If only I could *express* what I most certainly feel, with as much clarity and intuitive perception as you do the moment you enter upon a subject, I would never in my life make another muddled speech.' He was amazed that, after only 'a single very imperfect hearing', his father had been able to put his finger on certain little weaknesses that he himself had taken many months to discover.

Abraham heard a good deal more of the oratorio in Düsseldorf in 1835, but he was never to hear it performed in public.

CHAPTER SEVENTEEN

Courtship and Marriage 1835-1837

Leipzig, though only the second town of Saxony (Dresden being the capital), had a population of some forty-five thousand and was then the centre of the German book trade. Its fairs were world-famous, and it was the most important musical centre in all Germany. Besides the Gewandhaus Orchestra, which had been founded in 1781, there was the Thomasschule where J. S. Bach had been Cantor, a Singakademie and a good theatre.

The Gewandhaus Orchestra, though small, was manned by experienced and reliable players who soon became loyal supporters of their new conductor. He fully deserved their confidence in him. As Werner has pointed out, he was to be in many respects a pioneer. A benevolent administrator, he took a personal interest in his musicians, established a pension fund, out of his own pocket helped – though always anonymously – any who were in financial difficulties, and eventually got their wages substantially increased. Further, whereas conductors in the past had been little more than 'time-beating concert-masters', he made himself an 'orchestral pedagogue and master interpreter' under whom the Gewandhaus Orchestra became a model for all Europe. In this he was much assisted by Ferdinand David,[1] a friend of long standing and a brilliant young violinist and teacher, a Jew also, whom he was soon able to appoint as leader of his orchestra.

All this he achieved in a building that was singularly inadequate and ill-suited for its purpose.[2] The English soprano Clara Novello, though satisfied with its acoustics, described it as 'small and frightfully painted in yellow, the benches arranged [so] that one sits as if in an omnibus – and no lady and gentleman are ever allowed to sit together here or in their churches. So that the women sit in rows opposite one another staring at each other's dress which is celebrated for being as ugly as the men and women – the men standing round looking at you through an immense eyeglass the whole night.' And the young music critic Henry Chorley adds the information that the men were 'crowded so thickly that any one going as late as half an hour before the music struck up, ran no small chance of being kneaded into the wall by the particularly substantial proportions of those before him, whom no good-natured wish to accommodate a stranger can make thin.' On the wall behind the platform were inscribed the monitory words 'Res severa est verum gaudium' – 'Seriousness is true joy'.

[1] Born a year after Felix, and, curiously enough, in the Mendelssohn's house in Hamburg.
[2] The old Gewandhaus (Cloth Hall) continued to be used for concerts until 1884, when a new Gewandhaus was built on another site. This was destroyed in the Second World War.

Mendelssohn's first concert, on 4 October, opened with his own *Calm Sea and Prosperous Voyage* Overture, followed by some Weber, a violin concerto by Spohr and the 'Introduction' to Cherubini's opera *Ali Baba*; the second part consisted of Beethoven's Fourth Symphony. Both Mendelssohn's overture and the Beethoven went splendidly, but a single rehearsal had proved inadequate for the other pieces.

Two days later Mendelssohn wrote a long letter to his family, telling them this and all his other news. Chopin had turned up on a very brief visit and in every moment that Mendelssohn could spare the two had made music together. 'His playing enchanted me afresh. . . . It is so completely original.' He could not understand how his father and Fanny had failed to appreciate his genius as a pianist. 'It was so delightful to be once more with a *real* musician – not one of those half-virtuoso half-classics who want to combine *les honneurs de la vertu et les plaisirs du vice*.' Chopin played his most recent *Etudes* and his new concerto, he his *St Paul*,

The Leipzig Gewandhaus. Wood engraving, c. 1840

while inquisitive Leipzigers stole into the hall to eavesdrop; 'and it was just as if a Cherokee and a Kaffir had met to converse'. While Chopin was in Leipzig there arrived the 'thirty-two great folios, bound in stout green leather', of the collected works of Handel that had been presented to Mendelssohn by the Committee of the Lower Rhine Festival.

Mendelssohn was delighted, he said, with Leipzig in general and with the Gewandhaus Orchestra in particular. 'You can see clearly enough that this is an institution that had been going for fifty-six years. Further, the people are extremely friendly and seem to like me and my music. The orchestra is very good and thoroughly musical, and in six months' time will I think be even better.' Then Moscheles arrived to give a concert. He stayed of course with Mendelssohn at his bachelor lodgings, in whose sitting-room he noted 'on the piano a delightful litter of scores and new music, yet cleanliness and neatness prevailing everywhere'. Mendelssohn found his old friend looking older but otherwise quite unchanged, 'as lively and as gay as ever, and playing superbly – another case of a perfect virtuoso and a master combined. . . . I am to play his piece for two pianos [his *Homage to Handel*] with him, and he is to play my new piano concerto.[1] My *Hebrides* has also managed to creep into the concert. This afternoon Moscheles, Clara Wieck and I are playing Sebastian Bach's Triple Concerto in D minor. . . .'

Clara Wieck, the brilliant sixteen-year-old daughter of the piano teacher Friedrich Wieck, was later to marry Robert Schumann[2] after four years of stubborn resistance on the part of her father – a man as selfish and as obstinate as Edward Barrett of Wimpole Street with regard to another Robert. The story of their long and bitter battle with Wieck belongs to the biography of Schumann rather than to that of Mendelssohn. Here it is only necessary to say that Wieck's objection to his daughter's marrying any man stemmed largely from the fact that he had given the best years of his life to creating a work of art – to making his daughter as concert pianist a 'vestal virgin of music'; he feared that matrimony, with its consequent household chores and family cares, might ruin her musical career. But if marry she must, then at all events she should not marry an impoverished self-indulgent and neurotic musician with a damaged finger which ruled out the possibility of his becoming a professional pianist.

Mendelssohn had first met Schumann and Clara immediately upon his arrival in Leipzig, and though Schumann was only one year younger than Mendelssohn he at once accepted him as his master. 'I take off my hat to him as to a superior,' he wrote, and praised his compositions extravagantly in the musical journal, *Neue Zeitschrift für Musik*, of which he was editor and principal contributor. (He was much given to saluting his heroes thus, having several years earlier cried, 'Hats off, Gentlemen! a genius!' when writing of Chopin.) Indeed his adoration of Mendelssohn, both as a composer and as a man, can fairly be described as a *Schwärmerei* – a 'crush'. Schumann found in Mendelssohn those qualities that he knew he himself lacked, both musically and in the everyday management of his life, though he himself possessed qualities that Mendelssohn did not. Mendelssohn was 'the Mozart of the nineteenth century' and 'a real god. . . . Not a day passes without his producing at least one or two thoughts that might straightway be engraved on gold.'

---

[1] This must have been the 'Munich' Concerto of 1831, for Mendelssohn's second concerto was not yet written.
[2] According to a recent programme on B.B.C.'s Radio Four, dealing with the courtship of Clara and Robert, 'their eyes first met over the ivories'. Polko rides again!

Clara and Robert Schumann

Mendelssohn, for his part, treated Schumann with affection, even with respect, and welcomed in him another Bach enthusiast; but where his music, and perhaps also his Bohemian way of life, were concerned, he had reservations. These he must have discussed openly, for Schumann, writing to Clara in 1838, says:

> I haven't been often to Mendelssohn; he has come more often to me. . . . I am told that he is not sincere with regard to me. That would hurt me, because I am consciously loyal to him and have proved it. But tell me some time what you know. . . . I know exactly how I compare with him as a musician, and for years to come I could learn from him; but he could also learn something from me. Had I been brought up as he was, destined for music from childhood, I should outsoar you all – the energy of my ideas makes me feel this.

★   ★   ★

Rebecka and her husband, who had been in Ostend, came to Leipzig in the middle of October and carried Felix and Moscheles off to Berlin for a brief surprise visit. They found Abraham now almost blind but otherwise very well; his death therefore a month later, almost without warning, came as a terrible shock to the whole family. So unexpected was it that, only half an hour before he died, peacefully in his sleep, the doctors had decided that there was no need whatever to send for Felix.

Hensel at once left for Leipzig to break the news personally, returning two days later with Felix, who was 'broken and stunned', too wretched at first even to find relief in tears. Two or three weeks later he wrote to Schubring, 'I was ten days in Berlin, so that my mother might have us around her. . . . I loved my father with all my heart, and during my long absences from him hardly an hour passed without my thinking of him'; and to another friend, Pastor Bauer, 'My one wish, night after night, has been that I might not survive this loss. . . . I so utterly clung – still cling – to my father that I don't know how I can go on living. I have lost not only a father . . . but also one who latterly was my only true friend, my teacher in art and in life.'

Abraham undoubtedly died of a stroke, and it may well be that this was precipitated by the recent publication of the correspondence between Goethe and Zelter. The letters had been written with no thought of publication and, wrote Werner, contained 'many observations of Zelter concerning the Mendelssohn family and their friends which hurt Felix and made his family look ridiculous'. Their tactless editing by Professor Friedrich Riemer – 'a narrow-minded, embittered schoolmaster, a poetaster and factotum of Goethe's' – wounded Abraham deeply; only a couple of days before his death he had drafted a sharp letter to Riemer.

Lea could find support in the love of her children, Fanny and Rebecka in that of their husbands and families; but Felix, back in his bachelor rooms in Leipzig, was completely alone. His father had always hoped that he would not follow in the footsteps of his Uncle Bartholdy and remain unmarried, and since Abraham's death the hopes of the father had virtually become obligations for the son. Even before leaving Berlin, Felix had told Fanny that he intended to find himself a wife, and in Leipzig there now began what can only be described as the search for a bride.

In March (1836) Mendelssohn was made an Honorary Doctor of Philosophy and Master of Fine Arts of Leipzig University – a most unusual distinction for so young a man after so short a residence in the town. In March, too, Lea and Fanny paid him a visit, no doubt partly in the hope that they would be shown and asked to vet a potential bride. But Leipzig, it seemed, had nothing suitable to offer; nor, apparently, did his thoughts turn to either of the two very musical Woringen girls at Düsseldorf, to each of whom he dedicated a volume of his *Songs Without Words*. Delighted as he must have been to see his mother and sister, he was at that moment desperately busy, for his *St Paul* was to be given its première at the Lower Rhine Festival at Düsseldorf in May and there was still much work to be done on it. Fanny's criticism was, however, always valuable to him, though he did not always find himself able to adopt her suggestions.

In April Mendelssohn received from the twenty-three-year-old Wagner, who was then at Magdeburg, the score of his Symphony in C major – a juvenile work which had been performed at Leipzig three years earlier. This was the last that was ever heard of it, and forty years later Wagner told his wife Cosima that he believed that Mendelssohn had destroyed it,

The small vegetable market at The Hague. Detail of a watercolour by Mendelssohn, August 1836

Das Gewandhaus.

'perhaps because he detected in it a talent that was disagreeable to him'. This is hardly to be credited; but the fact remains that the score was not among Mendelssohn's papers after his death. The symphony was, however, reconstructed from the orchestral parts, which were found in a trunk in Dresden when Wagner fled the town in 1849, and eventually published.

The general subject of oratorio in the nineteenth century will be discussed when we come to consider Mendelssohn's major work in this field, his *Elijah*; and for a detailed analysis of the individual numbers of the *St Paul* the reader must turn to the biographies by Werner or Radcliffe.

It will be remembered that Mendelssohn had undertaken to write an oratorio for Schelble and his Cäcilienverein at Frankfurt, and he had gladly agreed to the theme of St Paul because of the appeal of the converted Jew. But as the result of the serious illness of Schelble he had been obliged to turn to the Lower Rhine Festival for its first performance. The libretto had been provided by Julius Schubring, and in spite of the enormous amount of trouble taken by both him and Mendelssohn it proved to be very defective. Dramatic opportunities had been missed – for example, what might not have been made of the rescue of Paul and Silas from prison, or of the great trial scene at Caesarea? – and as the work proceeds the action steadily weakens. Musically the oratorio is of course inspired by Bach and Handel, and, writes Radcliffe, we can see Mendelssohn 'trying to emulate the introspective profundity of the one and the dramatic force of the other'. Bach's influence is most obvious in the use of chorales. Wholly original and very successful was the choice of a women's chorus, accompanied by wind instruments, to represent the voice of Jesus speaking from heaven: 'Saul, why persecutest thou me?'; several critics, however, objected, and one proposed the substitution of 'a powerful blast on the trombone'.

Among the best-known numbers is the chorus, 'How lovely are the messengers', and another chorus, 'Happy and blessed are they', has been described as 'the most beautiful choral elegy before Brahms'. But, as a whole, the work – which Schumann called a 'chain of beautiful thoughts' – seems today as faded and as difficult of fair appraisal as are the major allegories of George Frederic Watts, and Bernard Shaw observed that he would 'as lief talk Sunday-school for two hours and a half to a beautiful woman with no brains as listen to *St Paul* over again'. It is therefore hard for us to understand the astonishing success that it had when first produced. Within eighteen months of its publication it had been performed no less than fifty times in forty-one different German cities, and within two years it had reached England, Holland, Denmark, Switzerland, Poland, Russia and America.

Lea, Fanny, and Paul and his wife Albertine (*née* Heine), came to Düsseldorf to hear the *St Paul*, and, needless to say, Frau Polko has found a little story to tell about the performance:

> One trifling passage alone did not go steadily; one of the 'false witnesses' made a mistake.
> Fanny Hensel, who was seated with the *contralti*, became as pale as death, bent forwards,

The Leipzig Gewandhaus. Watercolour by Mendelssohn, 23 February 1836. The painting, dedicated to Fräulein Henriette Grabau, includes a brief quotation from the Introduction to Cherubini's Ali Baba *which Mendelssohn had conducted at his first concert there*

*Wagner. Drawing by
E. B. Kietz. Paris, 1842*

and, holding up the sheet of music, sang the right notes so steadily and firm that the culprit
soon got right again. At the close of the performance, in the midst of all the jubilation,
Felix tenderly clasped the hand of his helper in need, saying, with his sunny smile, 'I am
glad it was one of the *false* witnesses!'

★   ★   ★

While in London in June 1833 Mendelssohn had heard a seventeen-year-old pianist,
William Sterndale Bennett, play a piano concerto of his own composition at a pupils' concert
at the Royal Academy of Music; he was much impressed, and urged the boy to visit him in
Germany, 'not as my pupil but as my friend'. Bennett and another young musician, J. W.
Davison, had now turned up, in the company of Klingemann, for the festival.

The boy had already been at the Academy for seven years when Mendelssohn first heard
him play. At the age of fourteen he had appeared at the King's Theatre as Cherubino in
The Marriage of Figaro; but after unfavourable press notices – one critic described him as
'in every way a blot in the piece' – he wisely sang no more but developed instead his considerable talents as pianist and composer of music very like Mendelssohn's. Later he was often in
Leipzig, where (he told Davison in February 1837) he had met 'a very nice fellow, who is
named *Schumann*. . . . He is very clever; plays the pianoforte beautifully when he likes,
composes a great deal, although his music is rather too eccentric'. The admiration was

mutual, for Schumann wrote of Bennett: 'From the cocoon of the schools so brilliant a butterfly has taken wing that we would fain follow its flight with outstretched arms as it bathes in the ether and gives to and takes from the flowers.'

A number of Bennett's works were performed at Gewandhaus concerts, often with himself as soloist or conductor. But Mendelssohn's prediction, that at long last England was about to produce a really great composer, was not to be fulfilled; for Bennett's creative talent was soon drowned in a sea of administration, a tragedy for which a knighthood and a funeral in Westminster Abbey were inadequate compensations. His friend Davison became music critic of *The Times*, a post which he held for more than thirty years. To the end of his life he used to recall with pride and emotion how, having arrived at Düsseldorf with a severe headache, he was soothed by Mendelssohn who 'stroked his head, and said, with his German accent, "Poor fallow, poor fallow!"'

From Düsseldorf Mendelssohn went for six weeks to Frankfurt to keep the Cäcilienverein on a steady keel during Schelble's absence through illness. Hiller who was then living in Frankfurt, tells us that Mendelssohn made the choir sing Handel and Bach, that he 'electrified' them by his enthusiasm, and 'won all hearts by his invariable good-nature and kindness'. Hiller's mother, an ardent admirer of Mendelssohn, used sometimes to provide a carriage so that he and her son could make excursions in the neighbourhood, and Hiller mentions an occasion during one of their drives when he saw Mendelssohn lose his temper: 'The coachman did or said something stupid, upon which Mendelssohn jumped out of the carriage in a towering rage, and after pouring a torrent of abuse upon the man, declared that nothing would make him get in again. It was *we* who suffered, and my mother was quite worried when we arrived late in the evening, hot and exhausted, having had to walk the whole way home.'

Rossini arrived in Frankfurt while Mendelssohn was there – dragged thither by the Parisian banker, Lionel Rothschild, to be the lion at his wedding to a Frankfurt cousin. He had now, wrote Hiller,

> reached the highest pinnacle of his fame, and was also at the height of his personality, if I can put it so. He had lost the enormous corpulence of former years: his figure was still full, but not disproportioned, and his splendid countenance, which displayed both the power of the thinker and the wit of the humorist, beamed with health and happiness. . . . His long residence in Paris, where he moved in the highest society, had transformed him from a haughty young Italian into a man of the world, dignified, graceful and charming, who enchanted everybody by his irresistible amiability.

Mendelssohn found him one day at the Hillers', and was completely captivated by the man whom he had previously dismissed as a mere windbag. 'I really know very few people who can be so amusing and clever as he can when he wants to . . .', he wrote. 'He says he is enchanted with Germany, and when he once gets the list of wines at the Rhine Hotel in the evening, the waiter has to escort him to his room or he would never manage to find it. . . . Anyone who doesn't think him a genius ought to hear him holding forth, and he'd soon change his mind.'

But then came a mild rebellion. 'If your Rossini goes on muttering the sort of things he did yesterday,' Mendelssohn said to Hiller, 'I won't play him anything more.' 'What did he mutter? I didn't hear anything.' 'But I did. While I was playing my Capriccio in F sharp minor [op. 5] he muttered between his teeth, "Ça sent la sonate de Scarlatti."' 'Well, that's nothing so very dreadful.' 'Ah – bah!' There was more of Scarlatti in Mendelssohn's early piano compositions than he cared to admit.

In order to help out his friend Schelble, Mendelssohn had sacrificed a much-needed holiday that he had planned to take in Switzerland and Italy; this generous act was to be spectacularly rewarded.

Living in Frankfurt was a certain Mme Elisabeth Jeanrenaud (*née* Souchay), the widow of the Pastor of the French Reformed Church there, and her two daughters, Julie[1] and Cécile. Both the Jeanrenauds and the Souchays were old Huguenot families, the former from Neuchâtel and the latter from Geneva, who had intermarried with the patriciate of Frankfurt; Mme Jeanrenaud and her formidable mother, Mme Souchay, were what we would call 'very county'. Elisabeth Jeanrenaud, widowed within five years of her marriage, was at this time in her fortieth year; Cécile, the younger daughter, was nineteen, and there was also a son, Charles.

All Frankfurt was soon aware that Mendelssohn was spending a good deal of his spare time with the Jeanrenauds. The family had, of course, long known of him by repute, though Cécile confessed that she had always pictured him as a morose old man who wore a skull-cap and played interminable fugues; she was agreeably surprised. It was, however, generally believed, and at first even by Cécile herself, that what drew Mendelssohn to the Jeanrenaud house near the Fahrtor was the still very pretty mother rather than either of the equally charming daughters. On 13 July Mendelssohn mentions in a letter to his mother 'a particularly beautiful girl' of whom he hoped to see more; and this information, vague though it was, was enough to make her almost ill with apprehensions of every kind. She must have confided in Fanny, who was not in Berlin at the time, for soon afterwards the latter wrote to her, 'Dear Mother, I do beseech you not to worry, at the age of sixty, because you think that Felix is in love! Couldn't Dr W. give you a sedative to calm such youthful feverishness? I feel just as you do, and the suspense is upsetting me too; but we mustn't worry: Felix has good taste. I've got a vague idea that it may be a Mlle Jeanrenaud or a Mlle Souchay. . . .'

Fanny tells Felix that she is deeply interested in the girl, now referred to by her as his 'bride'. She will be highly 'disappointed' – she writes the word in English – if it turns out to be nothing serious, and adds, 'It occurs to me that I have never seen you truly in love. All your great amours were . . . superficial.'[2] Meanwhile, however, Felix had told Rebecka a good deal more than he had cared to tell his mother or Fanny (whose jealousy he feared), though he still does not mention Cécile by name:

> I am more desperately in love than I have ever been in my life, and I don't know what to do. . . . But I haven't any idea whether or not she likes me, and I don't know what to do to make her like me. . . . One thing is, however, certain; that to her I owe the first real happiness I have enjoyed this year, and now for the first time I feel fresh and hopeful again. . . . O Rebecka! what shall I do? I can't settle to anything all day long. I can't compose or write letters or play the piano; all I can do is to sketch a little. . . .

It was poor Hiller (who at this time did not even know Cécile) and a Dr Speiss, a Frankfurt

[1] To Julie, Mendelssohn was to dedicate his op. 34 – six songs which included the most famous of all, '*Auf Flügeln des Gesanges*' ('On Wings of Song').
[2] Unpublished letter of 30 July, quoted by Marek.

Madame Jeanrenaud, Cécile's mother. Pencil drawing by Wilhelm Hensel

physician, who were at the receiving end of most of the lovesick young man's monotonous outpourings. 'Lying on the sofa in my room after dinner,' wrote Hiller, 'or taking long walks in the mild summer nights with Dr S. and myself, he would rave about her charm, her grace and her beauty. . . . He would pour out his heart about her in the most charmingly frank and artless way, often full of fun and gaiety; then again with deep feeling, but never with any exaggerated sentimentality or uncontrolled passion.' Hiller mentions that all Frankfurt was now watching Mendelssohn's courtship, and that he overheard many remarks which showed him that 'to possess genius, culture, fame, amiability, and fortune, and to belong to a family of much consideration as well as celebrity, is in certain circles hardly enough to entitle a man to raise his eyes to a girl of patrician birth. But I don't think that anything of this sort ever came to Mendelssohn's ears.'

Everyone was agreed that Cécile was very pretty. Frau Polko wrote: 'Her figure was slight, of middle height, and rather drooping, like a flower heavy with dew, her luxuriant golden-brown hair fell in rich curls on her shoulders, her complexion was of transparent delicacy, her smile charming, and she had the most bewitching deep blue eyes I ever beheld, with dark eyelashes and eyebrows.' Then, dipping her pen in purple ink, she added that the mere sight of her produced an intoxication like that which results from the taking of opium, but without the distress of a hangover. However, many people considered Cécile cold, and apparently her nickname locally was 'the fair Mimosa'.

Yet, if truth be told, she was really a rather ordinary girl with conventional tastes and, as was then the fashion, an atrocious handwriting; not (in spite of her name) particularly musical, nor widely read, but quite reasonably talented as an artist; silent often because she had little to say, yet far from stupid; rather exhaustingly pious; but an excellent housekeeper, gracious hostess and charming companion. Mendelssohn would never have been happy with a flirt, a bluestocking or a girl as highly strung as himself. For him, life with a George Sand or a Harriet Smithson would have been a torment. No – Cécile was exactly what he needed: someone restful and gentle and soothing to whom he could turn for comfort and support when things went wrong or his nerves were frayed.

But Mendelssohn had not yet proposed, far less been accepted. Indeed, in love though he undoubtedly was he was not yet *absolutely* sure that he had found the ideal partner for life. He had, after all, decided almost in cold blood that it was time he got married, and Cécile was the first candidate to appear since that decision had been taken. Had he been quite as infatuated as he led Hiller to believe, he would probably have declared his passion and learned his fate. Instead he did something very sensible but very bourgeois: at the beginning of August he went off to Holland for several weeks to take the sea-water cure at Scheveningen and think things over. Before he left he was presented by the choir of the Cäcilienverein with a small token of gratitude – a dressing-case inscribed with agreeable ambiguity: 'F.M.B. and Caecilia'. But it seems that Cécile was by now pretty sure of her man, for when Mendelssohn came to leave she wrote to one of her cousins, 'Mother and I have made a little bet . . . I hope I win!'

Mendelssohn went to Scheveningen with his friend Schadow and his young son, and all three of them were bored to distraction. In Holland even the sea was boring. For some reason or other Mendelssohn acted as nursemaid-tutor to the child: 'I have to teach S.'s boy,' he told Hiller, 'help him with his Latin construing of Cornelius Nepos, mend his

A Dutch steamboat. Drawing by Mendelssohn

pens, cut his bread-and-butter, and make tea for him every morning and evening; and today I had to coax him into the water because he always screamed so with his father and was so frightened.' Then, to make matters worse, Mendelssohn sprained his ankle while bathing.

But at last the prescribed twenty-one baths – the minimum treatment – had been taken, and he was able to return to Frankfurt. His mind was made up. He had already sounded his mother and extracted her approval in principle; during a picnic in the Taunus he now proposed and was accepted. To his mother he wrote on 9 September: 'I have only this moment returned to my room, but I can't settle to anything until I have told you that I have just become engaged to Cécile Jeanrenaud. I feel quite dizzy after all that has happened today. It is very late, and I can't say more; but I simply had to write to you. Oh, how wonderful and how happy I feel!'

Among innumerable friends who were delighted to hear the news was Frau Moscheles, who recalled with amusement a letter she had received from Mendelssohn four years earlier and dutifully kept. In it Mendelssohn had written, 'Klingemann still remains a Knight of the Order of Bachelors, and so do I; thirty years hence we shall both want to get married, but then no girl will take us. When you burn this letter, cut the prophecy out and preserve it carefully, and in thirty years' time it will be seen whether it was worthy of credit.'

Almost immediately after this, Mendelssohn was obliged to return to Leipzig to conduct the first of the winter season of Gewandhaus concerts. One of these concluded with the finale from *Fidelio*, and the appropriateness of the words '*Wer ein holdes Weib errungen*' ('Who has won a lovely bride') was not lost on the audience, who went on applauding until Mendelssohn satisfied them by extemporizing on the theme. Over Christmas, however, he was back in Frankfurt, laboriously paying with his fiancée the hundred and sixty-three calls upon all and sundry that etiquette prescribed.

Relations between the families of the young couple were, unfortunately, by no means satisfactory. The Souchays, like the Mendelssohns, were a clan, and each felt at heart that its beloved child might have made a better or a more suitable match. As for Fanny, she was – as he had feared – frankly jealous, while Lea Mendelssohn fretted, and tiresome old Madame Souchay made as much trouble as she could. Three times the visit of Mme Jeanrenaud to Berlin was cancelled because of her alleged illness, and though Lea did meet some of her future daughter-in-law's family in Leipzig at the beginning of March (1837), she did not attend the wedding at the Reformed Church in Frankfurt on the 28th of that month; indeed, none of Felix's family was present except his splendid old aunt, Dorothea Schlegel – now in her middle seventies and still much disapproved of by Lea, who called her 'that Schlegel woman'. The service was conducted in French, and if the young couple could not leave the church to the strains of the famous 'Wedding March' from the incidental music to *A Midsummer Night's Dream*, which had yet to be written, they were at least greeted in the bride's house by a marriage song specially composed by Hiller and performed by a choir of young ladies under his direction.

The honeymoon was spent chiefly in the Upper Rhineland and Swabia, and excerpts from the diary that they jointly kept and illustrated are to be found in Petitpierre's *The Romance of the Mendelssohns* and Marek's biography of the composer. It was a protracted affair – a two-month honeymoon proper, followed by a month in Frankfurt and two further months of summer holiday together. Petitpierre, loyal always, described it as a 'fairy-tale journey of unforgettable happiness', which no doubt it largely was; but Marek has spotted and deciphered a little lovers' tiff which took place at Freiburg towards the end of April. It seems that Cécile had caught Felix turning round several times to admire a very pretty flower-girl, and that this, together with one or two tactless little remarks on his part, had made her insanely jealous and unhappy. She behaved, she admitted, very badly: burst into tears, but refused to give any explanation. They returned in utmost misery to the inn, where suddenly Cécile brought herself to confess the cause of all her 'crazy thoughts'. Dutifully she entered

Two pages from Felix and Cécile's honeymoon diary: TOP *A late breakfast, including a sample of Cécile's depressing handwriting* BOTTOM *At the milliners*

Another page from the honeymoon diary

the whole story in their diary, and beneath it Felix penitently added, 'Don't be angry with me, dear Cécile!'

The original diary is now in the Bodleian Library, Oxford, and with it a little withered nosegay of violets which Cécile picked near Ebenach. 'It was I who saw them first,' she wrote, 'and I picked all I could reach through the bars of a gate. They were for his buttonhole. But Felix climbed over the gate and gathered little bunches which he offered me. They were exquisite, but no more so than the delightful allegretto which he composed for me on this theme.' Petitpierre reproduces the two pages of the diary on which this otherwise unpublished little piece is written.

During his honeymoon Mendelssohn found inspiration for a number of compositions. His setting of Pslam XLII (op. 42) was considered by Schumann to be his finest religious work to date, and his Quartet in E minor (op. 44, No. 2) anticipates in its first movement the famous violin concerto of 1844, which is in the same key. His second piano concerto, in D minor (op. 40), written like its predecessor in honour of a woman with whom he was in love, has been much abused; even Schumann condemned it as being 'among his most casual productions', and Mendelssohn betrayed his own uncertainty when he told Hiller that he feared he would not like it. Yet when played by a great pianist such as John Ogdon it is enormously impressive, and it was not for nothing that a London audience applauded for ten minutes after a performance of it there by the composer in 1843.

The honeymoon had, perhaps, been too prolonged, for by the beginning of July Cécile, now some two months pregnant, was often unwell, swallowing medicine 'with horrible grimaces' and amazed how 'so little a creature' could cause her so much inconvenience. Probably neither of them was sorry when the time came for them to return to Leipzig.

Towards the end of August Mendelssohn had to go to England to fulfil a long-standing engagement to direct the Birmingham Festival. This was at the invitation of Joseph Moore, a music-lover and philanthropist who had made a fortune in the button trade, and who, although in his seventies, was still a lively promoter of music in the Midlands. Mendelssohn did not want to go, and half hoped that the death of the King in June would have caused the festival to be cancelled; he longed to be sitting happily at home with Cécile, and increasingly he longed to be able to devote himself more to composition and less to performing in public in any capacity. To Hiller he wrote soon after his arrival in London on what was his fifth visit to this country:

> Here I sit in the fog – very cross – without my wife – writing to you because your letter of the day before yesterday needs an answer; otherwise I should hardly do so, because I am much too bad-tempered and gloomy. It's nine days since I parted from Cécile at Düsseldorf. The first few were quite bearable though very exhausting; but now I have got into the whirl of London – great distances – too many people – my head crammed with business and accounts and money matters and plans – and it's becoming unbearable, and I wish I were sitting with Cécile and had let Birmingham go hang. . . .
>
> I have heard nothing from my family in Berlin for so long (more than five weeks) that I'm beginning to get anxious – and this adds greatly to my unhappiness. I composed a lot while we were on the Rhine, but I don't mean to do anything here but curse and pine for my Cécile. What's the good of all the double counterpoint in the world when she isn't with me? . . .
>
> It seems that Chopin came over here quite suddenly a fortnight ago, paid no visits and saw nobody, played very beautifully one evening at Broadwood's and then took himself off again. They say he is still very ill and miserable. . . .

While in London Mendelssohn again played the organ at St Paul's, and with such success that no one would leave the building until the organ-blowers, in desperation, bolted in the middle of a Bach fugue. He also conducted a performance of his *St Paul* given at the Exeter Hall by the Sacred Harmonic Society, which subsequently showed its appreciation by the gift of a silver snuff-box. A great sorrow at this time was the sudden death of his dear friend Rosen at the age of only thirty-two. He had always been delicate, but he succumbed, after an illness of only three days, to a mysterious form of blood poisoning then beyond the reach of medical skill. Mendelssohn had had to leave his bedside to conduct at the Exeter Hall, and on his return several hours later he found Rosen already dead.

Naturally Mendelssohn saw a good deal of the Horsleys, but unfortunately their letters of this time seem to have disappeared; in 1841, however, Sophie Horsley came to stay with the Mendelssohns in Leipzig and formed a close friendship with Cécile. Then, too, there was Klingemann, anxious now as to his future because with the death of King William IV the

Hanoverian Chancellery threatened to become superfluous. With Klingemann Mendelssohn discussed the possibility of an oratorio on the subject of *Elijah*; the composition of this great work was not to be completed until the summer of 1846, only a year before Mendelssohn's death.

Of the four-day festival at Birmingham, which was held in the new Town Hall, Mendelssohn told his mother that he had never had 'so brilliant a success'. On the first day came Handel's *Solomon* and Mozart's D major Symphony (on whose themes he improvised that evening on the organ), and his *A Midsummer Night's Dream* Overture. The second day was devoted to his *St Paul*; on the third he played his new piano concerto, and on the last displayed his unsurpassed skill as an interpreter of Bach on the organ. Then, almost before the last chords had died away, he left for London, probably by the recently opened railway. By 1 October he was back in Leipzig, with only four hours in hand before the first Gewandhaus concert of the new season. Not surprisingly he was (as he told his mother) 'a bit *kaput*' by the end of the evening.

CHAPTER EIGHTEEN

Leipzig: Music and Family Life 1837-1839

On his marriage Mendelssohn had given up his bachelor lodgings and moved to a flat on the second floor of a large building near the town gates of Leipzig called Lurgensteins Garten. Hiller, who stayed there in 1839, described the rooms as having a pleasant view over the Thomasschule and Thomaskirche, 'once the sphere of the great Bach's labours'. The flat, he said, consisted of 'a kind of hall, with the dining-table and a few chairs; to the right of this a large sitting-room and one or two bedrooms, to the left my friend's study with his piano. Opening out of this came a fine big salon. . . .' By then the Mendelssohns had two small children, so that a bed for Hiller, and a piano for his use, were put in the salon.

Fanny Hensel had still to meet her new sister-in-law. Why she did not attend the wedding is not known; but in the end curiosity overcame what may well have been jealousy, and in a letter to Cécile on 5 October 1837 she paved the way for a visit to Leipzig. 'What a pity it is', she wrote, 'that fate should have decreed that we are to live so far apart, and that [Felix] should have had a wife these eight months whom I have never seen. I tell you frankly that now, when anybody talks to me about your beauty and your eyes, it makes me quite cross. I have had enough of hearsay, and beautiful eyes were not made to be heard.'

Her chance came – and no doubt she saw it coming – almost immediately, when the Woringens, who had been staying in Berlin, 'persuaded' her to travel with them to Leipzig. The encounter, awaited with some apprehension by all concerned, was apparently a complete success, for back in Berlin Fanny wrote to Klingemann, her regular confidant:

> At last I know my sister-in-law, and I feel as if a load were off my mind, for I cannot deny that I was very uncomfortable and ill at ease at never having seen her. She is amiable, childlike, fresh, bright, and even-tempered, and I think Felix is very lucky; for though inexpressibly fond of him she does not spoil him, but when he is moody treats him with an equanimity which will in time probably cure his fits of irritability altogether. Her presence produces the effect of a fresh breeze, so light and bright and natural is she.

That the attraction was mutual may be gathered from a letter which Fanny wrote to Cécile that November: 'The kind things you say to me, dear Cécile, have made me very happy, for seldom in my life have I been *more* anxious to make a favourable impression than I was on you; and your kind words, which I believe to be sincere, allow me to hope that this has been the case. . . . How I look forward to a visit from you!' In the course of time the relations between Cécile and the Mendelssohns in Berlin were to deteriorate.

Lurgensteins Garten. Drawing by Frau S. Hauptmann, the wife of Mendelssohn's colleague at the Leipzig Conservatoire

Hiller, who was now in Milan, had written to Mendelssohn asking him how matrimony suited him, and on 10 December the latter replied:

You want to know whether I like it here as much as ever? Living as a married man in a pretty, new and convenient flat with a fine view over gardens and fields and city towers; enjoying such comfort, happiness and peace as never before since I left home; and having, too, enough to live on and good will on every hand – with all this, how could I be otherwise than content here? I really think that this is the job for me – this, or none; but I often feel that no regular job would be best of all. Conducting ceaselessly for two months has taken more out of me than composing all day long for two years would have done, and in the winter I hardly get any time at all for composition. . . . Yet having the direction of a musical institution does have its attractions.

Soon after Christmas, when the musical season was at its height, Mendelssohn suddenly had a sharp recurrence of ear trouble—brought on, he thought, by the exceptionally cold winter. To Hiller he wrote on 20 January, 'I am suffering, as I did four years ago, from total deafness in one ear, with pains on and off in my head and neck. . . . As I have had to conduct and play in spite of it . . . you may imagine my agony at not being able properly to hear either the orchestra or myself on the piano! Last time it passed off after six weeks, and pray God it may do the same this time!' But the possibility of permanent deafness, which in spite of his doctor's reassurances he could not get out of his head, terrified him.

His letter to Hiller continued, 'Besides this, there is another still greater anxiety from which I hope daily to be released and which does not leave me for a moment. My mother-in-law has been here for a fortnight. . . .' This is not as sinister as it sounds, for he adds, 'You know why' – and Hiller did: Cécile was expecting her first child. On 7 February a son and heir was born, and named Karl Wolfgang Paul in honour of Klingemann and Zelter, Goethe and Mozart, and his brother and the Apostle of his oratorio; he become a professor of history at Heidelberg University, and died in 1897. Four other children followed in due course: Marie (b. 1839), Paul (b. 1841), Felix (b. 1843) and Lili (b. 1845).

Two days after the boy's birth, Mendelssohn concluded a hurried letter to Klingemann: 'Paper and time are both running out, and I wanted to tell you what it feels like when my little son cries, when Cécile suckles him and gazes so tenderly at him, when she smiles at him and maintains that he is already beating time with his fingers, and when she is so well and lovable and angelic. But how can I describe it? You must try to imagine it. . . .' But hardly had Mendelssohn written the word 'well' when Cécile became seriously ill, and several anxious weeks were to pass before he knew that she was out of danger.

Not until April was Cécile really herself again. 'What I went through at that time I couldn't put into words,' he told Hiller; 'but you, dear Ferdinand, will be able to understand. And now that all the anxiety is over, and my wife and child are well, I feel so happy. . . . It's absolutely glorious to see a tiny infant who has inherited his mother's blue eyes and retroussé nose, and who recognizes her so well that he laughs whenever she comes into the room. When he is lying at her breast and tugging away, they both look so happy that I hardly know what to do with myself for joy. . . .'

Meanwhile the winter season of Gewandhaus concerts, of quartet evenings (at which Mendelssohn played the viola) and of organ recitals had drawn to its close. The star of the Gewandhaus concerts had been a young English soprano of nineteen, Clara Novello – the fourth daughter of the fine musician and famous musical publisher, Vincent Novello.

Mendelssohn had known the Novello family for a number of years, and had heard Clara sing when he was in England with his father in 1833; on hearing her again in Birmingham, in 1837 he had immediately invited her to Leipzig. She arrived there with her parents towards the end of October and made her début at the Gewandhaus a few days later. In her diary Clara wrote: 'I sang *Non più di fiori* and *Casta diva*. Mendelssohn, who came to me after the concert, told me that such enthusiasm had never been witnessed before in Leipsic, although it appeared to me a very cold affair.' Cold it can hardly have been, for it was said that after she had sung the recitative to her first aria 'the applause was so great and continued that she could not proceed with the air for some minutes. . . . Multitudes of compliments were showered on her, one gentleman declared she brought "the tear to his eye", another that he had had no sleep all night. . . .'[1]

---

[1] An English contemporary of Clara's, renowned for associating colours with voices, saw hers as 'a cold glaring tomato-colour'.

A fortnight later she sang (in German) in Handel's *Messiah* at the Pauluskirche, and afterwards Mendelssohn wrote a long letter, in English, to her brother Alfred in London, describing her triumph. But with an irony that apparently missed its mark, he added:

> I am sometimes afraid she must find the place [Leipzig] so very small & dull, & miss her splendid Philharmonic band & all those marchionesses, & duchesses and lady patronesses who look so beautifully aristocratically [sic] in your concert-rooms, 'of whom we have a great want'. But if being really and heartily liked & loved by a public, & being looked on as a most distinguished & eminent talent, must also convey a feeling of pleasure to those that are the object of it – I am sure that your sister cannot repent her resolution of accepting the invitation to this place.

Alas! as Werner comments, 'From every page of her memoirs there speaks the soul of a silly, often unbearable snob.'

Among those present in the church were the actor Charles Kemble (whom Mendelssohn had seen in London as Hamlet) and his daughter Adelaide,[1] described by Clara as 'all nose'. Adelaide made herself very much at home at the Mendelssohns', insisted (Cécile is said to have told Clara) on singing '*à casser les vitres*, to Felix's intense distress', and at a reception given by Mendelssohn for Kemble created a sensation by 'flinging herself full length at her father's feet during his Shakespeare readings'.[2] All this is 'the gospel according to Clara' – a biased observer; Moscheles, however, writing four years later, spoke of Adelaide's 'glorious voice', great linguistic powers and 'extraordinary musical memory'.

The Novellos left for Weimar in the middle of December, but returned to Leipzig at Christmas for Clara to sing at two further concerts in January which, in spite of Mendelssohn's deafness, were again brilliantly successful. Then came Berlin, where Lea Mendelssohn and the Hensels (whom they had already met at Leipzig in November) gave them a warm welcome. Of Lea, Clara wrote that she was 'my ideal of a beneficent fairy. I was awed by her, as she sat with her everlasting knitting, looking like one of the Fates, yet felt intimate at the same time.'

Soon the almost royal progress through Europe was resumed; but though Clara sang again for Mendelssohn at Leipzig in the following autumn and at the Düsseldorf festival in 1839, her association with him seems then to have come to an end. In October 1838 he had told Moscheles that her recent concert had stirred up 'a vast amount of rivalry and created a lot of artistic bad blood. . . . When *good* musicians begin to belittle one another, to be malicious and backbiting, then I feel like giving up music (or rather, musicians) altogether.' He had previously imagined that only third-rate artists behaved like that. But a further reason for his rejection of Clara may perhaps be found in a letter that he wrote in January 1838 to Klingemann, to whom he could always speak his mind. The sting is in the tail:

[1] Later Mrs Sartoris. She became a very close friend of Lord Leighton.
[2] A. Mackenzie-Grieve, *Clara Novello, 1818–1908* (London, 1955).

Clara Novello at the age of fifteen. Oil painting by her brother Edward, painted in 1833 when he was twenty. A career of brilliant promise was cut short by his death three years later

Her farewell concert yesterday provoked all the enthusiasm of which Leipzig is capable. They applauded the moment she came into the hall; her chair was festooned with garlands, and at the end there fluttered from the boxes rosy poems in which, believe it or not, she was compared to a nightingale. . . . She has become a popular favourite here; I often got great pleasure at our concerts from her fresh and musical singing, and I have nothing whatever against any of her family; and yet it is a curious fact that ever since I first met her eight years ago I have had a certain inner antipathy to everything about her – an antipathy I can't always explain, but which never leaves me.

But Clara had no more need of Mendelssohn to further her spectacular career, and when, some years later, she hooked and landed her Italian Count, Countess Gigliucci's cup of happiness was full.

Besides giving first performances in the Gewandhaus of many works by contemporary composers, Mendelssohn also revived those of earlier composers which he considered to be unjustly neglected. To his sister Rebecka he wrote in February 1838 that he was putting on a series of 'historic concerts':

> At the last but one we had the whole of Bach's Suite in D major, some Handel and Gluck, etc., and a violin concerto of Viotti's; in the last, Haydn, Righini, Naumann, etc., ending with Haydn's 'Farewell' Symphony in which, to the great delight of the public, the musicians literally blew out their lights and went off one by one till the first violins alone remained and finished in F sharp major. It's a curious, melancholy little piece. Earlier on we played Haydn's Trio in C major, and everyone was amazed that anything so beautiful could exist; yet it was published long ago by Breitkopf and Härtel. Next time we have Mozart, whose C minor Concerto I am to play, and also for the first time a quartet from his unfinished opera, *Zaïde*. Then comes Beethoven, and to complete our set of twenty concerts we are left with two for every possible kind of modern work.

So great was the demand for tickets that often the doors from the ante-rooms had to be left open for the benefit of those who could not get seats in the hall itself.

In May, Mendelssohn went with Cécile to Berlin to pay the visit that Fanny had long been awaiting; probably Cécile was rather apprehensive, for she was never to feel quite at ease with her mother-in-law. They stayed for about two months, though Mendelssohn was away for a time directing the Lower Rhine Festival, which was held that year in Köln. Among the works given at it were Handel's *Joshua* and the Symphony in C minor by Beethoven's pupil Ferdinand Ries,[1] who had died in January. A severe epidemic of measles was raging that summer in Berlin, and most of the Mendelssohns became victims. Felix caught it (it was his second attack) soon after his return to Leipzig, and it left him for a time feeling 'rather lazy'. But for his summer's work he had three string quartets (op. 44) to show, and a cello sonata (op. 45) written for his brother Paul.

Mendelssohn's first composition of the year 1839 was an overture hastily written for a charity performance of Victor Hugo's *Ruy Blas* – a play which he considered 'absolutely detestable'.

[1] See p. 166.

Paradise Street, Birmingham. Detail of a watercolour by Charles Rudd, 1845. The Town Hall, on the left, is the building in which Elijah *was first performed*

'I intend to call it,' he told his mother 'not the overture to *Ruy Blas*, but to the *Theatrical Pension Fund*.' This *pièce de circonstance*, though thrown off in the matter of a day or two, is often heard today and is still very effective.

In May, Mendelssohn again directed the Lower Rhine Festival at Düsseldorf, where (wrote Frau Polko) 'a triad of female singers was united, such as could be rarely met with in similar perfection. The fair-haired Auguste von Fassmann, the most aristocratic "Countess" in Mozart's *Figaro* that ever sang the lament of "*Dove sono*"; the enchanting Clara Novello, whose voice was as fresh and redolent of spring as her face and her disposition, and the nightingale of contraltos, Sophie Schloss. . . . Clara Novello on that day sang like a harbinger of spring, or a glad exulting lark. . . .'

After the festival, Mendelssohn went with Cécile to Frankfurt for his sister-in-law Julie Jeanrenaud's wedding, and in August he wrote to Klingemann from Hochheim, near Koblenz:

> The summer months I have just passed in Frankfurt have thoroughly refreshed me. In the mornings I worked, then bathed or sketched; in the afternoons I played the organ or the piano and afterwards walked in the woods, then went into society – or home, where I always found the most charming society of all. . . .
>
> The new pieces I have completed are a Piano Trio in D minor, a book of four-part songs to be sung in the open air, some songs for one voice, some organ fugues, half a Psalm, etc. I intend to go on with these four-part songs and have given a good deal of thought to what can be done in this field. The most natural of all music is that which comes from the heart when four people are strolling together through the woods or out in a boat. . . .

These songs to be sung alfresco were composed for a delightful musical party, given in the remotest depths of the forest near Frankfurt, which Mendelssohn describes in rapturous terms in a letter to his mother (3 July 1839). Pretty girls, charming singing, strawberries and cherries, ices and wines, and finally a splendid supper by torchlight at tables which appeared as if from nowhere and were almost smothered with flowers: nothing was lacking to make the party idyllic. The guests did not get home until midnight; the hosts were busy until two in the morning packing up and loading the wagons, then lost their way, and ended up in Isenburg, many miles from Frankfurt.

The Mendelssohns returned to Leipzig at the end of August, travelling at a leisurely pace because Cécile was shortly expecting her second child. His wife stood the journey well, Felix told Fanny, and 'the little one [Karl] was a pattern of goodness in the carriage and only got one slap the whole way. He screamed frightfully then, but soon fell asleep; and when he awoke he kissed me as tenderly as if he had not been slapped, and I had not been the person who slapped him. Well, thank God we are safely back home!'

The Hensels, who were just off on a long visit to Italy with their nine-year-old son Sebastian, spent a week in Leipzig on their way south, reaching Rome at the end of November. Here old 'Papa' Ingres had succeeded Vernet as Director of the French Academy; but Vernet was still around, now wearing native dress (in which he sat for Hensel) and looking most convincingly the Arab. Fanny describes Ingres as 'awkward for a Frenchman' but 'a great fiddler before the Lord', prouder of his violin playing than of his painting;[1] she often

---

[1] Hence the well-known phrase, 'C'est son violon d'Ingres', meaning that it is a hobby in which a man takes more pride than in his real work.

Leipzig. Engraving by J. Poppel after L. Rohbock, 1840

played chamber music with him. His taste was severely classical, and the young listened sadly to the tales of gay parties and balls in the days when Vernet was Director.

Young Gounod was at the Academy as a student, usually excellent company but very immature, and talking one evening at the Hensels such arrant nonsense about Beethoven that his friends felt obliged to carry him off home to bed. Soon afterwards he fell into the clutches of a proselytizing priest and very nearly gave up music for the cowl. And then, of course, there were the inevitable English – silent and morose until the music began, whereupon they always broke into the most animated conversation. 'The national pride,' wrote Fanny, 'which enables them to do such great things as a nation, seems intolerable arrogance in the individual, and even when they take pains to be kind they are generally as clumsy as bears.'

On 2 June, after having been very publicly and very embarrassingly over-embraced by Ingres, Fanny left Rome with her husband and son for Naples. Here Hensel was more fortunate than Felix had been, in that he succeeded in getting to Sicily, though Fanny,

fearing the heat, preferred to remain behind with Sebastian. By the beginning of September they were all back in Leipzig, to find Cécile 'in good health and unaltered loveliness, and sweet and amiable as ever, while the children, Karl and Marie, were growing up and thriving'.

In September 1839 Mendelssohn directed a three-day festival at Brunswick. Among those present was a young English critic named Henry Chorley (1808–72), who was to become an ardent champion of the composer, and who has left a full account of his experiences.[1]

Mendelssohn must have been expecting Chorley, for soon after the latter's arrival at the Blue Angel there appeared a 'clean, civil little boy' sent to conduct him to the Aegidienhalle, a former Gothic church used at that time as a concert hall, where he found Mendelssohn rehearsing Beethoven's Fifth Symphony. This at an end, 'a weak and tame contralto singer, with a profusion of fair ringlets, went through the delicious arioso in *St Paul*, "But the Lord is mindful of his own"; and then the conductor, hitherto a personal stranger, came down to me, and gave me a friendly welcome to Germany.'

The two men were immediately attracted to one another, and Chorley, who was to spend a good deal of time in Mendelssohn's company before the festival ended, expressed the opinion that his face was 'one of the most beautiful which has ever been seen' and one to which no artist had ever done justice. What others described as a lisp in Mendelssohn's speech, Chorley considered to be 'a slight cloud (not to call it thickness) on his utterance, which seemed like the voice of some friend'.

Soon after dawn the next morning the town was alive with 'cargoes of pleasurers' arriving for the festival, and by nine o'clock, according to Chorley, the hall was already three-quarters full:

A gaily varying sight was the audience. Elegantly dressed girls, in the transparent and gay toilettes of an English ball-room, might be seen sitting side by side with the gipsy-coloured, hard-handed peasant women of the district, in their black caps gracefully displaying the head, and picturesquely decorated with pendent streams of ribbon. Here, again, was a comely youth, tight-laced in his neat uniform, and every hair of his moustache trimmed and trained to an agony of perfection, squeezed up against a dirty, savage, half-naked student, with his long, wild hair half-way down his back, and his velveteen coat confined at the waist with one solitary button, letting it be seen that neither shirt nor waistcoat was underneath.

　　The orchestra, on the other hand, had an effective appearance of uniformity. The lady-singers, though all serving gratuitously, both amateur and theatrical artists, had wisely agreed to merge all individual fancies in an inexpensive, but delicate and pretty uniform of white, with large nosegay by way of ornament. The whole assembly of orchestra and audience, thus heterogeneously composed, was cemented by one sympathetic desire to honour a great musician. All eyes awaited Mendelssohn's (not the Duke of Brunswick's) coming. His conductor's desk was wreathed with a fresh garland of flowers. Upon it, beside the score of his oratorio, was laid another more delicate bouquet, and for his refreshment, a paper, if I mistake not, of those dainties in which every good German housewife is so skilful.

[1] *Modern German Music*, London, 1854.

Henry Chorley in later life

The first concert was devoted to Mendelssohn's *St Paul*, the second to works by Weber, Spohr (a native of Brunswick), Handel, Beethoven, and one or two now forgotten composers. At the second concert, after the conclusion of Beethoven's Fifth, 'a *feu de joie* of splendid bouquets, carefully hidden till then, was discharged upon the conductor by the ladies'. The same evening came a ball:

> The scene of this festive ceremony, which ended with the apotheosis of Mendelssohn, was the theatre, which had been gaily decorated for the occasion, though not sufficiently lighted. A suite of rooms had been temporarily added for supper. At the further depth of the stage, a stately pavilion, draperied with white, had been erected. This was at first concealed by the curtain, which was kept down till the right moment – the arrival of the composer. When he entered the theatre, according to preconcerted signal, he was met by two young girls, who led him gently forward, the curtain slowly rising, to this shrine of honour: six other young ladies, dressed as genii, there awaited him; and after a brief address from one of them, a laurel-crown was placed on his head.

The final concert of the festival included several of Mendelssohn's own works, among them his Piano Concerto in D minor and a serenade for piano and orchestra, and Beethoven's Seventh Symphony. There was also an organ recital in the Cathedral, given on a much-neglected instrument in a 'dolefully worm-eaten' case. Chorley discusses Mendelssohn's capabilities both as performer and as composer, and it is interesting to read that in his opinion 'Mendelssohn's is eminently manly music, and loses effect beyond that of almost any other of his contemporaries, when attempted by female hands.'

An important event both for Mendelssohn personally and for Leipzig musically was the arrival there in December of Ferdinand Hiller. Mendelssohn and David met the coach and conducted him to Lurgensteins Garten, where he soon felt completely at home:

> Our way of life was regular and simple. We breakfasted at about eight on coffee and white bread and butter. Felix never ate butter, but dunked his bread in his coffee like any school-boy, as he had always done. At one, the table was brought out of the anteroom. . . . Though Mendelssohn despised butter he always liked a glass of good wine, and sometimes we had to sample a special vintage, which our host would produce with great delight and swallow with immense satisfaction. We generally wasted little time over lunch, but in the evenings we often used to sit round the table for hours chatting (not smoking), unless we moved to the pianino which had been given to Frau Mendelssohn by the directors of the Gewandhaus.

It was Mendelssohn's idea that he and Hiller should sit and compose together at the same table, but both soon realized that this would not work; after a fortnight, therefore, Hiller moved to rooms nearby which Mendelssohn had occupied in his bachelor days. Here he was to work and to sleep, but he continued to take his meals and spend the rest of his time with Felix and Cécile. Naturally they made much music together, and one day Mendelssohn played him his new Piano Trio in D minor (op. 49) – one of the loveliest things he ever wrote:

> I was tremendously impressed by the fire and spirit, the flow, and, in short, the masterly character of the whole thing; but I had one small misgiving. Certain piano passages in it, constructed on broken chords, seemed to me – to speak candidly – rather old-fashioned. I had lived for many years in Paris, seeing Liszt often and Chopin every day, so that I was thoroughly accustomed to the richness of passages which marked the new piano school. I said something on the subject to Mendelssohn and suggested certain alterations, but at first he wouldn't listen to me. . . .

In the end, however, Mendelssohn was persuaded that Hiller was right, and the latter 'enjoyed the small triumph' of seeing Mendelssohn rewrite the piano part '*exactly* as I had suggested', saying as he played it, 'That is to remain as a remembrance of you.'

During that winter Hiller witnessed 'a curious example of Mendelssohn's almost morbid conscientiousness with regard to the possible perfection of his compositions'. One evening he came round to Lurgensteins Garten to find his friend in such a feverish state of excitement that he was genuinely alarmed. It appeared that Mendelssohn had been wrestling for four hours with a few bars of a part-song which would not come right, though scattered on his desk were twenty different attempts most of which would have satisfied almost anyone else. Hiller implored him to sleep on it, saying that what four hours had failed to produce that evening would come to him in as many minutes next morning. But Mendelssohn could not sleep, and whether or not he solved his problem next morning we do not know; during the night, however, he did compose a setting of Eichendorff's 'The Huntsmen's Farewell' ('*Wer hat dich, du schöner Wald!*') which was to become almost a national folk-song, thus (wrote Ernst Wolff) 'making its creator immortal among a whole section of society who perhaps do not even know his name'.

CHAPTER NINETEEN

Leipzig: A Busy Year 1840

In March 1840 Liszt arrived at Leipzig fresh from his triumphs in Vienna and Prague; he was now in his twenty-ninth year, and at the height of his fame as a virtuoso pianist. In letters to his mother, to Fanny and to Moscheles, Mendelssohn gives three very similar accounts of his visit; and in addition to these we have the reviews of Schumann, and the personal impressions of Hiller which, though recorded many years later, had remained vivid in his memory.

A good deal of unpleasantness was created at the very outset when, because of the greed of Liszt's manager, a pianist named Kermann, the prices of seats for the concerts at the Gewandhaus had to be increased; but after some initial hissing, which broke out again when Kermann appeared in the role of accompanist, a part at least of the performances brought Liszt the kind of ovation to which he had become accustomed. Hiller wrote:

> At his first concert, as he glided along the platform of the orchestra to the piano, dressed in the height of fashion and as lithe and slender as a tiger-cat, Mendelssohn whispered to me, 'There's a strange spectacle – the nineteenth-century virtuoso!' I need hardly describe the impression made by his playing. When he played Schubert's *Erlkönig*, half the audience stood on their seats; and the *Lucia* [*di Lammermoor*] Fantasy sent them quite crazy. But one or two other pieces were less successful – for example Mendelssohn's new D minor Concerto, which he could neither sight-read nor find the time to study properly; many people thought the composer played it better himself.
>
> His performance of a part of the 'Pastoral' Symphony, in the same hall where it had so often been heard with full orchestra, did not meet with general approval. In his foreword to his transcriptions of the Beethoven symphonies Liszt boldly declares that every effect can be reproduced on the modern piano. When Mendelssohn read this, he said, 'I'd just like to hear the first eight bars of Mozart's G minor Symphony, with that delicate figure on the violas, played on the piano as they sound in the orchestra, and then I'd believe it.'

Mendelssohn was once again dazzled by Liszt's amazing virtuosity, deep musicianship and astonishing memory; unlike Hiller, he makes no criticism of his performance of the D minor Concerto, which one would have thought Liszt could have taken in his stride. 'Moreover, when one gets beneath his fashionable French veneer [*neufranzösische Oberfläche*] he is a really good, genuine artist whom one can't help liking even though one can't always agree with him. There is, as I see it, only one thing he lacks: he has no talent as a composer. . . .' In this connection it must be remembered that almost all of Liszt's greatest compositions had yet to be written; it is, however, unlikely that they would have caused Mendelssohn to alter his opinion. Liszt's great rival as a virtuoso pianist, Sigismond Thalberg, whom he had successfully challenged in Paris to a musical duel,[1] had also been heard in Leipzig, and comparing the two men, Mendelssohn admitted that Liszt was the more brilliant; no other virtuoso could have played 'incomparably' (as Joachim recalls) the piano arrangement of the orchestral accompaniment of the last movement of Mendelssohn's violin concerto *while holding a lighted cigar between his middle and forefinger!* Yet Mendelssohn considered that Thalberg 'with his composure, was, within his more limited sphere, the more perfect virtuoso . . .'. What was certain was that in this field the two men were in a class by themselves.

Unhappily the dissatisfaction over the high price of the seats, which had led to 'discussions in the newspapers, explanations and counter-explanations, criticisms, and complaints', continued to poison the air. Mendelssohn wrote:

> It now occurred to me that this unpleasantness might be most effectively allayed by people seeing and hearing him in private. So on the spur of the moment I decided to give a soirée for him at the Gewandhaus, with three hundred and fifty guests, orchestra, choir, mulled wine and cakes, my *Meeresstille*, a Psalm, a triple concerto by Bach (Liszt, Hiller and I), choruses from *St Paul*, and the devil and his grandmother. All were delighted, played and sang with the utmost enthusiasm and vowed they had never passed a more enjoyable evening. . . .

Schumann adds the information that the whole programme of this 'half rout, half concert' consisted of works previously unknown to Liszt, and that 'the devil and his grandmother' included Schubert's C major Symphony (the 'Great C major'), which had recently been found by Schumann in the possession of Schubert's brother in Vienna and given its first performance under Mendelssohn at a Gewandhaus concert in March 1839. 'We passed three happy hours of music such as sometimes does not come one's way for years, and at the end Liszt played alone and marvellously.'

Hiller also helped by entertaining Liszt at a 'rather pompous' dinner at a very smart hotel, and invited all the heads of the local musical societies to meet him. 'Some time afterwards, when we were talking over these heroic social deeds of ours, Mendelssohn was infinitely amused to hear that my private fête for a mere handful of people had cost me far more than his grand display. He had such a childishly naïve and good-natured way of laughing at anything of that sort, and really was never so amiable as when he was able to make fun of something.'

At his second concert Liszt played with astonishing fire Weber's *Conzertstück*, a great favourite of Mendelssohn's, and returned from a flying visit to Dresden to give a third concert in aid of the pension fund for aged and invalid musicians. His programme tactfully included works by Mendelssohn, Schumann and Hiller, played almost at sight; and Liszt noted with indignation that 'the musicians, as well as the so-called musical experts', for the most part failed to appreciate the 'jewelled' beauty of Schumann's *Carnaval*.

There was also informal music-making at the Mendelssohns'. Young Max Müller,[2] later to become world famous as an Orientalist and philologist, was among those present one

---

[1] See p. 149.

[2] Friedrich Max Müller (1823–1900), son of the poet of Schubert's *Die Schöne Müllerin*, godson of Weber (and named 'Max' after the hero of *Der Freischütz*), and pupil of Mendelssohn. The quotation is taken (in slightly modified form) from Marek's *Gentle Genius*.

Friedrich Max Müller, aged fourteen

evening when Liszt, dressed in Hungarian costume and looking 'wild and handsome', announced that he had prepared something special for his host:

> He sat down at the piano and played first a Hungarian folk-song and then three or four variations on it, each one more incredible than the other, all the while swinging to and fro on the piano stool. We stood around, completely spellbound. After praising the hero of the hour, one of Mendelssohn's friends said to him, 'Well, Felix, now we can pack up! Nobody can play like that. . . .' Mendelssohn smiled, and when Liszt approached him, saying that it was now his turn, he burst out laughing and replied that he wasn't going to play – certainly not tonight.

But Liszt would not take No for an answer, and after some parrying Mendelssohn said, 'Well, I will play; but you mustn't get angry with me.' With that he sat down at the piano and played – what? First the Hungarian folk song and then all the variations, reproducing them so accurately that only Liszt himself might have discerned a difference. We were all afraid lest Liszt might feel rather put out, because Mendelssohn, like a regular tease, couldn't prevent himself from imitating Liszt's grandiose movements and extravagant gestures. But Liszt laughed, applauded enthusiastically, and admitted that nobody else, not even he himself, could have managed such a piece of bravura.

Mendelssohn's astonishing powers of memorizing music at a single hearing, and moreover of storing it permanently in his mind, never ceased to amaze people. Shortly after Mendelssohn's death, King Friedrich Wilhelm IV of Prussia asked Rellstab (who, it may be recalled, was present when young Felix had played to Goethe in 1821) whether the stories of the composer's remarkable memory were really true. Rellstab replied, 'He knew by heart not only his own works, but almost *all* the works of the great masters; he retained in his memory, note for note, lengthy pieces of music after hearing them once, even when they did not please him particularly and he had not listened to them very attentively. Because of this gift, he was accustomed not to write down his larger compositions until and unless he had completely perfected them in his mind.'[1] To a young English composer who once asked him whether he knew much of Handel's music, Mendelssohn replied, 'Every note.'

Johann Christian Lobe – a Weimar musician who had also been present when Felix played to Goethe – met him again at a performance of *St Paul* in Weimar in April. His senior by twelve years and also something of a hypochondriac, Lobe happened to say, regretfully, that he would never live to hear most of Mendelssohn's later works. Mendelssohn immediately interrupted him: 'O, my dear friend – you will long outlive me!' Lobe tried to pass this off as a joke, but Mendelssohn repeated, '*I shall never make old bones*'; then, as though regretting what he had said, he began an animated conversation about the rehearsal that had just finished. Looking at the 'handsome young man, still in his early thirties, and the picture of health', Lobe thought it inconceivable that this prophecy could so soon be fulfilled. Lobe, who published his autobiography in 1869, died in 1881.

In fact, soon after this conversation had taken place Mendelssohn was for several weeks seriously ill and remained in poor health throughout the summer. The trouble resulted from bathing for too long in a very cold river, after which he had been unconscious for many hours and had continued for a time to suffer from cramps, severe headaches, and general lassitude. 'Now I know what it's like to be *really* ill,' he told Klingemann. But he refused to allow his work to suffer, and as soon as he was on his feet again he began to make preparations for the celebration in June of the quatercentenary of the invention of printing by Gutenberg.

Many German cities were commemorating the event, and naturally Leipzig, as the centre of the book trade, took the occasion very seriously. Lortzing's specially composed opera, *Hans Sachs*, was staged in the theatre, while Mendelssohn wrote what (at Klingemann's suggestion) he called a symphony-cantata, *Lobgesang* ('Hymn of Praise'), for performance in the Thomaskirche, and a *Festgesang*, or Festival Chorus for double male choir, to be sung at the unveiling of a statue of Gutenberg in the market-place.

---

[1] Rellstab, *Zwei Gespräche mit Sr. Majestät König Friedrich Wilhelm IV*, Berlin, 1849 (quoted by Werner).

The market-place, Leipzig. Engraving by G. M. Kurz after L. Rohbock, 1840

The *Festgesang*, though fittingly pompous, was in reality a poor thing, remembered today only because one tune from it was adapted by Dr W. H. Cummings to provide the well-known setting of 'Hark! the herald angels sing'.[1] Fifty years ago, ribald schoolboys used to parody, 'Hark! the herald angels sing, Beecham's pills are just the thing'; in fact, the text praised 'Gutenberg, der deutsche Mann', and 'Gutenberg is just the thing' might not be too far-fetched a paraphrase. One cannot help wondering whether those Church of England clergy-men who, according to recent newspaper reports, refuse to allow Mendelssohn's 'Wedding March' in their churches on the grounds that it is secular or even pagan music, are aware of the origin of what is possibly the most popular tune in the English hymnal.

The *Hymn of Praise*, like Beethoven's Ninth, is a kind of choral symphony; but here resemblance ends, for in the Mendelssohn work a relatively brief orchestral introduction in three linked movements is followed by the cantata that constitutes the bulk of it. Mendelssohn himself described it to Chorley as 'a kind of universal thanksgiving on the words of the last Psalm, "Let every thing that hath breath praise the Lord"'. Its success was instantaneous, though one or two critics felt that the composer was treading dangerously near holy ground.

[1] Charles Wesley, amended by George Whitefield.

Schumann singled out for especial approval the duet 'I waited for the Lord', which at the première was succeeded by 'a whispering that counts for more in a church than does loud applause in a concert hall. It was like a glimpse of a heaven filled with Raphael Madonnas. . . .' Werner probably voices the general opinion today when he writes of the duet's 'unpleasantly unctuous tone'; he does, however, find merit in certain other numbers.

In the autumn the *Hymn of Praise* was repeated, for the benefit of the King of Saxony, at an extra subscription concert at which Mendelssohn and David also played, at the King's request, Beethoven's 'Kreutzer' Sonata. King Friedrich August II thought very highly of Mendelssohn and had recently appointed him a Court conductor. Mendelssohn, for his part, had appealed to the King to devote to the foundation of an Academy of Music in Leipzig a substantial sum of money bequeathed by a certain Dr Heinrich Blümner for a purpose of this kind; he was still awaiting a decision.

Writing to his mother, he tells her that the command performance 'went off famously':

> The King had already sent for me during the interval, which obliged me to pass between a double row of ladies (you know the arrangement of our concert hall) in order to get to where the King and his Court were sitting. He talked to me for some time in the most amiable and friendly way, and spoke very shrewdly about music.
> The *Hymn of Praise* came in the second half, and at the end, just as I had left my music desk, I suddenly heard people round me saying, 'The King is coming to him this time.' He was in fact passing through the rows of ladies, and came up to my desk. You may imagine how delighted everyone was. He spoke to me with such vivacity, with so much cordiality and warmth, that I did indeed feel it to be a great pleasure and a great honour. He mentioned the particular passages that had pleased him most, and, after thanking the singers, took his departure while all the orchestra and the whole audience made the finest bows and curtsies they could manage. . . . Perhaps the King will now give us for our music here the twenty thousand thalers which I long ago petitioned for; if that were to happen, then I really could honestly say that I had done Leipzig music a good turn.

After conducting a small festival at Schwerin in July, Mendelssohn broke his journey home at Berlin in order to spend a few days with his mother and Rebecka. That at least one of the Mendelssohns had now accepted Cécile is shown by a letter written to her at this time by Rebecka: 'I don't say that there are not husbands who love their wives as much as Felix loves you, but *I* have never seen one so much in love before. However I can understand it, for though I am not your husband I am a little bit in love with you myself.'

In November 1839 Mendelssohn had expressed himself very forcibly, in a letter to Moscheles in London, on the subject of the modern craze in Germany for erecting monuments to great musicians. Little men, he said, tried to win for themselves a kind of reflected glory in this way, while allowing living musicians to remain so grossly underpaid that many orchestras did not attract the best talent:

> If only [he wrote] they would make a decent orchestra for Handel in Halle, for Mozart in Salzburg and for Beethoven in Bonn – orchestras capable of understanding and playing their works – then I would be all in favour [of monuments]; but I am not for stones where orchestras are more dead than stones, not for *conservatoires* where there is nothing to conserve.
> My hobby-horse at the present moment is our poorly paid orchestra and how to get them better wages. I have now – after untold running around, writing innumerable letters and

ABOVE *The Bach Memorial at Leipzig. Engraving, 1843* OPPOSITE *View of the Thames. Drawing by Mendelssohn, 2 October 1840. It was later given to Moscheles*

meeting with endless vexations – succeeded in getting them an extra five hundred thalers, and before I leave here they have got to get double that amount more. If the town does that – then it can also put up a memorial to Bach in front of the Thomasschule. But first the extra money!

However, by the summer of 1840 he had decided that the scandal of there being no memorial in Leipzig to its most illustrious citizen could not be allowed to continue any longer. He had at least won rather better conditions for his orchestra; he therefore now made up his mind to raise the money necessary for the erection of a memorial to Bach by giving two recitals of his music on Bach's own organ in the Thomaskirche. The first took place on a golden summer evening in August, and Mendelssohn, writing to his mother a few days later, said: 'I gave it *solissimo* and played nine pieces, winding up with an extempore fantasia. . . . Although my expenses were considerable, I cleared three hundred thalers. I mean to try this again in the autumn or next spring, and then we should have enough money to put up something very handsome. I practised so hard for a week beforehand that really I could hardly stand upright, and walked nothing but pedal passages in the street.'

Schumann, who was present, was enthusiastic, wishing for 'letters of gold' in which to describe the experience. The Polko was also there – also, of course, in ecstasies; and very properly, for Mendelssohn was undeniably the greatest organist of his day. 'It was no modern musician who sat up there in the organ loft,' she wrote. 'No! it was wonderful old Sebastian Bach himself who was playing! Sacred awe pervaded the souls of the hearers, and tears rushed to eyes that had long since ceased to weep. Worthy old Rochlitz [the doyen of the Leipzig critics] . . . embraced the young master at the close of the concert, saying, "I can now depart in peace, for I shall never hear anything finer or more sublime." In my opinion, neither Mendelssohn's piano nor his organ playing has been sufficiently highly esteemed. . . .'

A second recital followed, and three years later, on Bach's birthday, a bust was placed on the Promenade, under the windows of his rooms in the Thomasschule.

Mendelssohn's doctors had at first tried to dissuade him from fulfilling an enagement to conduct a performance of his *Hymn of Praise* (with English text) in Birmingham in the autumn; but in the end they agreed that he was well enough to take the risk. It was his sixth visit to England and he had hoped this time to have Cécile with him; but she was again pregnant (their second son, Paul, was born in the following January), and it was considered inadvisable for her to make so long and tiring a journey.

So Mendelssohn went alone. He reached London on 17 September after a shocking crossing and a day later than he had intended, stayed for two nights with Klingemann and then travelled with Chorley and Moscheles by train to Birmingham. Once again Birmingham welcomed him with open arms, the whole audience rising spontaneously to its feet for the final chorus of the *Hymn of Praise* as it had become the custom to do for Handel's 'Hallelujah Chorus'. After a week in London he returned to Leipzig, taking Chorley and Moscheles with him.

Chorley stayed only a week in Leipzig, but in that short time he seems to have fallen under the spell of the whole Mendelssohn family, even composing a sonnet praising the 'infantile grace' of little Karl ('O blooming, bright-haired Boy!'), who was equally devoted to his '*Onkel* Chorley'. For several days Chorley was tied to his hotel room by a bad foot, and it

was characteristically kind and thoughtful of Mendelssohn to have had an Erard grand piano sent up to him, on which he and Moscheles made music at his bedside.

Moscheles who also could stay no more than a week, lodged with the Mendelssohns, and it felt, said Felix, just as though they had been living together like that for twenty years. 'Every morning Karl went to his room to watch him shave and dress, and in the evenings we took turns to read the *Allgemeine Zeitung*, after which we made music, sometimes alone and sometimes in company. Moscheles played a great deal, and superbly, and at the end of his visit I gave a big soirée for him at the Gewandhaus.' Four hundred people were present and the programme, which might be described as 'the mixture as before', included Bach's Triple Concerto (with Clara Schumann at the third piano), Moscheles's *Homage to Handel*, two *Leonore* Overtures, and Mendelssohn's *Hebrides* Overture and Psalm XLII. 'Everyone was in the gayest mood, and Moscheles seemed to take pleasure in the pleasure he was giving to others. Next day he left for Prague, so besieged to the very last moment by publishers, friends and other visitors that Cécile had to hand him his unfinished helping of pudding through the carriage window as he drove off to the station; there hadn't been a moment for a proper meal.'

A month later Mendelssohn wrote again to Klingemann: 'I am once more living here in as complete peace and solitude as I could possibly wish. My wife and children are well, thank God! and I have plenty to do; what more could any man want?' At this time of year he always found some difficulty in avoiding tedious and time-consuming social engagements, but at last he had discovered how to dodge them. His *Hymn of Praise* was to be performed at the end of the month in aid of his musicians' pension fund, and he was determined to do the revision which his illness in the summer had prevented; this included, among other things, the addition of four new numbers – one of them the striking tenor solo and chorus, 'Watchman! will the night soon pass?' – and involved the scrapping of the plates that had been engraved in Birmingham. He also, he said, had serious thoughts of revising his *First Walpurgis Night*, extending, as he had originally intended, the orchestral introduction and so turning the piece into another symphony-cantata. In fact, two years later he rewrote the whole score, adding two new arias and making various cuts. It was published in 1843 and received 'with quite wonderful applause' when performed in London in 1844. It deserves to be heard more often today.

In the same letter Mendelssohn tells Klingemann that all Leipzig was ringing with a jingoistic anti-French song called '*Rheinlied*' or, familiarly, 'The Colognaise'. The press was pushing it, three or four composers had already set the poem to music, and one newspaper even announced that Mendelssohn had written the words as well as a tune for them! In fact, he considered the poem particularly silly. It began, 'They shall never have it, the free, German Rhine', and every verse repeated this sentiment. He thought that 'We intend to keep it' made better sense; but in any case he had no intention whatever of becoming involved. He was a Liberal; but he had more important things to think about than politics. 'Political discussions,' wrote Frau Polko, 'which in those turbulent times were scarcely to be avoided among men, were apt to annoy him'; curiously enough, however, he was deeply interested in English parliamentary affairs and always asked Klingemann for the latest news from the House of Commons.

CHAPTER TWENTY

Berlin 1841

It may be remembered that the Prussian Crown Prince, while at Düsseldorf in 1833, had jokingly reprimanded Mendelssohn for his desertion of Berlin. When in June 1840 his father died and he ascended the throne as King Friedrich Wilhelm IV, one of his first acts was to command the reorganization and expansion of the existing Academy of the Arts; and for the direction of the musical side of it he decided to acquire Mendelssohn. The endlessly protracted and complicated negotiations that ensued cannot but make tedious reading today; they will therefore be reduced here to the barest minimum.[1]

In school history books kings used sometimes to be dismissed as 'good' or 'bad'; Friedrich Wilhelm IV could best be classified as 'disappointing'. He meant well, he began well; his views were liberal and enlightened, and he was determined to encourage artists, scientists and scholars. He summoned Meyerbeer from Paris to replace Spontini. But as Prince Metternich wrote of him, 'I do not think I am wrong when I make a distinction between what the King still wants today and what he will do tomorrow';[2] in short, when the time came for action he almost invariably proved a broken reed. In some respects the new King resembled his great-nephew and godson, King Ludwig II of Bavaria; a romantic too at heart, he founded an Order of the Swan, and he ended his life with a mind completely clouded. It should, however, hardly be necessary to add that his relations with Mendelssohn were wholly unlike those that existed between Ludwig and Wagner.

The official entrusted with the delicate task of enticing Mendelssohn from Leipzig, where he was happy, to Berlin, where outside the family circle he usually was not, was H. E. von Massow – a worthy man who, unfortunately, was responsible to a 'dull, unimaginative and reactionary' departmental Minister, Karl von Eichhorn. Massow decided to act through Felix's brother Paul, the most practical member of the family, who accordingly went to Leipzig in November 1840 to put the King's proposal to Felix. The Academy of the Arts was to be divided into four schools – painting, sculpture, architecture and music – under four directors who would take it in turns to act as head of the whole institution. Mendelssohn's salary as director of the musical faculty would be considerably more than he was receiving at Leipzig – and naturally Paul stressed how much the family, especially their old mother and Fanny, would rejoice at having Felix back among them again.

[1] The glutton for every thrust and parry may consult the biographies by Werner and Jacob.
[2] Quoted by Werner.

In spite of endless correspondence and personal discussions with Massow in Berlin, Mendelssohn could never elicit precisely what his status or his duties would be. But by May 1841 some kind of an understanding had been reached, and Massow was able to report to the King that he had made the following proposition to Mendelssohn, who was ready to accept it. He was to establish himself in Berlin for a year, where his services would be at the King's disposal; he was to be appointed *Kapellmeister* but relieved of any duties in connection with the Royal Opera; and he was to receive a salary of three thousand thalers. At the end of this time, when the duties of a permanent appointment had been clarified, a further decision could be taken. Exchanging Leipzig for Berlin was, he told Klingemann, 'one of the sourest apples a man can eat; and yet eaten it must be'. His main reason for accepting the post had been to please his mother; but he must also have felt some satisfaction in showing the Berliners, who had previously rejected him, that after all he *did* count for something.

So in July, having arranged for David to act as his deputy during his absence, Mendelssohn moved with his family to Berlin; for the present they were to live in the garden house, but for greater comfort in the winter he had rented an apartment exactly opposite the family house. A fortnight later he reported to David:

> You wish to hear some news about the Berlin Conservatoire? So do I, but there is none. The affair is on the most extensive scale – if it is on any scale at all, and not merely in the air. The King seems to have a plan for reorganizing the Academy of the Arts; but it is hardly possible to do this without entirely reconstructing it, and this they can't make up their minds to do. And I am hardly likely to advocate it, because I don't see that music is likely to benefit much from the Academy in any shape or form.
>
> The musical part of the new Academy is, I believe, to become a Conservatoire; but it is absolutely useless to reorganize one part alone, so now it all depends on the other three. They haven't yet found a director for the architectural department, and the existing heads of the four departments can't (or won't) be superseded or have their powers curtailed – so we shall just have to wait until they die off. . . .
>
> So you will ask, what on earth do they want with me in Berlin at the moment? My answer is that I don't really know, but that I believe they intend to give during the winter a number of important concerts, using all the resources at their disposal, and that I am to direct them. Some will be in a church, some in a concert hall; but whether they will ever take place seems to me very doubtful. In any case, these are in my opinion the only projects which can or will be carried out at the moment.

As Mendelssohn became daily more and more convinced that the reformed Academy was a mere castle in the air, his mood grew ever blacker; and Devrient, who shared his doubts and fears, could do nothing but 'try to soothe him with generalities'. However, among the King's innumerable schemes was one that not only greatly appealed to Mendelssohn as a classical scholar, but that also had a chance of being carried out: a performance (in German) of Sophocles' *Antigone* for which Mendelssohn was invited to compose incidental music.

It was Tieck who had directed the King's attention to the *Antigone*, and immediately the monarch was like a child with a new toy. He saw himself as the rediscoverer of Greek tragedy, and determined to have the play produced in his private theatre in the New Palace at Potsdam. On 21 October 1841 Mendelssohn wrote to David:

> There was a lot of talk about it [*Antigone*], but nobody would get started. They wanted to put it off until late next year; but the magnificence of the piece so fascinated me that I got

ABOVE *Title-page of the score of* Antigone
BELOW *The Antigone Medal, 1841*

hold of Tieck and said, 'Now or never!' And he was very nice and said, 'Now.' So I composed music for it to my heart's content. We rehearse twice a day, and the choruses are sung with such precision that it's a real pleasure to hear them. Of course all Berlin thinks that we are very cunning and that I composed the choruses in order to become a court favourite, or a court *musicus*, or a court fool. . . .

Composition was begun early in September 1841 and the première took place at Potsdam on 28 October. On the dramatic side Mendelssohn received much help from Devrient, who played Haemon. Fanny Hensel, who was among the distinguished invited guests at Potsdam, noted in her journal that her brother had 'deliberately disavowed all intention of writing in the antique style; his music was rather intended to form a sort of connecting link between the antique drama and the modern audience'. And the great classical scholar, August von Boeckh, found the music[1] 'perfectly in harmony with his conception of Greek life and character, and with the muse of Sophocles'. The play was, however, staged in the classical manner, and Fanny thought that it looked 'quite beautiful. I cannot say how much nobler this arrangement appears to me than our stupid changes of scene and absurd footlights. Who ever saw light *coming from below*? Then the curtain sinking instead of rising, so that the heads of the actors are seen *first*, is much more sensible than our fashion of making acquaintance with them feet foremost, so to speak.'

The private performance of the *Antigone* was commemorated by a medal struck at the command of the King. A public performance took place in the following April at the Berlin Schauspielhaus, and was soon repeated in many other cities. In 1845 the play ran for forty-five nights in London, and to Fanny in Rome Mendelssohn wrote on 25 March of that year:

> See if you can get hold of *Punch* for 18 January. It contains an account of *Antigone* at Covent Garden, with illustrations, especially a view of the chorus which has made me laugh for three whole days. The chorus-master, with his plaid trousers showing beneath his robe, is a masterpiece. . . . I hear wonderful things of the performance, particularly of the chorus. Would you believe it – during the Bacchus chorus there is a regular ballet with ballet-girls and all!

One remarkable composition for the piano also dates from the year 1841 – the *Variations Sérieuses* in D minor (op. 54), written in Leipzig just before Mendelssohn moved to Berlin and by a man who had complained to Hiller that where the piano was concerned he had nothing new to offer. On 15 July Mendelssohn told Klingemann 'Can you guess what I've just been composing – and passionately? Variations for piano! Eighteen of them on a theme in D minor, and I had such enormous fun with them that I immediately went on to some on a theme in E flat, and now I'm on my third on one in B flat. It's just as though I had to make up for lost time in never having written any before.' In an age when 'variations' usually meant empty brilliance, Mendelssohn deliberately chose a humble and plaintive little chromatic tune – he even called it 'peevish' – and embroidered it in a sober but completely novel way that was to influence later nineteenth-century composers such as Brahms and César Franck. The other variations to which he refers break no new ground and were only published posthumously; they are rarely played today.

[1] Why is it never heard today?

OPPOSITE 'Antigone *Analysed*'. A cartoon from Punch, *18 January 1845*

ANTIGONE ANALYSED.

A MODEST young gentleman,
bâton in hand,
Walks up to the stool in the
midst of the Band ;
Apparently awed by the
numbers around,
He looks at the ceiling and
then at the ground.

His collar turned down his pretensions assert,
For Genius ever is known by the shirt.
A Symphony solemn is slowly gone through,
The instruments making a blunder or two,
Which causes the youth with the collar turned down
To crush an unfortunate Flute with a frown,
Or make at the Drum some exceeding wry faces,
As if the *grosse caisse* was the grossest of cases.

The curtain ascends, and discovers a view
To classic authority perfectly true ;
A stage—whose five different door-ways bespeak
That the scenic arrangement is thoroughly Greek.
Two ladies now enter—*Antigone's* one,
And when the applause at her entrance is done,
She gracefully turns to *Ismene*—the other,
And says she's determined to bury her brother.
In *that* there would nothing particular be,
Except that it's death by a certain decree.
As a tragedy lady is likely to view it—
The deed being dangerous, prompts her to do it.

Ismene's her sister, and tries to dissuade her ;
Though her sister, she'll neither assist her nor aid her.
Antigone says to her plan she'll adhere,
And the ladies through opposite doors disappear.
A feeling of classical rapture comes o'er us,
Which is smash'd when there enters a queer-looking Chorus,
With sheets on their shoulders and rouge on their cheeks ;
Though Greek in their guise, they are sad guys of Greeks.
Their fleshings, which ought to fit close to their shapes,
Are clumsily fasten'd with ill-conceal'd tapes ;
And if the theatrical text be relied on,
The skins of the Greeks were most carelessly tied on.
A chorus they sing—which is rather a long one—
But still in a musical point 'tis a strong one.
We don't very often hear anything finer
Than the beautiful change from the major to minor.

Unable to make head or tail of their shout,
We learn by the book what they're singing about.
They sing of a fight 'twixt a brother and brother,
In which one killed the one, and the other the other ;
At which we ejaculate mentally, " That's
Exactly the case of Kilkenny's famed cats."
Nor e'en to the end does the simile fail,
For nothing remains of them now but their tale.
The Chorus, expecting that *Creon* will enter,
With energy point to the door in the centre.
They say that he's summoned of sages a host
By *Herald* ! But why not by *Times* or by *Post* ?
Of the summons they're hoping to get at the cause,
When *Creon* walks in to a round of applause :
To the nobles assembled he tells his decree,
That poor *Polynices* unburied shall be.
They nothing reply, though they p'rhaps think it hard ;
When all of a sudden there enters a Guard—
He's full of alarm, and his toga and tights
Conduce to his looking the queerest of frights.
(*King Creon* was surely uncommonly needy,
If we judge by his guards, who are awfully seedy.)
The sentinel states, though he's watched night and day,
The body by somebody's taken away ;
The *King* in a truly monarchical fashion
Soon works himself into a towering passion,

And swears, if the culprit's not found in a trice,
That in killing the Guard he won't be o'er-nice ;
A volley of threats at the fellow he fires,
And having exhausted his fury, retires.
The nobles, suspected of having a share
In this job, that has much of a black job the air,
In asserting their innocence take a wide scope,
By singing an Essay on Man, *à la* POPE.
King Creon comes in when the Chorus is done,
And hears that *Antigone's* self is the one
Who buried her brother. The deed she avows,
And then there ensues the most awful of rows !
Her sister *Ismene* is sent for, who cries
That *she* will die *too* if *Antigone* dies :
An assertion that's much more heroic than wise !

CHAPTER TWENTY-ONE

Queen Victoria and Prince Albert 1842

In March 1842 Mendelssohn went to Leipzig for the first performance of his 'Scottish' Symphony, which later in the year he was given permission to dedicate to Queen Victoria. Conceived in 1829 during Mendelssohn's visit to Edinburgh and the Highlands, the work had languished for a dozen years before being taken in hand again and completed. Scottish ballads – though nobody can point to a particular one – are believed to have played a part in it, Scottish mists have tinged it here and there with a gentle melancholy, and Benedict noted that in the scherzo 'the familiar tones of the bagpipes at once indicate the rude merriment of a mountaineer's feast'. Though known as the Third Symphony it was Mendelssohn's last, his longest and, in the opinion of many, his finest; Bernard Shaw called it 'a work which would be great if it were not so confoundedly genteel'. The posthumously published 'Reformation' Symphony (No. 5) was, of course, written earlier.

After conducting the Lower Rhine Festival in Düsseldorf, Mendelssohn, accompanied now by Cécile, left for England to take part in several concerts of the Philharmonic Society, at one of which his 'Scottish' Symphony was to be given. Devrient wrote that in London Mendelssohn 'was greeted with storms of applause, not only at the concerts in which he was taking part, but also at others at which he appeared only among the audience, where the cry, "Mendelssohn is here!" caused the entire public to rise from their seats, and ministers of state to take precedence in showing him marks of their enthusiastic esteem'. Natalia Macfarren, who made the English translation of Devrient's *Recollections*, saw fit to add a footnote to the effect that the whole of this passage seemed 'a little overwrought'; but the fact remains that by now Mendelssohn had become for the English a national hero, and his own account of the incident, in a letter to his mother, shows that Devrient was hardly exaggerating:

The other day I went to a concert in Exeter Hall,[1] one in which I was taking no part, and was sauntering in quite coolly with Klingemann – in the middle of the first part, and an audience of about three thousand present – when, just as I entered, such a clamour and clapping and shouting and standing up ensued that at first I had no idea that it had anything to do with me. But when I reached my seat I discovered that it was, for near me were Sir Robert Peel and Lord Wharncliffe who went on applauding with the rest until I made my bow and thanked them. I was enormously proud of my popularity in Peel's presence. When I left the concert they gave me another hurrah.

[1] On the site now occupied by the Strand Palace Hotel.

There was, however, an unpleasant incident during the concert at which the 'Scottish' Symphony received its première. The symphony was followed by a performance by Thalberg of his Fantasia on *La Sonnambula*, which was also wildly applauded and had to be repeated. 'Thereupon Macfarren and Davison[1] hissed so vigorously as to become the observed of all observers and draw down upon themselves the scorn of the "Times", "Athenaeum" and "Morning Post".' Thalberg behaved extremely sensibly; but at the next rehearsal of the Philharmonic, 'Mendelssohn was just about to begin his D minor Concerto when he was startled by a volley of hisses from the orchestra, followed by cries of "turn him out". The object of this demonstration was Macfarren walking up the room to his place.'

Mendelssohn had been provided by the King of Prussia with a letter in his own hand to Prince Albert. This led to a formal meeting with the Prince, followed by two informal sessions of music-making at Buckingham Palace. Curiously enough, Mendelssohn's brother-in-law, Wilhelm Hensel, had as it were beaten him to the palace, for in 1838, shortly before the coronation, he had shown some of his paintings to the young Queen in the Picture Gallery, where to his embarrassment they were displayed for inspection among the Rembrandts and Van Dycks. The Queen had been sufficiently impressed to purchase his *Miriam* for the Royal Collection and later both she, Prince Albert, and the child who was one day to become King Edward VII, sat for portrait drawings in pencil.

Many of the Hanoverian monarchs and princes had shown an interest in music which ranged from the merely polite to the entirely genuine. George III had encouraged Handel and J. C. Bach; George IV when Prince of Wales, and his brother Frederick, Duke of York, patronized Haydn, who wrote, perhaps with more tact than truth, 'The Prince of Wales is the most handsome man on God's earth. He has an extraordinary love of music and a lot of feeling, but not much money. . . . He played with us on his violoncello quite tolerably.'[2] One cannot but regret that the tape-recorder and the camera were not invented in time to preserve for us the occasion when George IV and Rossini sang duets together.

Queen Victoria enjoyed music and sang very agreeably. Shortly before her accession she had taken lessons from the great operatic bass, Luigi Lablache (1794–1858), famous for his astonishing breath control. An ear-witness recalled an occasion when at a dinner-party Lablache 'sang a long note from piano to forte and back to piano; then drank a glass of wine without having breathed; then sang a chromatic scale up the octave in trills, still in the same breath; and finally blew out a candle with his mouth open.' Though it is improbable that the Queen ever attempted to emulate this *tour de force*, she did acquire excellent breath control. But it was Prince Albert, a really competent musician, who developed and widened his wife's taste, which previously had been principally for Italian music. Mendelssohn was to become their god.

Of a concert at Buckingham Palace in 1840, Guizot, the French Ambassador, wrote that 'the Queen took a more lively interest in it than the greater part of her guests. Prince Albert slept. She looked at him, half smiling, half vexed. She pushed him with her elbow. He woke up, and nodded approval of the piece of the moment. Then he went to sleep again, still

---

[1] (Sir) George Macfarren (1813–87), composer and later Principal of the Royal Academy of Music; he married the German contralto Natalia Andrae in 1845. For Davison see pp. 184–5.

[2] Quoted from an article, 'Music and the Monarch', written for the programme of the Festival of Windsor by R. Mackworth-Young. The Prince of Wales's cello, ornamented with a large royal coat of arms, is now in a glass case in Hill's in Bond Street.

nodding approval, and the Queen began again.' However, it was the Queen who, on another occasion, recorded in her diary after hearing a performance of Bach's *St Matthew Passion*: 'Though so fine, it is a little fatiguing to listen to, there being so much sameness.'[1]

The Queen is our best authority for what took place at her first meeting with Mendelssohn, in anticipation of which (according to Kupferberg) she and Albert, 'for all their exalted station, were quite fluttery':

> June 16, 1842[2] . . . After dinner came Mendelssohn Bartholdy, whose acquaintance I was so anxious to make. Albert had already seen him the other morning. He is short, dark, & Jewish looking – delicate – with a fine intellectual forehead. I should say he must be about 35 or 6. He is very pleasing & modest, & is greatly protected by the King of Prussia. He played first of all some of his *Lieder ohne Worte* after which, his Serenade & then, he asked us to give him a theme, upon which he could improvise. We gave him 2, 'Rule Britannia', & the Austrian National Anthem. He began immediately, & really I have never heard anything so beautiful; the way in which he blended them together & changed over from one to the other, was quite wonderful as well as the exquisite harmony & feeling he puts into the variations, & the powerful rich chords, & modulations, which reminded one of all his beautiful compositions. At one moment he played the Austrian Anthem with the right hand he [*sic*] played 'Rule Britannia' with his left! He made some further improvisations on well known themes & songs. We were all filled with the greatest admiration. Poor Mendelssohn was quite exhausted, when he had done playing.

Mendelssohn's second visit to the palace, again made without Cécile, is fully described in a delightful letter that he wrote to his mother after his return to Germany. Though it has been often quoted, it would be impertinent to attempt to paraphrase it, and, long though it is, a pity to abbreviate it more than very slightly:

> . . . As Grahl says, the only really nice, comfortable house in England, one where one feels completely at home, is Buckingham Palace. . . . But to be serious: Prince Albert sent for me on the Saturday [9 July] at half past one, so that I could also try his organ before I left England. I found him by himself; but while we were talking, in came the Queen, also alone and dressed quite informally. She was just saying that she had to leave for Claremont in an hour's time, when she looked round and exclaimed, 'Heavens,[3] how untidy!' – for the wind had scattered some sheets of music from a large portfolio all over the room and even among the organ pedals. Down she got on hands and knees and started picking them up. Prince Albert joined in, and I too did not remain idle. Then Prince Albert began to explain the organ stops to me, and the Queen said she would do the rest of the tidying-up herself.
>
> I begged the Prince to begin by playing me something, so that I could boast of it in Germany. He played a chorale by heart, with the pedals – and so charmingly, precisely and accurately that it would have done credit to a professional. Meanwhile the Queen, who had

---

[1] This and other passages from Queen Victoria's diary are quoted by gracious permission of Her Majesty the Queen.
[2] Yet Mendelssohn, in a letter to his mother dated 21 June, refers to the visit to the palace as having taken place 'yesterday'.
[3] Mendelssohn writes 'Mein Gott!' Since he speaks of the Queen's excellent command of German, presumably the conversation was in that language.

OPPOSITE *Cécile Jeanrenaud. Oil painting by Eduard Magnus, made in 1836 at the time of her engagement to Mendelssohn* OVERLEAF *The drawing-room of the Mendelssohn's home in Leipzig, with Cécile and their two eldest children. Watercolour by Mendelssohn, 1840. The figures were added by Cécile, who seems to have been even more incompetent at them than Felix*

finished what she had been doing, came and joined him, listening with pleasure. Then it was my turn, and I began with the chorus from *St Paul*, 'How lovely are the messengers'. Before I had come to the end of the first verse they both began singing the chorus, and Prince Albert managed the stops so cleverly for me . . . that I was quite enchanted.

Then the Hereditary Prince of Gotha came in, and we talked for a while. The Queen asked me whether I had written any new songs, because she was very fond of singing my published ones. 'You ought to sing one to him,' said Prince Albert; and after a moment's hesitation she said she would try the 'Spring Song' in B flat – 'if it's still here, because all my music is packed up for Claremont'. Prince Albert went in search of it, but returned saying that it was already packed. 'Couldn't it possibly be *un*packed?' I ventured. 'We must send for Lady ——', said the Queen – I didn't catch the name. So the bell was rung and servants dispatched, but to no avail. At last the Queen went herself, and while she was out of the room Prince Albert said to me, 'She begs you will accept this gift as a memento', and gave me a case containing a beautiful ring on which was engraved 'V.R., 1842'.

Then the Queen returned and said, 'Lady —— has gone and she's taken all my things with her; it's really most annoying.' (You can imagine how that amused me!) I now begged her that I might not be the loser by this mischance, and hoped she would sing another song. She consulted her husband, who then said, 'She will sing you something by Gluck.' Meanwhile the Princess of Gotha had come in, and all five of us proceeded through various rooms and corridors to the Queen's boudoir, where there stood near the piano a very plump rocking-horse and two large bird-cages. . . . The Duchess of Kent also came in, and while they were all talking I rummaged about among the music on the piano and soon discovered my first set of songs; so of course I asked the Queen to sing one of these instead of the Gluck, and she agreed.

Just as we were about to begin, she said, 'But first we must get rid of the parrot, or he will scream louder than I can sing.' Prince Albert rang the bell and the Prince of Gotha said '*I*'ll take him out'; so I came forward and said, 'Please allow me!' and lifted up the big cage and carried it out to the astonished servants.

And which of my songs did she choose? '*Schöner und schöner schmückt sich*'[1] – and sang it quite charmingly, strictly in time and in tune, and very nicely enunciated. Only when it came to the line 'Der Prosa Last und Müh', where it goes down to D and then rises again chromatically, each time she sang D sharp; and since I gave her the note the first two times, in the third verse she sang D where it ought to have been D sharp! But except for this little mistake it was really charming, and I've never heard an amateur sing the last sustained G better, more purely or more naturally.

Then I had to confess – I found it very hard, but pride goeth before a fall – that Fanny had written that song, and would she now sing one of mine? She said she would gladly try, so long as I gave her plenty of help, and then she sang '*Lass dich nur nichts dauern*'[2] really quite faultlessly and with much feeling and expression. I thought that this wasn't the moment to indulge in extravagant compliments, so I merely thanked her several times. But when she said 'Oh, if only I hadn't been so frightened! I generally have a pretty long breath,' then – and with the clearest conscience – I praised her warmly, because it was precisely that particular passage at the close, with the long-sustained C, that she had managed so well. . . .

After this Prince Albert sang '*Es ist ein Schnitter*'[3] and then said that I must play him

[1] 'Italy' (op. 8, No. 3). Three of the songs in the first set were in fact by Fanny, and this was one of them.
[2] 'The pilgrim's maxim' (op. 8, No. 5).
[3] 'Harvest Song' (op. 8, No. 4).

Mendelssohn. Oil painting by Eduard Magnus, 1845. Painted for Jenny Lind

ABOVE *Mendelssohn playing to the Queen and Prince Albert. After a painting by Car Rohling* OPPOSITE *Prince Albert playing the organ before the Queen and Mendelssohn at Buckingham Palace, 1842*

something before I left, and gave me as themes the chorale which he had played on the organ and the song he had just sung. Usually when I particularly want to improvise well I do it very badly – and that would have spoilt my whole morning. But it was as if everything conspired to make it perfect, for I never improvised better. . . . I played for a long time, and enjoyed it so much myself that, besides the two given themes, I brought in quite spontaneously the two songs that the Queen had sung. . . . The Queen said several times, 'I hope you will come back to England again soon and pay us another visit.' Then I took my leave; and down below I saw the beautiful carriages waiting, with their scarlet outriders, and a quarter of an hour later the flag was lowered and the Court Circular announced, 'Her Majesty left the Palace at thirty minutes past three.' I walked back in the rain to Klingemann's, and the best moment of all was when I gave him and Cécile a stop-press [*brühwarm*] account of everything.

In old age the Queen was sometimes heard to make the proud but exaggerated claim that Mendelssohn had been her singing teacher.

During this visit to England Cécile seems to have won the hearts of Felix's friends the Horsleys, as also of Klingemann and the Moscheles. Before returning to Germany the

Mendelssohns went to Manchester, where they passed 'two quiet days with Cécile's uncles and aunts. On our return to London we were plunged once more into the whirl. I will tell you when we meet of Sir Edward Bulwer's shocking flirtation with Cécile, and how old Samuel Rogers the poet shook hands with her and begged her to bring up her children to be as charming and to speak as good English as herself. . . .' There was also a party by boat to Greenwich for a fish dinner (with whitebait and speeches) given in Mendelssohn's honour by the directors of the Philharmonic Society.

A few days were spent on Denmark Hill with the Beneckes, cousins of Cécile's, where there were charades at which Klingemann acted a West Indian planter and Sir Walter Scott. One day, when everyone else had gone off to Windsor, Mendelssohn stayed behind and composed

At Interlaken. Drawing by Mendelssohn, 1842

his 'Spring Song' (op. 62, No. 6), the most popular of all his *Songs Without Words*, massacred since by a million maidens. Not far from the Beneckes, and about to become almost their next-door neighbour, lived a clever young man of twenty-three, who had just been given an honorary double-fourth at Oxford: his name was John Ruskin.

The Mendelssohns left England for Frankfurt on 10 July, and in August set out to take a holiday in Switzerland, where they were joined by Paul Mendelssohn and his wife Albertine. Exhausted by all the social life and music-making in London – for besides his Philharmonic Society concerts he had given several organ recitals – Felix needed to relax; and once again he found new strength in revisiting old haunts in the country he so much loved, and whose

Lausanne. Drawing by Mendelssohn, 7 August 1842. A thoroughly professional piece of work

grand scenery he once, to the indignation of another tourist, referred to as *hübsch* (pretty) – a word which in his vocabulary stood for the highest praise. From Interlaken he wrote to his mother recalling their visit there twenty years before: 'The Jungfrau with her silver horns is, still as virginal as ever, still as delicately, elegantly and sharply silhouetted against the sky. But the landlady has grown old, and it was only by her gait that I recognized her.' He composed nothing; but he drew 'furiously' every day, 'till fingers and eyes ached', and an admirable facsimile edition of his sketch-book was published in Basel in 1966.

Busy too that summer in Switzerland were three artists who surpassed him in talent though hardly in enthusiasm: Turner, Corot, and young Ruskin.

CHAPTER TWENTY-TWO

Retreat from Berlin 1842-1844

Mendelssohn had now been resident in Berlin for more than a year, and once again he had come to find the city intolerable. He felt like a fish out of water; he was constantly frustrated by procrastination and red tape and bureaucratic interference; he had no choir or orchestra at his regular disposal, and plans for the Academy of the Arts had been shelved. Moreover, there was trouble on the home front, for it soon became apparent that Cécile and Fanny could not live in such close proximity without friction. So, though he knew how much it would pain his mother, he decided that there was no other course open to him but to request the King to release him. He therefore wrote to Massow, explaining the situation and asking him to procure an audience with the King. At the same time he broke the news to his mother, who wept bitterly.

The audience, which took place at the beginning of November 1842, is fully described by Mendelssohn in a letter to Klingemann. Massow, always a good friend to Mendelssohn, had warned him that the King was extremely annoyed, but in the event he proved to be in the sunniest of moods and prepared to make fullest use of what Karl Marx once described as his 'commercial-traveller's persuasiveness'. He could not, he said, force Mendelssohn to stay, but he would deeply regret his going because without him there would be an end to all his schemes for the regeneration of music in Berlin. Mendelssohn maintained that he was far from being irreplaceable; but this the King strenuously denied, and then proceeded to put forward his new plan. A choir of about thirty first-rate singers and an orchestra composed of the cream of the players at the Royal Theatre were to be formed. These would be responsible for music both in the Cathedral and in concert halls; they would perform oratorios and other works specially composed for them by Mendelssohn, who would have complete charge of them.

Mendelssohn was amazed and delighted; the lack of such an instrument, he said, had been the principal obstacle to his remaining in Berlin. The King then repeated that he would make it his business to provide the choir and the orchestra, but that he must have Mendelssohn's promise that once they were there he would use them; this, he said, could only be assured by Mendelssohn remaining in his service. In the meantime the composer was to be free to go wherever he liked – back to Leipzig, 'Or to Italy,' the King added, 'for I'm told you are very fond of travelling.' He did not want an immediate answer; Mendelssohn was to think the matter over and then let Massow know his decision. Massow, who was also present at the audience, 'was quite flushed with excitement as we left the room, and kept on repeating,

"You can't possibly consider deserting us now!" But to tell the truth I was thinking more of my dear old mother than of anything else.'

Two days later Mendelssohn wrote to Massow accepting the King's generous offer; and, knowing well that at the palace intention and action were by no means the same thing, he took the precaution of putting down in black and white the terms that had been mutually agreed. He said that he would be returning to Leipzig, and he asked that for the time being his salary might be halved. 'If something really comes of it in Berlin,' he told Klingemann, 'then I can settle there with a clear conscience. But if they go on temporizing, then I shall very likely remain here [in Leipzig] on half pay for a year or even longer and just carry out any particular commands of the King.' Soon afterwards Mendelssohn was appointed *Generalmusikdirektor* of church music and awarded the *Pour le mérite*, the highest Prussian order. He never coveted honours for their own sake, but knew that he needed them for the prestige they brought him.

Though Mendelssohn had several times visited Leipzig during the year he had been residing in Berlin, it was the faithful David who had been bearing the brunt of the work there. It is, indeed, remarkable how ready the authorities in Leipzig seem to have been to allow him to absent himself for long periods, leaving one of his colleagues to deputize for him. During the winter season of 1843/44 it was Hiller who held the fort, and in the following winter it was to be the young Danish composer Niels Gade.

Soon after his return Mendelssohn went briefly to Dresden to resign from the post of *Kapellmeister* to the King of Saxony, it being impossible for him to continue to hold this after his appointment as *Generalmusikdirektor* to the King of Prussia. At his audience with King Friedrich August, Mendelssohn heard the exciting news that at long last Dr Blümner's twenty thousand thalers were to be put at his disposal to found a Conservatoire in Leipzig. 'During the two days that I was in Dresden,' he told Fanny, 'I was as frisky as a rabbit.'

He had also arranged to go to Berlin on 17 December in order to settle one or two outstanding details about his duties to the King; but a sad event was in fact to call him there sooner. On 11 December Lea had given one of her regular Sunday parties for the family and close friends. She seemed extremely well and was in high spirits; but suddenly she collapsed, and early next morning she died. 'A more happy end could not have been desired,' wrote Fanny in her diary. 'She was taken just as she told Albertine last summer she would like to be – knowing nothing about it and without a long illness, but busy to the last in the ordinary course of her pleasant daily life and in the full enjoyment of her intellectual faculties.' She was sixty-five. Round her the whole family had revolved; and though Felix had felt the death of his father more deeply, that of his mother left the survivors without a rallying-point. The big house in the Leipzigerstrasse now became his, but he handed it over to his sisters.

Back in Leipzig Mendelssohn was endlessly busy. There were the regular weekly Gewandhaus concerts and various others to rehearse and conduct, and the commissioned works to be composed for Berlin. He was rewriting his *Walpurgisnacht* 'from A to z', composing a cello sonata and some *Songs Without Words*, and preparing his *Antigone* and 'Scottish' Symphony for the press. Visitors pursued him incessantly, and there was always 'a frightful pile of letters' to be answered. But no appeal for help was considered unworthy of his attention; he even took up the cudgels on behalf of the landlord of the Krone at Meiringen, the excellent inn where he had stayed in the previous summer, who begged him to use his influence to get his establishment included in Murray's *Handbook to Switzerland*.

But of course his most demanding task was the foundation of the Conservatoire, and the appointment of the staff. He himself would take charge of piano and ensemble, to which was later added composition; Schumann was also to teach piano and composition, and David of course violin. To other distinguished musicians were allotted the theory of music and counterpoint, solo and choral singing, and organ; and there were two other piano teachers. The Conservatoire was formally opened on 3 April 1843 in the Gewandhaus, and by the summer there were thirty-three male and eleven female students – 'strictly segregated'. Initially six scholarships were made available, and later this number was increased.

In that same spring, Berlioz, finding himself in Weimar in the course of his first German concert tour, considered whether he should take the opportunity to visit Mendelssohn in nearby Leipzig. Though the two men had been on friendly terms in Rome twelve years earlier, since then, wrote Berlioz, 'our artistic paths had diverged so far that frankly I feared I would not find him sympathetic'. However, he decided to write to Mendelssohn, from whom he received a most warm reply. Mendelssohn would, he said, treasure as long as he lived the memory of 'our Rome friendship'. He would arrange a concert for Berlioz at the Gewandhaus which might well bring him a profit of six or seven hundred crowns. He could hardly wait to see his friend again, to shake his hand and 'bid him *willkommen* to Germany'.

'Could I resist an invitation couched in such terms?' wrote Berlioz to his friend the composer Stephen Heller. But before Berlioz died, Paul Mendelssohn had published the selection of his brother's letters in which, though much that was unfavourable to Felix had been excised, he had tactlessly retained the wounding passage about Berlioz ('not a spark of talent') already quoted;[1] and when the Frenchman came to include his letter to Heller in his *Memoirs* he added in a footnote the sad comment, 'I now see what his "Rome friendship" for me amounted to.'

Berlioz arrived in Leipzig on 1 February and went straight to the Gewandhaus, where he found Mendelssohn rehearsing his newly revised *Walpurgisnacht* which was to receive its première on the following day. He was enormously impressed, and as Mendelssohn came down into the auditorium to greet him he asked for the baton with which he had just been conducting. 'Gladly,' replied Mendelssohn, 'provided you'll give me one of yours.' Next day Berlioz sent him his 'heavy oak cudgel', together with a letter which he hoped the Last of the Mohicans would not have disowned:

> *To Big Chief Mendelssohn*: Great chief! We have promised to exchange tomahawks. Here is mine; it is rough-hewn, yours too is plain. Only squaws and palefaces like ornate weapons. Be my brother; and when the Great Spirit sends us to hunt in the Land of Souls, may our warriors hang our tomahawks side by side at the door of the Council Chamber.

So wrote Berlioz. But Fanny, who was in Leipzig at the time, provides a rather different version of what happened, adding that 'Berlioz's odd behaviour gave so much offence that Felix was continually being called upon to smooth ruffled feathers.'

[1] See p. 127.

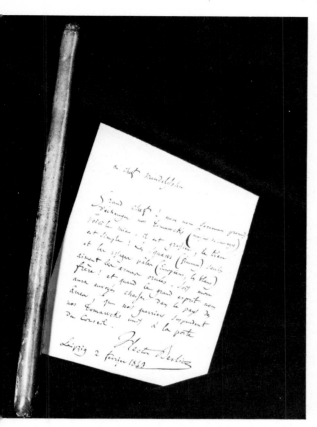

LEFT *Berlioz's baton and his letter to Mendelssohn* RIGHT *Berlioz conducting. Engraving by Dumont after a drawing by Gustave Doré, c. 1850*

Though there were difficulties over the augmented orchestra that Berlioz needed – a harpist could not be found in time, and the only available ophicleide (an instrument also favoured by Mendelssohn) was denounced by Berlioz as worthless – in general the latter was much impressed by the way the works he had chosen, which included such difficult pieces as his *King Lear* and *Francs Juges* overtures and *Symphonie Fantastique*, were performed after only two rehearsals. At a second concert, given several weeks later in aid of charity, the finale of *Romeo and Juliet* had to be omitted, after a week of rehearsals, because the bass soloist proved (wrote Berlioz) to belong to 'that large and flourishing class of musicians who are ignorant of music'. The 'Offertorium' from his *Requiem*, however, won Berlioz 'the priceless approval of Robert Schumann, one of the most justly renowned composer-critics in Germany'.

When the Frenchman came to leave Leipzig he noted that Mendelssohn had treated him 'like a brother', and doubtless, comments Petitpierre, 'the two composers drank together a few of the two dozen bottles of champagne which the Veuve Clicquot[1] – whether out of

[1] Madame Clicquot (1778–1867), of whom it was written, 'If she found no *Veuve-Clicquot* in heaven, we imagine this formidable woman sent God out to get some.'

admiration or as a piece of intelligent publicity – never failed to send Felix every year.' Berlioz had only one regret: Mendelssohn, he said, 'is rather too fond of the dead'. In his friend's album he wrote, 'Donec eris Felix, multos numerabis amicos' – 'As long as you are *Felix* [prosperous] you will have plenty of friends.'[1]

Mendelssohn was not to see Berlioz again; but in April 1846 the latter wrote to him from Prague:

> I'm afraid I shan't be able to shake you by the hand on my way through Leipzig. I'm terribly sorry about this. May I say that I heard your *A Midsummer Night's Dream* at Breslau and that I have never heard anything so profoundly Shakespearean as your music. On leaving the theatre I would gladly have given three years of my life to have been able to embrace you.
> Adieu, adieu!
> Believe me when I say that I love you as much as I admire you, and that is saying a lot.

★   ★   ★

Young Gounod, whom Fanny had met in Rome in 1840, came to Berlin in the spring of 1843. He spent most of his time there with the Hensels; to see them was, in fact, the principal object of his visit. Fanny, who had always rather liked him, found him much more mature now, and was greatly impressed, not only by his musical gifts but also by his general intelligence and 'infinite tenderness and delicacy'. He was still considering becoming a priest.

In 1842 and 1843 Mendelssohn met Wagner on a number of occasions in Berlin and elsewhere, and in the summer of the latter year each composed a *pièce de circonstance* for the unveiling in Dresden of a statue to the late King of Saxony. Outwardly the two men were polite to one another, but temperamentally they were so different that any real *rapprochement* was impossible. Of a performance of *The Flying Dutchman* in Berlin in January 1844, Wagner wrote in his highly tendentious and unreliable autobiography, *My Life*:

> Mendelssohn . . . was present in the stage box during this performance. He followed its progress with a pale face, and afterwards came and murmured to me in a weary tone of voice, 'Well, I should think you are satisfied now!' I met him several times during my brief stay in Berlin, and also spent an evening with him listening to various pieces of chamber music. But never did another word concerning the *Fliegender Holländer* pass his lips, beyond inquiries as to the second performance, and as to whether Devrient or someone else would appear in it. I heard, moreover, that he had responded with equal indifference to the earnest warmth of my allusions to his own music for the *Midsummer Night's Dream*.

Yet in a letter to his wife, Wagner wrote at the time that after the performance Mendelssohn had come on the stage and embraced and congratulated him most warmly![2]

In October 1845, after reading the score of *Tannhäuser*, Schumann told Mendelssohn that Wagner, 'though undoubtedly a clever fellow and full of bold and original ideas', couldn't write four consecutive bars that were melodious or, indeed, even correct. Only to Mendelssohn could he speak thus plainly, because in Dresden (where Schumann was now living) any criticism of Wagner was believed to stem from jealousy. On hearing the opera Schumann

---

[1] Ovid. The quotation continues, 'but when your sky is cloudy, you will be left to yourself.' Berlioz was of course not invoking the cynical sense of the verse, but purely playing with the verbal coincidence. Some years later, he wrote the same line in the album of Mendelssohn's godson, Felix Moscheles, who attributed it to Horace.
[2] Quoted by Werner.

Joachim accompanied by Clara Schumann. Drawing by Adolf van Menzel, 1854

somewhat revised his adverse opinion; but Leipzig could never allow that the 'music of the future' had any merits, and an 'ostentatiously ill-humoured' performance by Mendelssohn of the *Tannhäuser* Overture at the Gewandhaus in February 1846 merely served to widen the breach between the Mendelssohnians and the Wagnerians.

Mendelssohn had never liked accepting commissioned works, but the great success of *Antigone* showed him that it was not impossible for him to write 'to order'. In fact, further commissions – or rather, royal commands – soon followed for church music, and for incidental music to Sophocles' *Oedipus at Colonus*, Racine's *Athalie* and Shakespeare's *A Midsummer Night's Dream*. The *Oedipus* music is rarely if ever heard today, that of the *Athalie* remembered only for the once-famous 'War March of the Priests' of which Radcliffe wrote, rather acidly, that it 'does not now sound either warlike or priestly, and the chorus that follows . . . comes perilously near to *The Pirates of Penzance*'.

With the incidental music to *A Midsummer Night's Dream*, however, we come to an undisputed masterpiece and one which, like the violin concerto of 1844, gives the lie to those who maintain that Mendelssohn never really fulfilled his prodigious promise. Like Wagner, who after a break of twelve years in the middle of his *Siegfried* picked up the threads so cunningly that the seam is invisible, so Mendelssohn now exactly recaptured the youthful romantic mood of his overture written more than sixteen years earlier. The work was dedicated to an old friend, the gifted amateur musician Dr Conrad Schleinitz.

The première took place at Potsdam on 18 October 1843, and Fanny, writing to Rebecka, reported that among those who had come from Leipzig to attend it were Hiller, David, Gade, and 'a delightful little Hungarian, Joachim, who, though only twelve, is such a clever violinist that David can teach him nothing more, and such a sensible boy that he travelled here alone, and lives by himself in the Rheinischer Hof, all of which seems quite natural and proper'. The play was an outstanding success, perhaps the only anxious moment being when Moonshine's dog bit Lion; in subsequent performances a stuffed dog was substituted. Fanny's one thought as she witnessed her brother's triumph was, 'If only Mother could have been there!' The evening ended with a banquet given by the King, at which one of the guests observed to Mendelssohn, 'What a pity that your glorious music should have been wasted on such a silly play!'

There had been eleven full rehearsals and four performances of *A Midsummer Night's Dream* within a fortnight, and Mendelssohn was utterly exhausted; as soon, therefore, as he was free he returned to his family in Leipzig to relax. 'You will be glad,' he told Rebecka, 'to hear that I am now living on larks and apple-sauce, playing billiards at the café, and strolling about all day long in the delightful summer air which for the last few days has been reviving us all.' His children, too, were a constant joy to him; but he never spoiled them and did not hesitate to give Paul (aged two and a half) a spanking for striking his nurse and refusing to apologize. In the summer he had written to Rebecka:

> Here come Cécile and Karl, the latter with a live crayfish which he sets crawling on the floor while Marie and Paul scream with delight. The other day I heard Paul making a tremendous noise in the next room, and Karl calling out 'Encore! Encore!' When Cécile went in to see what it was all about, Karl said, 'Mummy, I wanted to know what kind of voice Paul had, so we are having a rehearsal.' Marie was standing by, and said quite seriously, 'Paul has really a very strong voice for singing.' They are all dear good children and a great blessing, and even the baby looks about quite intelligently with his blue eyes.

★   ★   ★

After a good deal of *va-et-vient* between Leipzig and Berlin during the autumn, at the end of November Mendelssohn left Leipzig 'with wife and children, tables and chairs and piano; in short, the lot', and established himself in Berlin for the winter; he really had no choice, for the King was constantly making fresh demands of him. Some of these were unreasonable, and Mendelssohn was soon to give much offence by his refusal to provide incidental music for the *Eumenides* of Aeschylus because he felt himself 'unequal to the sublimity of the subject'.

Busy though he was, life in Berlin that winter was peaceful enough – in spite of Fanny's smart Sunday concerts, at one of which she recorded 'twenty-two carriages in the court, and Liszt and eight princesses in the room'. Of her brother at this time, she wrote, 'I admire him afresh every day, for this quiet life together is new to me, and his mind is so many-sided, so unique, so interesting in every way, that one never gets accustomed to him. I do believe that he grows more lovable, too, with every year that passes. . . .' Felix was doing all he could to avoid social engagements. 'You would laugh,' he told Rebecka, 'to see me plunging about to escape the nets of the English Ambassador.' This was Lord Westmorland – a keen amateur musician who had been largely responsible for the foundation of the Royal Academy of Music in London, but who perpetually badgered Felix to perform his trite compositions. Fanny mentions a '*soirée monstre*' at which her brother conducted the Ambassador's 'ridiculously childish symphony with an almost imperceptible smile of sarcasm on his lip, but with the utmost politeness'.

However, with each day that passed Mendelssohn became increasingly aware that he could never find permanent happiness or satisfaction in Berlin:

> His position there [wrote Sebastian Hensel] was too intricate and too confined; he could hardly turn without coming into collision with one or other of the departments – now with the Singakademie and its conductor, now with the managers of the theatre, now with the ecclesiastical authorities. It became, too, more and more evident that the difficulties were not mere accidents, but incidental to the artificial nature of the position, that he was hemmed in on all sides by other officials who had a broader and more definite sphere of action, and that therefore there was no hope that the lapse of time would tend to make things run more smoothly, but the contrary, for the more conscientiously he fulfilled his duties, the more opposition would be roused on all sides.

★   ★   ★

In May 1844 Mendelssohn, taking with him an old family servant Johann, went to London to conduct a series of concerts of the Philharmonic Society. At one of these his young protégé Joseph Joachim – at this time on his first visit to England, where he had arrived in March with a letter of warm recommendation from Mendelssohn – played Beethoven's violin concerto and was instantly hailed as a master; exactly sixty years later he was to play it again at Queen's Hall at a concert at which he also conducted his own overture to *Henry IV*. But an unpleasantness marred for Mendelssohn what was otherwise perhaps the most successful of all his visits to Britain. He had again included in one of the concerts Schubert's C major Symphony, which Schumann had unearthed in 1839, and the greatness of which had been immediately recognized when Mendelssohn had performed it at Leipzig. During its rehearsal in London, however, certain members of the orchestra were so convulsed with mirth by the repeated triplets in the final movement that Mendelssohn angrily cancelled its performance. He further registered his displeasure by removing his own *Ruy Blas* Overture from the programme.

In London Mendelssohn was, to his great joy, once more the guest of his old friend Klingemann. While there he met Dickens, and again made music with the Queen and Prince Albert at Buckingham Palace. On 10 July he left England – crossing to Antwerp in the *Soho* and, though not actually sick, feeling, he told Klingemann, 'decidedly "skuiemisch" (as you call it)' – and joined his family at Soden, a spa in the foothills of the Taunus Mountains near Frankfurt. Here, but for a flying visit to Zweibrücken to conduct a two-day festival at the end of July, he remained until the autumn. And perhaps there was never a time when he was happier; he always, he said, felt 'at home among cows and pigs: my equals!' To Rebecka he wrote a few days after his arrival:

> After my crazy, absolutely crazy, life in England – for we never got to bed before half past one, and every hour of the day was filled with engagements three weeks in advance, and I got through more music in two months than in all the rest of the year put together – this life at Soden, with its eating and sleeping, without morning coat, without piano, without visiting-cards, without carriage and horses, but with donkeys, with wild flowers, with music-paper and sketch-book, with Cécile and the children, is doubly refreshing.

Soden was to witness the birth of a masterpiece that had been gestating for more than six years: the Violin Concerto in E minor. In the summer of 1838 Mendelssohn had told David, 'I want to write a violin concerto next winter. One in E minor is running in my head, and the

The family at Soden. Pencil drawing by Mendelssohn, 23 September 1844

beginning of it never gives me a moment's peace.' The advice of David, for whom it was written, had often been sought, and no doubt Soden merely saw the commitment to paper of a work already note-perfect in the composer's mind. It was first performed, with David as soloist, in Leipzig on 13 March of the following year, and Mendelssohn, who was again enjoying a *villegiatura*, was not present.

The concerto – one of the most popular of all Mendelssohn's major compositions – is too well known to call for description; written only three years before the composer's death, it provides, as had already been said, the most substantial refutation of the myth of his failing powers in the latter part of his life. The honeyed sweetness of the lyrical passages becomes cloying only in the hands of a sentimental soloist, the bravura passages in the last movement degenerate into empty virtuosity only when played without feeling or understanding. By general consent the concerto has taken its place in the little handful of master works in this field composed in the nineteenth century. At a party given for Joachim in 1906, on his seventy-fifth birthday, the great violinist who did so much to popularize it said, 'The Germans have four violin concertos. The greatest, the one that makes fewest concessions, is Beethoven's. The one by Brahms comes close to Beethoven's in its seriousness. Max Bruch wrote the richest and most enchanting of the four. But the dearest of them all, the heart's jewel, is Mendelssohn's.'[1]

In the autumn Mendelssohn came to a decision about Berlin. 'To stay on such slippery ground under such perplexed circumstances' was, he wrote, impossible; and as he did not want to be 'an indifferent, doubtful, secretly discontented servant to the King', the affair must come to an end. On 30 September he went to Berlin, where the King reluctantly agreed to his being released from all definite duties beyond occasional special commissions. His salary would in future be one thousand thalers.

Devrient had recently been offered the post of Director of the Royal Court Theatre, Dresden, and he had asked Mendelssohn whether he advised him to accept. 'Mendelssohn replied, "There's only one question: have you enough trunks and packing-cases for all your things? If not, I'll lend you some. Dearest Devrient," he added affectionately, with the old drawl, and stroking my head, "the first step out of Berlin is the first step towards happiness!"'

[1] Quoted by Jacob.

CHAPTER TWENTY-THREE

Jenny Lind 1845-1846

In December 1844, having entrusted the Gewandhaus Orchestra to his colleague Niels Gade, Mendelssohn retired to Frankfurt, undertaking no engagements there and composing only when the urge to do so proved irresistible. During the autumn his youngest son, Felix, had been dangerously ill, but had now turned the corner. Writing on 10 January 1845 to his sister Rebecka, who was also seriously ill in Italy, he reports on the state of his family and then continues:

> I myself am what you know me to be; but what you do not know is that I have for some time felt the necessity for complete rest – *not* travelling, *not* conducting, *not* performing. . . . So I want to stay here quietly through winter, spring and summer, *sans* journey, *sans* musical festival, *sans* everything. Unless we are obliged for health's sake to go to one of the Taunus spas we shan't even do that. Consequently I've refused all invitations (including a very flattering one to a musical festival in New York). I grew so fond of our quiet uneventful life at Soden last summer – and the few days after our child got better and could breathe freely again did me so much good too – that these refusals cost me nothing. . . .
>
> Fanny has told you that I was obliged to give up the Berlin appointment. I couldn't with a clear conscience remain at the head of a public institution for music whose organization I considered bad but had no power to alter, as that rested *solely* with the King, who had, indeed, other things to think of. . . .

A young English musician named William Rockstro, who visited him several months later on his way to Leipzig, has left a happy account of Mendelssohn's carefree existence with his family at Frankfurt:

> Reaching Frankfort, at the beginning of the bright spring weather, we[1] found him living out of doors, and welcoming the sunshine, and the flowers, with a delight as unaffected as that of the youngest of his children. On the evening of our arrival, after taking us to see Thorvaldsen's lately finished statue of Goethe, and the poet's birthplace in the Hirschgraben, he playfully proposed that we should go to an 'open-air concert', and led the way to a lonely little corner of the public gardens, where a nightingale was singing with all its heart.
>
> 'He sings here every evening,' said Mendelssohn, 'and I often come to hear him. I sit here, sometimes, when I want to compose. Not that I am writing much, now; but, sometimes, I have a feeling like this '– and he twisted his hands rapidly, and nervously, in front of his breast – 'and when that comes, I know that I must write. I have just finished some sonatas for the organ; and, if you will meet me at the Catherinenkirche, at ten o'clock tomorrow, I will play them to you.'

[1] Rockstro uses the royal 'we'.

St Catherine's Church, Frankfurt. Lithograph after a drawing by Heinzlmann, c. 1830

Rockstro went next morning to the church, where Mendelssohn's playing deeply impressed him, and then returned with him to family lunch. 'He was full of fun, with a joke for each of the little ones; and made us all cover up the lower part of our faces, to see what animals we were like. "Ich bin ein Alder,"[1] he said, placing his hand in a position which made the likeness absurdly striking. Madame Mendelssohn was pronounced to be a hare; Karl, a roebuck, Paul, a bullfinch; and we ourselves a setter.' The following evening came an informal musical party at which Mendelssohn, David and an excellent cellist performed Mendelssohn's new Piano Trio in C minor – one of his most brilliant chamber works.

David, who had been playing at the Lower Rhine Festival, was on this way back to Leipzig, and Rockstro travelled with him, to spend a year there at the Conservatoire. In the autumn he attended Mendelssohn's piano and composition classes, which he thus describes:

> The first pianoforte piece selected for study was Hummel's Septett in D minor: and we well remember the look of blank dismay depicted upon more than one excitable countenance, as each pupil in his turn after playing the first chord, and receiving an instantaneous reproof for its want of sonority, was invited to resign his seat in favour of an equally unfortunate successor. Mendelssohn's own manner of playing grand chords, both in *forte* and *piano* passages, was peculiarly impressive; and now, when all present had tried, and failed, he himself sat down to the instrument, and explained the cause of his dissatisfaction with such microscopic minuteness, and clearness of expression, that the lesson was simply priceless.
>
> He never gave a learner the chance of mistaking his meaning; and though the vehemence with which he sometimes expressed it made timid pupils desperately afraid of him, he was so perfectly just, so sternly impartial in awarding praise, on the one hand, and blame on the other, that consternation soon gave place to confidence, and confidence to boundless affection. Carelessness infuriated him. Irreverence for the composer he could never forgive. 'Es steht nicht da!'[2] he almost shrieked one day to a pupil who had added a note to a certain chord. To another, who had scrambled through a difficult passage, he cried, with withering contempt, 'So spielen die Katzen!'[3] But, where he saw an earnest desire to do justice to the work in hand, he would give direction after direction, with a lucidity which we have never heard equalled. . . .

After the breakdown of Mendelssohn's health in the autumn of 1846 his class was taken over by Moscheles, who sacrificed his splendid position in London in order to help his friend and serve the cause of music; but by this time Rockstro had returned to England.

The summer of 1845 was again spent at Soden. Here Mendelssohn composed his String Quintet in B flat major (op. 87) and again allowed his thoughts to dwell on a possible opera; he wanted a libretto on a theme that was 'German and noble and cheerful'. He consulted Devrient, who, though he was desperately busy and also knew the task to be hopeless, once more did what he could to help. 'Besides Heiling,' he wrote,

> I had proposed to him the legends of Bluebeard, of King Thrushbeard, the Musk Apple, the Loreley, a plot of my own . . . and then Kohlhaas, Andreas Hofer, and an episode of the Peasants' War; in each of these I had done my best to bring the musical points in relief, yet not one could win his entire sympathy.

★   ★   ★

[1] 'I am an eagle.'
[2] 'It's not there!'
[3] 'That's how cats play!' On another occasion he said to Rockstro (in English), 'I call that modulation very ungentlemanlike.'

What had revived Mendelssohn's interest in opera was his meeting with Jenny Lind, then at the beginning of her spectacular career. He had first made her acquaintance in October 1844 at the house of the Berlin sculptor, Ludwig Wichmann. The attraction was immediate, and mutual.

The Swedish Nightingale, like the Arabian Lawrence, is one of those mysterious figures about whose true character there will always be argument. Joan Bulman, in a recent biography of Jenny,[1] approves the traditional image of the pure and simple country girl whose apparition (wrote Chorley) 'was indeed a godsend among the clumsy and exaggerated women who strode the stage, screaming as they strode.' The verdict of Henry Pleasants,[2] on the other hand, is very different. In his opinion, which would carry more weight had he provided some evidence, the 'insignificant, snub-nosed, plain, simply dressed, hesitant, unassuming poor-little-me, pining for the northern homeland, pure of heart and noble of thought, was the greatest of her roles'. He calls her 'smug' and 'prim' and asserts that 'her whole life was a series of pious, sanctimonious attitudes, relieved, when she chose to turn it on, by compelling charm' which conquered everyone who was at the receiving end of it.

That she fell in love with Mendelssohn is beyond doubt. He for his part called her 'as great an artist as ever lived, and the greatest I have known'. Inevitably Cécile was alarmed by the enthusiasm that he could not conceal; but she had no serious cause for jealousy, though whether Jenny really 'clamped down on her feelings', nobly refusing 'to indulge in forbidden fruit' (as Joan Bulman maintains), or whether she realized that Mendelssohn the married man was not to be had, we cannot tell. 'A less honorable man than Mendelssohn', writes Werner, 'might have made an "affair" out of this love and entered into an adventure with the adoring young girl.' And he adds, 'Who knows whether, in the interests of music, we should not regret Mendelssohn's integrity.'

In December of the following year Jenny appeared for the first time with Mendelssohn at a Gewandhaus concert, where she scored a sensational triumph. The price of the seats had been doubled, and when the usual free list for Conservatoire students was suspended a red-haired young Jewish student named Otto Goldschmidt was chosen to protest to the management. He failed, bought his own ticket, was swept off his feet, and after touring America in 1851 as Jenny's accompanist he married her. Frau Polko, inevitably among the audience, described the entry of a 'slender girlish form, with luxuriant fair hair, dressed in pink silk, and white and pink camellias on her breast and in her hair, in all the chaste grace of her deportment, and utterly devoid of all pretension'. She could never remember how she got home after the concert: 'I only know that I trembled and wept, and never closed my eyes all night.' She adds that Jenny 'only looked beautiful when she sang'.

A second concert followed – given at Jenny's suggestion in aid of Mendelssohn's pension fund for members of the orchestra – and after it was over a crowd of grateful musicians and students, the latter completely reconciled by her generous gesture, almost stormed the house where she was staying, presented her with a silver salver, and clamoured for a speech. Jenny adopting her favourite role of the shy country girl, drew back and begged Mendelssohn to thank them on her behalf, and this he gracefully did.

[1] *Jenny Lind*, James Barrie, 1956.
[2] *The Great Singers*, Gollancz, 1967.

Whenever the opportunity offered, Mendelssohn and Jenny made music together, and she was the principal attraction at the Lower Rhine Festival in 1846, held that year at Aachen under Mendelssohn's direction. Mendelssohn joined her at Frankfurt, from where the two of them, properly chaperoned, travelled together by steamer down the Rhine to Aachen. At the festival Jenny sang the soprano solos in Haydn's *Creation* and Handel's *Alexander's Feast*, and scored her final triumph with Mendelssohn's 'On Wings of Song' and one of his innumerable 'Spring Songs'. The festival was remembered ever after as the 'Jenny Lind Festival'. When it was over there came a further chaperoned *Rheinfahrt* to the Drachenfels, Königswinter and Köln.

For Jenny, Mendelssohn now began to write, to a libretto by Emanuel Geibel, an opera entitled *Loreley*. Devrient, when shown the text, felt obliged to say that he thought it inadequate, and at the time of Mendelssohn's death only three numbers had been composed. Nor did anything come of the attempt by Benjamin Lumley (alias Levy), the director of Her Majesty's Theatre, to collaborate with Scribe on a libretto based on Shakespeare's *The Tempest*. Mendelssohn nibbled at the bait, and indeed for a time so eagerly that Lumley rashly advertised the opera as a forthcoming attraction. Then Mendelssohn backed out. Thus, to the end, opera was to elude him.

CHAPTER TWENTY-FOUR

Elijah 1846

Oscar Wilde was never able to decide whether it was the fogs that were the cause of there being so many dull people in London, or the dull people who caused the fogs. Similarly, as Ernest Newman has pointed out, it still remains undetermined whether the British have been so fond of oratorios because Handel and Mendelssohn wrote them, or Handel and Mendelssohn wrote oratorios because the British have a natural taste for them.

Oratorio, like opera, had its origins in Italy, though it too was derived from the miracle plays and 'moralities' of the Middle Ages. It was of course Handel who started the cult in England, where his oratorios were primarily designed for use in Lent when theatrical performances were forbidden by law; and so instantaneous was their success that by the end of the eighteenth century William Mason could write, in his *Essays on English Church Music*, 'The rage for oratorio has spread from the capital to every market town in the kingdom.' 'The large majority of the British oratorios of the later eighteenth and nineteenth centuries,' said Percy Scholes, 'were mere academic exercises, or popular examples of what may (now that the composers are dead) be called choir-fodder. They served their day and generation and then fell on sleep. . . .' He adds that the new order of thought initiated by Darwin and Huxley had probably, more than any other single cause, been responsible for the death of oratorio in Britain. 'Death' is a strong word; but by comparison with her twin sister, opera, oratorio was until recently in relatively poor health.

A century or so ago the situation was very different, as Wagner noted after attending several concerts given by the Sacred Music Society at Exeter Hall in 1855:

> It was here that I came to understand the true spirit of English musical culture, which is bound up with the spirit of English Protestantism. This accounts for the fact that an oratorio attracts the public far more than an opera. A further advantage is secured by the feeling among the audience that an evening spent in listening to an oratorio may be regarded as a sort of service, and is almost as good as going to church. Everyone in the audience holds a Handel piano score in the same way as one holds a prayer-book in church. . . .[1]

He adds that the custom of rising at the beginning of the 'Hallelujah Chorus', which had originated in a spontaneous expression of enthusiasm, was now carried out at each performance of *Messiah* 'with painful precision'.

As Mendelssohn had already understood from the warm reception given to his *St Paul* in Birmingham, the English soil was right, and the English climate was right, for the growth

[1] *My Life*, Vol II, p. 635.

Elijah. *Title-page of the score*

and flowering of his oratorios, which came to our shores 'not as strangers, but as the younger brothers of the *Messiah* and *Judas Maccabaeus*'. For the English, Berlioz once said, Mendelssohn was 'a Handel and a half'.

But so far there was only the *St Paul*; the greater *Elijah* was yet to come, and the composer's early death robbed the world of his *Christus*, of which only a few numbers were ever written. However, within a month or two of the première of *St Paul* at Düsseldorf in 1836, and even before it had been heard in England, Mendelssohn began to consider following up its success with a second oratorio. He hoped that Klingemann, whom he consulted, would provide him with a libretto, and was open to suggestions as to a suitable subject. *St Peter*, perhaps? Or, he jokingly added, *Og of Bashan*? While in London in 1837 he talked the matter over with Klingemann, and even proposed that a libretto for *St Peter* or, possibly, *Elijah*, would make an acceptable, if perhaps unconventional, wedding present. But Klingemann, though in due course he put a sketch for *Elijah* on paper, could not conceal the fact that his heart was not in it, and soon Mendelssohn was obliged to turn elsewhere for help. In fact, he turned to Schubring, his collaborator with the *St Paul*.

Mendelssohn sent Schubring what Klingemann had jotted down, and an exchange of correspondence continued for some months; by February 1839, however, Schubring had to confess that, though he had thought that his *Elijah* would 'turn out all right', in fact it had not, and regretfully he asked Mendelssohn to look for another librettist. But Mendelssohn, enormously busy with a hundred other things, decided to shelve his oratorio, and for nearly seven years there is no more than an occasional passing reference to it in his letters. Then in the summer of 1845 came an invitation from Joseph Moore for an oratorio for the Birmingham Festival the following summer. So Mendelssohn 'began once again to plough up the soil'.

And once again he appealed to Schubring, who agreed to make a further attempt to help his friend. After some correspondence the two men met in January 1846, and with the performance less than seven months away the final attack on words and music was launched. Feverish activity followed, and it is not too much to say that the great strain of these months, during which Mendelssohn 'lived the life of a marmot', was in part responsible for his death in the following year.

It so happened that in February Devrient was for two days a guest of the Mendelssohns, who were now living in a first-floor apartment in the Königstrasse. He wrote sadly of the change that had come over his old friend, whose 'blooming youthful joyousness had given place to a fretfulness, a satiety of all earthly things'. Business and public appearances of any kind had become intolerable to him, and he spoke of leaving the conducting of all the next season's concerts to Gade. He was bored with the Conservatoire and had handed over all his piano pupils to Moscheles. He was completely out of sympathy with all his composition students, none of whom, he said, had a grain of talent or gave the slightest hope for the future of German music.

But composition had become an obsession, and he was working ceaselessly – not only on *Elijah* but also on church music:

> He called it 'doing his duty'; it seemed to me, however, that quite apart from considerations of health, he would have done his duty better by writing less and waiting for moments of inspiration – which now came less frequently than in the past. I had noticed lately that he

had begun to repeat himself in his composition, and to copy older masters, especially Bach, and that his writings exhibited certain mannerisms. I told him these things, and he received what I said without any irascibility, because he believed I was completely wrong. . . . I have not been able to alter this opinion in the face of his later productions, even of *Elijah*.

So it was a sick man who was embarking upon a suicidal venture with all the frenzy of one who knows that his time is running out. Letters now sped to and fro between Mendelssohn and Schubring, who in the past had had some rather wild ideas. 'It seemed to me', he had written, 'that as Elijah appeared to Christ on the Mount of Transfiguration (Matthew XVI), so Christ might come to Elijah, transfigure him, and show him from afar the streams of peace which flow over the heavenly Canaan.' Mendelssohn himself was now hardly less whimsical: might Elisha, he asked, be a soprano, since perhaps he was only a boy? Schubring replied, 'Your inquiry whether Elisha may sing soprano is comical. . . . One who ploughs with twelve yoke of oxen (I Kings XIX, 19) is no child.'[1] Finally there emerged a libretto, compiled from the Lutheran Bible, which Werner contemptuously dismisses as a 'weak potpourri of religious fanaticism and sanctimonious piety'.

An English translation was necessary for the Birmingham performance, and for this Mendelssohn turned, as often before, to a remarkable man whom he once called his 'translator *par excellence*' – William Bartholomew: poet, chemist, violinist and botanical artist. The job was a difficult and a finicky one, for it was essential, while respecting the music, to keep as close as possible to the text of the Authorized Version; moreover, it was the harder for being a race against time, Bartholomew not receiving the first fragments of the text until May, and thereafter a succession of small instalments until the very last moment. That he did a brilliant job is generally acknowledged. It was Bartholomew who spotted that Mendelssohn's setting of 'O rest in the Lord' was dangerously like a Scotch air, 'Robin Gray', and begged him to alter it so as to spare him the 'impertinence of the saucy *boys* of the musical press'. Mendelssohn changed one or two notes and so disguised the resemblance. At a later date, when the oratorio was being revised, it was Mendelssohn who objected to the widow singing 'I water my couch'; 'I do dislike this so very much,' he wrote, and begged him to substitute 'something in which no "watering of the couch" occurred, but which gave the idea of tears, of the night, of all that in its purity.' Bartholomew amended it to 'I lie down and weep at night'; but what Tovey described as 'the all too lifelike tiresomeness of the widow' was not only conserved but actually extended.

For a detailed account of the *Elijah* the reader is once again referred to the biographies of Werner and Radcliffe. Though probably not a year passes without an opportunity to hear, somewhere or other in England, a performance of what has been called 'Mendelssohn's *chef-d'œuvre*' and 'the greatest oratorio of the nineteenth century', the work, noble though it is, no longer commands the crowds. Moments of great drama – for example, Elijah's divinely inspired maledictory weather forecast which (a most original idea, proposed by Schubring) *precedes* the overture, and some of the choruses – still appeal today; there are, too, numbers which have true lyrical beauty, such as the trio 'Lift thine eyes' (which at the

---

[1] In fact, Elisha had charge of only one of these yoke.

OPPOSITE *Jenny Lind at the piano. Oil painting by J. L. Asher, 1845*

first performance was arranged as a duet); but elsewhere the music is not always free from a sentimental sweetness which the modern concert-goer finds hard to stomach.

Nor is the libretto free from that brand of Old Testament vengeance which is even more distasteful, and which *Og of Bashan*, had it been chosen, would have provided in even richer measure. Bernard Shaw wrote that it was strange that Mendelssohn, who was shocked by the mild eroticism of an Auber opera,[1] 'was himself ready to serve up the chopping to pieces of the prophets of the grove[2] with his richest musical spice to suit the compound of sanctimonious cruelty and base materialism which his patrons, the British Pharisees, called their religion'. Comparing *Elijah* with the oratorios of Handel he was even more withering: 'Set all that dreary fugue manufacture, with its Sunday-school sentimentalities and music school ornamentalities, against the expressive and vigorous choruses of Handel and ask yourself on your honour whether there is the slightest difference in kind between Stone him to Death and Under the Pump with a Kick and a Thump from *Dorothy*.'[3]

At the end of May, as has already been told, Mendelssohn was at Aachen with Jenny Lind for the Lower Rhine Festival, and in June he went to Liége to hear a new work of his, the fine but little-known *Lauda Sion*. From Liége he travelled to Köln to conduct another new work, his *Festgesang an die Künstler* for men's voices and brass. Then Spohr and Wagner came to Leipzig, and Spohr mentions in his egotistical autobiography that Mendelssohn and Wagner performed 'with enormous pleasure' his latest quartet.

On 18 August Mendelssohn arrived in London, where he conducted private rehearsals at Moscheles' house of the soloists who were to take part in *Elijah*, and two orchestral rehearsals at the Hanover Square Rooms. 'He looked very worn and nervous,' wrote Rockstro, 'yet he would suffer no one to relieve him, even in the scrutiny of the orchestral parts.' Five days later he and the orchestra left in a special train for Birmingham, where two full rehearsals took place. The reporter of the *Birmingham Journal*, who was present at one of these, wrote:

> Mendelssohn was received by the performers with great enthusiasm, renewed again and again as his lithe and *petit* figure bent in acknowledgment of these spontaneous and gratifying tributes to his genius, personal affability and kindness. . . . His manner, both in the orchestra and in private, is exceedingly pleasing. His smile is winning, and occasionally, when addressing a friendly correction to the band or choir, full of comic expression. . . . He possesses a remarkable power over the performers, moulding them to his will, and though rigidly strict in exacting the nicest precision, he does it in a manner irresistible – actually laughing them into perfection. Some of his remarks are exceedingly humorous. . . . At its conclusion the whole band and chorus broke into a torrent of enthusiastic acclamation. . . .

The performance took place on the morning of 26 August, and among the large audience was the ever-faithful Benedict, who wrote: 'The reception Mendelssohn met with on stepping

---

[1] See pp. 147–8.
[2] The artist G. F. Watts, not noted for his sense of humour, when asked by a lady how God could have given this vindictive order, is said to have replied, 'Isn't it nice that God has got so much nicer!'
[3] Quoted by Wilfrid Mellers, *Man and his music*, vol. 4, p. 29. *Dorothy*, produced in the 1880s was a 'comedy-opera' by Cellier.

Elijah and the Widow's Son. Watercolour by Ford Madox Brown, 1868. The subject was probably inspired by Mendelssohn's oratorio

Mendelssohn conducting Elijah *at Birmingham*

into his place, from the assembled thousands, was absolutely overwhelming – whilst the sun, emerging at the moment, seemed to illumine the vast edifice in honour of the bright and pure being who stood there, the idol of all beholders!' Nor was the London correspondent of *Signals for the Musical World* less ecstatic: 'It was a noble scene, the hall filled with men, the galleries gay with ladies, like so many tulip-beds, added to the princely music, and these thundering bravos.'

Eight numbers (four choruses and four arias) had to be repeated, and even the critic of *The Times* dipped his pen into ink almost as purple as that habitually used by Frau Polko:

The last note of *Elijah* was drowned in a long-continued unanimous volley of plaudits, vociferous and deafening. It was as though enthusiasm, long-checked, had suddenly burst its bonds and filled the air with shouts of exultation. Mendelssohn, evidently overpowered, bowed his acknowledgments, and quickly descended from his position in the conductor's rostrum; but he was compelled to appear again amidst renewed cheers and huzzas. Never was there a more complete triumph – never a more thorough and speedy recognition of a great work of art.

Of the soloists, the Viennese bass-baritone Josef Staudigl (as Elijah) and a young English tenor named Charles Lockey surpassed all expectations. The weak spot was the soprano. Mendelssohn had hoped for Jenny Lind – had, indeed, written the part with her ringing high F sharp in mind; but Jenny had broken her contract with Alfred Bunn, the cantankerous

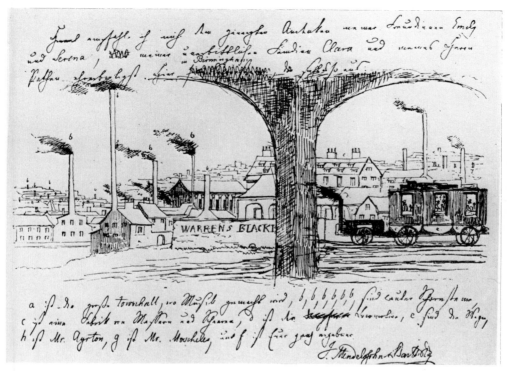

Birmingham. From a pen drawing by Mendelssohn

manager of Drury Lane, and nothing would induce her to risk a visit to England at that moment. So a certain Madame Caradori-Allan was chosen – a tiresome woman of nearer fifty than forty who had made trouble at the very first rehearsal of the soloists by trying to persuade Mendelssohn to rewrite 'Hear ye, Israel' a whole tone lower. Mendelssohn had responded with commendable brusqueness, telling her either to sing it as it was written, or be replaced. She came to heel.

Of her and her performance, Mendelssohn wrote that she was 'so pretty, so pleasant, so elegant, but also so out-of-tune, so soulless, so brainless, that the music acquired a sort of *amiable* expression which even today makes my blood boil when I think of it. The alto [Marie Hawes] had not enough voice to fill the hall . . . but her rendering was musical and intelligent, which for me is far more important than merely having a voice. I dislike nothing so much as such cold, heartless coquetry in music. . . .'

Chorley had also been present in the capacity of critic of the *Athenaeum*, and Mendelssohn had begged him in advance to be prepared to criticize frankly. 'Don't tell me what you like,' he said; 'tell me what you *don't* like.' After the performance he invited Chorley and one or two other friends to take with him what he called 'the prettiest walk in Birmingham.' And there, beside the coal and slag heaps that bordered the canal, a post-mortem was held at which criticism was frankly given and gratefully accepted.

CHAPTER TWENTY-FIVE

'Tired-Very Tired' 1846-1847

Soon after his return to Leipzig in the latter part of September 1846, Mendelssohn wrote to Fanny:

> After the exertions of this summer, and all the travelling I had to do, I'm now leading a vegetable existence. Ever since I got home, and saw at a glance that everyone was well and happy, I've done nothing all day long but eat and sleep and go for walks – and yet I never seem to get enough of any of these things. I *ought* to be preparing the *Elijah* for the press, *ought* to be sending the parts to Bonn to have the German text added . . . but, as I said before, I must indulge myself and be lazy a bit longer. . . .
>
> I was asked to go to Manchester for two concerts, but I refused and went to London instead, where my only engagement of any note was a fish dinner at Lovegrove's at Blackwall. After that I stayed for four days at Ramsgate for the sea air, and ate crabs, and enjoyed myself with the Beneckes. . . . Then I stayed a day at Ostend because I felt sleepy, and another at Köln with the Seydlitzes because I was too tired to go on. Then four more at Horchheim, where my uncle walked me about in his vineyards for an hour and a half in the broiling sun and at such a pace that again and again I was on the point of telling him I couldn't keep up with him, but felt ashamed and stopped my mouth by stuffing tepid purple grapes into it. Then I stayed at Frankfurt because I was worn out, and ever since I got back to Leipzig I've been resting.

In November Mendelssohn's faithful old retainer Johann – more a friend than a servant – died after a long illness. He and Cécile felt his loss deeply, and it was perhaps to give them both a change of scene that he now took his wife briefly to Dresden to show her the picture gallery, which she did not know. Here they met Devrient, who, like all their friends, was much struck by Mendelssohn's 'excessive touchiness, which approached the quarrelsome testiness of his father. He was particularly annoyed by the political ferment of the day. . . . It was evident that he was under the dominion of an irritation of the nerves of the brain. . . .'

Meanwhile the winter season of Gewandhaus concerts had started and the Conservatoire was in full swing; but Mendelssohn was in no condition to concern himself with either. Gade relieved him of most of the conducting, and Moscheles of his teaching at the Conservatoire. As for Mendelssohn, in the neurotic state he was now in he had a sharp attack of the 'dreadful disease' (as he called it) from which he suffered chronically and severely: his inability to stop revising, again and again, a work which seemed to others as near perfect as possible. Moscheles begged him to leave the *Elijah* alone and turn to new compositions; but he would not be persuaded, and it was not until the following summer that he considered the much amended score ready at last to go to Messrs Simrock.

It cheered him considerably to have the Moscheles in Leipzig, and the two families met constantly; David and young Joachim were also often in their company. On 3 February 1847 what proved to be Mendelssohn's last birthday was celebrated with a gay party of charades and amateur theatricals, thus described by Moscheles:

The proceedings opened with a capital comic scene between two lady's-maids, acted in the Frankfurt dialect by Cécile and her sister. Then came a charade on the word *Gewandhaus*. Joachim, wearing a fantastic wig *à la* Paganini, played a crazy impromptu on the G string; the word *Wand* [wall] was represented by the Pyramus and Thisbe wall-scene from *A Midsummer Night's Dream*; for *Haus*, Charlotte [Moscheles] acted a scene she had written herself, in which she was discovered knitting a blue stocking and soliloquizing on the foibles of female authoresses, advising them to attend to their domestic duties. By way of enforcing the moral she summons her cook – that was me, and my appearance in cap and dress was the signal for a general uproar. Mendelssohn was sitting on a large straw armchair which creaked under his weight as he rocked to and fro, and the entire room echoed with his peals of laughter. The whole word *Gewandhaus* was illustrated by a full orchestra, Mendelssohn's and my children playing on little drums and trumpets, Joachim leading with a toy violin, and my Felix conducting *à la* Jullien. It was splendid.

The house in Leipzig where Mendelssohn died. Engraving, 1849

ABOVE *Jullien's concert orchestra and four military bands at Covent Garden Theatre. Engraving, 1846* OPPOSITE *Queen Victoria at Exeter Hall. Engraving, 1845*

This Jullien, by the way, was a musical buffoon whose concerts had an undeserved success in London. His opera, *Pietro il Grande*, which he brought out on the most magnificent scale at his own expense, failed and was withdrawn after five performances. Chorley wrote of him: 'He had deluded himself (bystanders aiding in the folly) into conceiving that he had a real genius for composition. When the news of Mendelssohn's sudden death reached him at a rehearsal he stopped his band, smote his forehead with a tragical blow, in which there was a touch of genuine dismay and regret, and exclaimed to the bearer of the tidings, "This is what happens to all people of genius! I will never compose any more!"'

But for all Mendelssohn's gaiety at moments of relaxation, he was in fact a very sick man. He suffered constantly from severe headaches. To Klingemann, whom he calls his *one* friend ('for, as Montaigne says, a man can only have *one*'), he confessed his longing to put an end to public music-making, his longing to be able just to sit at home with his family and play and compose and let the whole mad world go by. And yet he had pledged himself to undertake in the near future a concert tour in England which would have taxed the strength of a man in the rudest of health!

He travelled to London with Joachim,[1] and between 16 and 30 April conducted no less than six performances of his revised *Elijah* – four at Exeter Hall, one in Manchester and one

[1] Petitpierre is mistaken in saying that Cécile went too.

in Birmingham. There was an amusing sequel to the Birmingham concert, which had been advertised by big posters pasted on the walls of many of the public buildings. According to an article in the *Musical World*,[1] 'A little after, other posters, relating to a Whitsun trip, were pasted over them but not covering the lower part. The combination read thus: "The *Odd Fellows* of Birmingham will make an extraordinary trip to Worcester, Gloucester and Bristol, returning next day. Leader: Mr Willy. Conductor: Dr Mendelssohn."'

Before leaving for Germany on 8 May Mendelssohn had also conducted and played at a Philharmonic Society's concert at which both the Queen and Jenny Lind were present ('so I wanted to play especially well'), had taken part in several formal and informal concerts of chamber music, had played the organ at a concert of ancient music, had met Mr and Mrs Gladstone at Baron Bunsen's, and had attended the performance at Her Majesty's of Meyerbeer's *Robert le Diable* in which Jenny (as Alice) had made her first bow to an English audience.[2] Of the opera, which was sung in Italian, the Queen (who was also present) wrote:

> The great event of the evening, however, was Jenny Lind's appearance & her *complete* triumph. She has a most exquisite, powerful, & really quite peculiar voice, so rounded & soft & her acting is charming & touching & very natural. Her appearance was very ladylike & sweet & though she is not beautiful, she has a fine tall figure, is very graceful, has fine blue eyes & fine fair hair. The storm of applause when she 1rst appeared, & during the singing of her 1rst air, was tremendous.

After the fall of the final curtain the Queen threw a bouquet at Jenny's feet.

Last, but not least, Mendelssohn had been summoned again to Buckingham Palace. Here, when the music was at an end the Queen had said to him, 'You have given me so much pleasure; now what can I do to give *you* pleasure?' On her insisting, he finally asked whether he might be allowed to see something which would particularly interest him as a family man: the royal children in their nursery. The Queen immediately took him there, 'all the while comparing notes with him on the homely subjects that had a special attraction for them both.'

The Queen and Prince Albert were also present at the second of the London performances of the *Elijah*, after which the Prince had sent Mendelssohn his copy of the libretto, in which he had written (in German):

> To the noble artist who, surrounded by the Baal-worship of debased art, has been able, by his genius and science, to preserve faithfully, like another Elijah, the worship of true art, and once more to accustom our ear, amid the whirl of empty, frivolous sounds, to the pure tones of sympathetic feeling and legitimate harmony: to the Great Master, who makes us conscious of the unity of his conception, through the whole maze of his creation, from the soft whispering to the mighty raging of the elements.
>
> Inscribed in grateful remembrance by Albert
Buckingham Palace, 24 April 1847[3]

★   ★   ★

When Mendelssohn came to leave England he was at the end of his tether – so wretched, indeed, that the faithful Klingemann decided to travel with him as far as Ostend. But it was on the following day that his support would have been of even greater value; for at the

[1] 1847, p. 351, quoted by Stratton.
[2] Her appearance at Her Majesty's, after breaking her contract with Drury Lane, was to cost her £2,500 in damages.
[3] As translated in F. G. Edwards, *The History of Mendelssohn's Oratorio* Elijah (London, 1896).

Jenny Lind and Josef Staudigl in Robert le Diable. *Engraving, 1847*

Prussian frontier-post of Herbesthal the composer, mistaken for an advanced liberal of the same name, was arrested, detained and cross-examined for many hours – long enough, he said, to have composed an overture – while vainly protesting his innocence.[1] This minor irritation was, however, soon forgotten in the happiness of being united once again with his wife and children in Frankfurt. But two days later came a crushing blow for which he was totally unprepared and from which he was never fully to recover. A messenger arrived with an urgent letter from Berlin; he opened it, read it, and 'with a loud, fearful shriek fell senseless to the ground'. His beloved sister Fanny was dead!

She had been rehearsing her choir for a performance of her brother's *Walpurgis Night*, when suddenly, as she sat at the piano, her hands had fallen limp at her sides. Leaving a friend to take her place, she went into an adjoining room to bathe them in hot vinegar. 'How lovely it sounds!' she said, and was just about to return to the music-room when she collapsed. Her son Sebastian ran for the doctor, who diagnosed apoplexy (cerebral haemorrhage), and at eleven o'clock that same evening she died the swift and merciful death of so many of the Mendelssohns.

When Felix had parted from Fanny for the last time, she had reproached him for not having for so many years past spent her birthday (14 November) with her. As he stepped into the carriage he had taken her hand and said, 'Depend upon it, the next I shall spend with you.' Before her next birthday he too was dead; and so – adds Devrient, who relates this – 'he kept his word'.

There was no question of Mendelssohn going to Berlin for the funeral; by June, however, he was considered sufficiently recovered to try a cure at Baden-Baden. He set out with his whole family, a governess and a tutor, and was joined there by Paul and Albertine, and the still-tearful Hensel and his seventeen-year-old son. But Cécile and Albertine bickered, and the waters availed nothing. So once again he thought of Switzerland, which often in the past had restored his peace of mind. The trunks were packed, and, travelling by way of Lucerne and Thun, in mid July the party reached Interlaken where they stayed at the Hôtel du Nord. From here, Paul, his wife and the Hensels soon returned to Germany; and, devoted though Felix was to his brother, he was perhaps not sorry that he no longer had to keep the peace between two incompatible women. To his sister Rebecka he wrote on 29 July:

> When your dear letter arrived I was just composing; I now force myself to keep very busy, in the hope that later I may feel like working and enjoy it. This, too, is 'composer's weather'. . . . Ever since Paul left, the sky has been so overcast and rainy that I have only been able to take one walk; and for the last two days it has been so cold that we have had a fire. . . . But I don't deny that I sometimes enjoy really wet days like these which keep one effectually house-bound; they give me a chance to spend all the time with my three eldest children. They write and learn arithmetic and Latin with me, paint or play draughts in their spare time, and ask a thousand wise questions that no fool can answer. . . .
>
> In September, God willing, I hope to come to Berlin, and Paul will probably have told you that I am seriously considering the idea of spending the rest of my life with you, my dear sister and brother. . . . One thought is ever uppermost in my mind: how short life is! May we soon be together, and long remain together.

[1] Incidentally, the Polko (pp. 149–52) touches a new nadir of glorious absurdity in describing this episode.

Fanny on her deathbed. Drawing by Wilhelm Hensel, 14 May 1847

So the days passed. When the weather and his recurrent headaches permitted there were long walks, and Mendelssohn made a few furious (*wüthend*) sketches in Indian ink while Cécile drew Alpine roses and other local wild flowers. He also composed a remarkable and deeply moving Quartet in F minor (op. 80) – a poignant cry of grief at the death of his sister which Chorley has called 'one of the most impassioned outpourings of sadness existing in instrumental music'. Occasionally a visitor known to them turned up at their hotel, among them the famous German traveller and author Johann Kohl, and the English historian Grote whom Jenny Lind once described as 'a nice old bust in a corner; you could go and dust him'. But for the most part Mendelssohn shunned the company of any but his family. However, at the end of August there appeared an old and welcome friend with business to discuss –

Henry Chorley; and it is to him that we owe the clearest picture of Mendelssohn at Interlaken.

Chorley wrote that Mendelssohn looked 'aged and sad, and stooped more than I had ever before seen him do; but his smile had never been brighter, nor his welcome more cordial'. Golden weather had suddenly returned, and on Chorley's first morning the two men set out early on a long walk through the woods above the Lake of Thun. The sound of cow-bells floated up to them from some pasture below. Mendelssohn immediately stopped, listened, and smilingly began to hum a few bars of the overture to *William Tell*, praising Rossini for so exactly catching the Swiss atmosphere. 'I wish I could make some Swiss music,' he said. 'I like the pine-trees and the very smell of the old stones with the moss upon them. . . . I have made up my mind that we will come here every year.'

The business that Chorley wanted to discuss with Mendelssohn was the composition of a work for him to conduct at the opening of the magnificent new concert hall at Liverpool. But again and again Mendelssohn repeated, 'I shall not live to see it; I must have quiet, or I shall die.' He must withdraw from public performance if he was to survive; and as he said this, Chorley saw 'the glow fade from his face, and the sad worn look come back, which it pained the very heart to see'.

A never-to-be-forgotten day was the one on which Mendelssohn took Chorley to a small church he had discovered at Ringgenberg, just above the Lake of Brienz, where the door was unlocked, the organ open, and there was nobody to prevent him from playing. They went there by boat and climbed up the rough flight of steps, overgrown with moss and maidenhair fern, that led to the little grey building. The gaily decorated organ was pretty enough, though naturally 'not super-excellent in tone', and a boy was soon found who for a small reward was willing to blow the bellows:

> It seems to me now as if [Mendelssohn] never could have played more nobly. After one or two movements by Sebastian Bach he began an improvisation in C minor, which took the canonical form of a prelude and fugue; his fancy kindling as he went on, and his face lit up by that serene and elevated smile, the highest and most beautiful of its many expressions, which all who knew him must remember. . . . I feel, when I think of this organ-playing, as if I had taken leave of the greatest music for ever. . . .

Chorley learned later that it was the last time that Mendelssohn ever played the organ.

That evening there was much talk of music, and Chorley was surprised to find Mendelssohn speaking 'with a good-natured cordiality' of Donizetti's *The Daughter of the Regiment*. ' "It is so merry," he said, "with so much of the real soldier's life in it. They call it bad; and to be sure," he continued, with a half-humorous tone of self-correction, "it is surprising how easily one can become used to bad music!" '

Next morning Mendelssohn drove with Chorley, whose time at Interlaken had come to an end, to Lauterbrunnen and the Staubbach Falls:

> Almost my last distinct remembrance of Mendelssohn is, seeing him standing within the arch of the rainbow, which, as every reader of *Manfred*[1] knows, the Witch of the Alps flings around the feet of the cascade – looking upward, rapt and serious, thoroughly enjoying the scene. My very last is the sight of him turning down the road, to wind back to Interlachen alone. . . . I thought even then, as I followed his figure, looking none the younger for the loose dark coat and the wide-brimmed straw-hat bound with black crape, that he was too

[1] Byron, *Manfred*, Act II, scene 2.

much depressed and worn, and walked too heavily. But who could have dreamed that his days on earth were so rapidly drawing to a close?

It must have been some time in early September, as Felix and Cécile were making their leisurely way back to Leipzig, that they stopped at Freiburg. Here Felix met the son of his old friend Ferdinand von Woringen and went with him to Badenweiler, where they climbed the tower of the old castle together. 'As we were coming down,' wrote Woringen, 'I suddenly shouted to Mendelssohn who was behind me, to try to catch me. We ran down the winding stairs at the risk of falling; but though I had a good start I only just managed to get to the bottom first. And when we were there, how we laughed – just as he used to – and, catching hold of me, said in the happy tone of days gone by, "We're just a couple of children!"'[1] Again for a moment he had managed to forget his misery.

Moscheles, when he saw Mendelssohn after his return to Leipzig on 17 September, thought him very much changed physically, though 'in mind the same as ever. . . . He is older and more feeble and his walk less elastic than before; but when he is at the piano or talking about art and artists he is all life and fire.' However, to Frau Moscheles, who asked him how he was, he replied, 'How am I? *Grau in grau!*'[2] And when Moscheles heard him play his new string quartet on the piano he confessed that he recognized in it a 'deeply agitated state of mind'.

Mendelssohn went briefly to Berlin to discuss a performance of the *Elijah* which he had agreed to conduct there in November; but the visit was a disaster, for at the sight of Fanny's old room, where nothing had been touched, he was so shattered that he at once cancelled the engagement. He still, however, hoped to go to Vienna for a performance at which Jenny Lind was to sing for the first time the part he had written for her.

Back in Leipzig, he went on the afternoon of 9 October to call on Frau Livia Frege, a fine artist who was shy of appearing in public, to beg her to sing in *Elijah*. 'I come today', he said, 'and I intend coming every day until you agree.' They then discussed the possible contents and suitable order of a new volume of six songs (op. 71) which Härtel was pressing him to prepare for publication. Among those under consideration was *Nachtlied* ('Night Song'; op. 71, No. 6) – a very moving setting he had made only a week before of a gloomy poem by Eichendorff about night and death. When she had finished singing it Mendelssohn shuddered and cried, 'Oh, that sounds so weary! But it's just how I felt.'

Again and again the songs were repeated, till finally Mendelssohn said, 'If you aren't too tired, let's try the last quartet of *Elijah*.' Frau Frege continues:

> I left the room to order lamps, and on my return found him in the next room on the sofa; his hands, he said, were so cold and stiff, and it would be better for him, and more sensible, to take a turn out of doors; he really felt too ill to make music. I wanted to send for a carriage but he wouldn't let me, and after I had given him a saline draught he left about half past five. . . .
>
> When he got home he sat down on the sofa, where Cécile found him at seven o'clock; his hands were cold and stiff as before. Next day he had such violent pains in the head that leeches were applied; the doctor thought the digestive organs were attacked, and it was only later that he pronounced the disease to be the result of an overwrought nervous system.

---

[1] The letter, was written to a friend of Woringen's after Mendelssohn's death, and is quoted by the (admittedly unreliable) Polko.

[2] Literally 'grey in grey' – the German for 'grisaille', or monochrome painting.

Ever since Fanny's death I had been struck with his paleness when he conducted or played; everything seemed to affect him more intensely than before.

But Mendelssohn rallied. Soon his friends found him outwardly cheerful, and he apologized to Frau Frege for the fright he must have given her. On 25 October he wrote to Paul, saying that his health was improving every day, but that any idea of his travelling in a week's time to Vienna to conduct his *Elijah* was out of the question; this, so far as is known, was the last letter he ever wrote. Three days later he felt well enough to go for a walk with Cécile, but on his return he collapsed from what was no doubt a slight stroke. Soon afterwards came a second and more severe one which left him partly paralysed and for a time in great pain. Then suddenly he began singing as if his heart would break. The doctor begged him to stop, saying that it was only exciting him; he paused a moment and smiled, then began again.

Paul had been hurriedly summoned from Berlin, and to Devrient, who did not arrive in time to see his old friend alive, he later described his brother's last hours. Devrient wrote:

On the 3rd [of November] Felix had spoken cheerfully with him [Paul] for several hours until midday, when he became restless. Paul and Cécile then took it in turn to sit beside his bed. About 2 o'clock Cécile ran in terror to call Paul, saying that she could not soothe the patient. Paul went to him and scolded him in jest, which Felix was still able to understand and respond to; but suddenly he started up as though seized with a frightful pain in his head; his mouth was open with an agonized expression. Then he gave one piercing cry and sank back on his pillow.

Now no more hope remained. From this moment he lay in a dull half-sleep, answering only 'Yes, and 'No' – except once, when to Cécile's tender inquiry as to how he felt, he said, 'Tired – very tired.' So he dozed peacefully until twenty-four minutes past nine, when his breathing ceased.

Ferdinand David, who was also among those who watched at Mendelssohn's bedside during his last hours, wrote to Sterndale Bennett in London an account which differs in certain respects from that given by Paul to Devrient; but he adds one small detail which finds confirmation in the death-mask and in drawings made by Hensel and other artists after Mendelssohn's death: that at the end his face wore 'the gentlest and most peaceful of smiles'.

When Devrient arrived he was taken to see the body, now lying in its coffin and wreathed in flowers. 'There lay my beloved friend . . .', he wrote. 'He looked much aged, but recalled to me the expression of the boy as I had first seen him; – where my hand had so often stroked the long brown locks and the burning brow, I now touched the marble forehead of the man. This span of time in my remembrance encloses the whole of happy youth in one perfect and indelible thought.'

All Leipzig mourned. 'An awful stillness prevails', wrote an English student at the Conservatoire; 'we feel as if the King were dead.' Indeed, half Europe mourned, and during the winter memorial concerts were given in Leipzig, Berlin, Vienna, Paris and London. At Buckingham Palace the Queen opened her diary to record her personal grief:

November 10, 1847. . . . We were horrified, astounded and distressed to read in the papers of the death of Mendelssohn, the greatest musical genius since Mozart, & the most amiable man. He was quite worshipped by those who knew him intimately, & we have so much appreciated & admired his wonderfully beautiful compositions. We liked & esteemed the

Felix on his deathbed. Drawing by Eduard Bendemann, November 1847

excellent man, & looked up to & revered, the wonderful genius, & the great mind, which I fear were too much for the frail delicate body. With it all he was so modest and simple. . . .

And three days later she added, 'We read & played that beautiful "*Lied ohne Worte*", which poor Mendelssohn arranged & wrote out himself for us this year. To feel, when one is playing his beautiful music, that he is no more, seems incomprehensible!'

Mendelssohn was buried in Berlin, but first a service was held in Leipzig for which Moscheles scored the composer's *Song Without Words* in E minor (op. 62, No. 3); the playing of it is not, however, mentioned in the account which appeared in the Berlin *Staatszeitung*:

On 6 November Mendelssohn's body was brought to the Pauliner [University] Church [in Leipzig], preceded by a band of wind instruments playing Beethoven's 'Funeral March'; the pall-bearers were Moscheles, David, Hauptmann and Gade.[1] The professors of the

---

[1] Also Schumann and Julius Rietz.

Conservatoire, with Mendelssohn's brother as chief mourner, and several guilds and societies from Leipzig and Dresden, followed the coffin. After the pastor's funeral oration in the church, an organ prelude and chorales from *St Paul* and Bach's *Passion* were played by the orchestra under Gade's and David's direction. During the service the coffin remained open, and the painters Bendemann, Hübner and Richard made drawings of the great man with the wreath of laurel upon his brow.

At ten o'clock at night the coffin was closed and carried by the pupils of the Conservatoire to the station of the Berlin Railway. A torchlight procession of more than a thousand persons followed the funeral procession through the crowded streets of Leipzig, and similar honours, accompanied by funeral music, were paid to the dead man at Köthen, Dessau, and other towns on the way to Berlin, which was reached between seven and eight o'clock in the morning.

There the coffin, adorned with ivy leaves and a large wreath of laurel, was carried on a hearse drawn by six horses draped in black to the cemetery of the Church of the Holy Trinity. Thousands of people followed the bier, and Beethoven's 'Funeral March' was again played. Two clergymen and other friends of the deceased pronounced orations at the grave, and a choir of six hundred sang a hymn by Groeber, 'Christ and the Resurrection'. It is impossible to describe that mournful scene; the men threw earth, and the women and children flowers, on the coffin when it was finally lowered into the grave. Mendelssohn sleeps near that beloved sister whose death so fatally affected him.

To Klingemann, Felix's brother Paul wrote, 'By Fanny's death our family was shattered [*zerstört*]; by Felix's it is annihilated [*vernichtet*].'

TOP *Lucerne, and* BOTTOM *'Souvenir of an excursion to Mürren'. Watercolours by Mendelssohn, July 1847*

Epilogue

In September 1850, three years after Mendelssohn's death, there appeared in the *Neue Zeitschrift für Musik* (the paper formerly edited by Schumann) an article entitled 'Über das Judentum in der Musik' – 'On Judaism in Music'. It was signed 'K. Freigedank' (Freethought), a pseudonym which deceived few; but in 1868 its still impenitent author republished it under his real name: Richard Wagner. In it the champion of the 'music of the future' openly attacked the dead Mendelssohn, whose work he had once loudly praised, and, more guardedly and with no name mentioned, the living and influential Meyerbeer[1] who often in the past had generously befriended him. The life and works of Mendelssohn, he wrote, clearly demonstrated that no Jew, however gifted and cultural and honourable, was capable of creating art that moved the heart and soul. In a word Wagner was saying (as Jacob puts it), 'Try your hardest – it's no use, for you're a Jew.'

So far Wagner, though offensive and lacking in gratitude, had not revealed himself as the fanatical precursor of the Nazis. In 1881–2, however, the *Bayreuther Blätter* contained an article from his pen, entitled 'Know Thyself!', which might have come straight from the pages of Streicher's *Stürmer*. In it, says Werner, 'he goes so far as to praise the massacres of Jews in Russia as an example worthy of imitation ("See how it succeeded in Kiev!")' and he ends his persecution with this tirade:

> Drive them out, German people – but not like the Egyptians, those Hamitic fools, who even gave them golden vessels for the journey. For they must go away empty-handed. Whither I know not, but I wish them all the same fate. May they find no shelter, no homeland; unhappier than Cain, may they seek and not find; may they descend into the Red Sea, but may they never, never emerge from it. German people, know thyself!

It is hardly surprising that Ellis preferred to omit this passage when publishing an English translation of the collected edition of Wagner's prose works.

Then, fifty years later, came Hitler, and soon after, and for more than a decade, the works of Jewish composers were no more to be heard in Germany. Musical history was rewritten and travestied by Nazi musicologists, and many of their tendentious judgments and puerile falsifications have been assembled in Joseph Wulf's monumental *Musik im Dritten Reich*

[1] Subsequently dismissed by Wagner as 'a Jewish banker who composes music'.

Mendelssohn's study, after his death. Copy by Ferdinand Schiertz of a watercolour by Felix Moscheles

('Music in the Third Reich'). This horrifying book also contains an account of Sir Thomas Beecham's rash visit to Germany with the London Philharmonic Orchestra in the early summer of 1936.

Even so late as that year Sir Thomas still persisted in considering the Nazis just a joke, and when his friend Ribbentrop suggested that he might give a series of concerts in Germany he saw no harm in accepting; he even meekly agreed to strike from his proposed programme Mendelssohn's 'Scottish' Symphony and replace it by a work of an Aryan composer. Accompanied by his German half-Jewish secretary Dr Berta Geissmar, whose safety Ribbentrop had assured, he drove through the streets of Berlin in a brash car adorned with swastikas and was received by the Führer at the Chancery. His itinerary then took him to Leipzig.

Since 1892 there had stood in front of the Gewandhaus in Leipzig a life-sized statue of Mendelssohn by Werner Stein. In May 1936, orders had been received from the Nazi local authorities that this memorial to 'the hundred per cent Jew Mendelssohn-Bartholdie [sic], which arouses public indignation', be removed. The Burgomaster, Dr Goerdeler,[1] had courageously opposed the order, claiming that such an act would seriously damage the reputation of Leipzig as an internationally famous centre of music. Meanwhile his deputy, a Nazi bigwig (Nazibonze) named Haake, perpetually pressed for action:

> Sir Thomas Beecham had inquired in advance whether Goerdeler would welcome it if he and a deputation of his orchestra were to lay a wreath at the foot of the memorial of Mendelssohn, who had built so important a bridge between the musical life of Leipzig and London. Goerdeler replied that he would much appreciate such a gesture. But as ill luck would have it, at the time of the concert (which was an outstanding success) Goerdeler was on holiday. Next morning Sir Thomas and his party went to the Gewandhaus to deposit their wreath. They searched in front of, behind, and on both sides of the building, which stands in the middle of a square: the monument had vanished! Deputy Burgomaster Haake had had it removed during the night to a cellar in one of the town's public buildings, where it had been hacked to pieces.[2]

This unpleasant experience seems to have given Sir Thomas an inkling that, musically at all events, the Nazis meant business, and by the summer of 1938 he was so far disillusioned as to announce that he would not revisit Germany.

In 1909 the centenary of Mendelssohn's birth had been no more than conventionally acclaimed, for, even in England, the reputation of the 'Victorian' master had sunk low; but in 1947, after the defeat of the Nazis, the centenary of his death was celebrated universally and with more genuine enthusiasm. In general, however, his music made then, and continues to make, more appeal to the man in the street than to the highbrow. Today, hardly a week passes without several of Mendelssohn's major works being heard on the B.B.C.'s Radio Three; yet how rarely does his name occur in the programmes of London concert halls!

Inevitably, Mendelssohn must in time find his true level. He will never again become the idol that he was in Victorian England, or, for many years, in America and Canada, where innumerable musical societies, glee-clubs and choirs were named in his honour. (A visit of the Toronto Mendelssohn Choir to the shores of Lake Erie once occasioned the improbable caption in a Canadian newspaper, BUFFALO SWEPT OFF FEET BY MENDELSSOHN CHOIR.)

---

[1] Goerdeler was later executed for his part in the July plot to assassinate Hitler.
[2] Wulf, J., *Musik im Dritten Reich* (Gütersloh, 1963), p. 407. Quoted from the manuscript account of a certain Kurt Sabatzky which is now in the Wiener Library, London.

Statue of Mendelssohn at Leipzig, destroyed in 1936 by the Nazis

Nor, however, will he remain the mere purveyor of sentimental trifles for the drawing-room, the composer of faded oratorios and of opiates for the masses who lack the intelligence to appreciate serious music. He will be seen to be an artist of high originality, one whose finest works (many still sadly unknown to those who reject him) entitle him to a place among the greatest composers of the nineteenth century.

So much for Mendelssohn's reputation as a musician; what became of his family?

Felix, the composer's youngest son, was never strong, and four years after his father's death he followed him to the grave. Cécile did not long outlive her Benjamin, dying of consumption in 1853 at the age of thirty-six. But the other four children flourished and married and multiplied. The eldest son, Karl (d. 1897), became a professor of history at Heidelberg University. The elder daughter, Marie, married Victor Benecke, whose son Paul

Cécile on her deathbed. Drawing by Wilhelm Hensel, 1853

was, during the First World War, Bursar of Magdalen College, Oxford, where he is said to have 'permanently ruined the digestion of his colleagues by his unnecessary injudicious economies'.[1] The composer's second son, Paul, was an able scientist and the creator of the famous firm of Agfa, and Paul's grandson Hugo (descended also through his mother from the composer) is the last direct descendant of Felix Mendelssohn Bartholdy who bears the family name. Of the younger daughter, Lili, who married a distinguished Prussian lawyer named Adolf Wach, Dame Ethel Smyth wrote that she was 'the only absolutely normal and satisfactory specimen I have ever met of that much-to-be-pitied *genus* the children of celebrated personalities'. A large number of the composer's great-grandchildren, and their children and grandchildren, are living today in Germany, Switzerland, England and the United States.

A year after Mendelssohn's death a memorial performance of *Elijah* was given at Exeter Hall, at which Jenny Lind sang the part that the composer had written for her. The proceeds, which amounted to more than a thousand pounds, were entrusted to a committee, under the chairmanship of Sir George Smart, to found a Mendelssohn Scholarship; its first winner (in 1856) was the fourteen-year-old Arthur Sullivan. In 1878 Mendelssohn's heirs handed

[1] Memoir of Paul Benecke by Margaret Deneke.

over to the Royal Prussian State Library all the composer's musical manuscripts,[1] in return for which two further musical scholarships were to be endowed. These were suspended in the early 1920s when the Mark made its Gadarene rush into the sea of inflation and were not resumed when it was stabilized. In 1961 a start was made to give to the world the most important of those of Mendelssohn's compositions which had not already been published by the composer himself or by the committee set up after his death by his widow.

The family letters, which miraculously survived the bombing of Dresden, passed eventually to two of Mendelssohn's great-nieces, who sold them in 1960 to the New York Public Library. The big collection of documents, sketch-books and relics (including some thousands of letters *to* Mendelssohn) now in the Bodleian Library, Oxford, were acquired between 1950 and 1960 through bequests or by purchase from descendants of Mendelssohn or their friends. The extensive Berlin holdings, including watercolours, sketch-books and manuscripts of the composer and his family, have, like the city, been divided into two – one part being in the Mendelssohn Archiv of the State Library, West Berlin, and the other in the Deutsche Staatsbibliothek, East Berlin.

After the Nazis gained power, the Mendelssohn banking-house was obliged to discontinue its activities, and those of the composer's descendants then still living in Germany were driven out and scattered over the face of the earth. Thus did a people who had once been great and generous repay their debt to one who had brought them world-wide honour and glory.

[1] Preserved over the years and carefully bound in forty-four volumes. It seems extraordinary that so meticulous a man as Mendelssohn should have died intestate.

Appendix

1. The Reverend H. R. Haweis, *Music and Morals*, 1871:

> That keen piercing intellect, flashing with the summer lightning of sensibility and wit, that full generous heart, that great and childlike simplicity of manners, that sweet humanity, and absolute devotion to all that was true and noble, coupled with an instinctive shrinking from all that was mean; that fierce scorn of a lie, that strong hatred of hypocrisy, that gentle, unassuming goodness – all this, and more than this, they know who knew Mendelssohn. . . .
>
> In this age of mercenary manufacture and art degradation, Mendelssohn towers above his contemporaries like a moral lighthouse in the midst of a dark and troubled sea. His light always shone strong and pure. The winds of heaven were about his head, and the 'STILL SMALL VOICE' was in his heart. In a lying generation he was true, and in an adulterous generation he was pure – and not popularity nor gain could tempt him to sully the pages of his spotless inspiration with one meretricious effect or one impure association. . . .

2. John Ruskin, Lecture on the 'Discourses' of Sir Joshua Reynolds (*Collected Works*, Vol. XXII).

While lecturing at Oxford in 1857 on the *Discourses* of Sir Joshua Reynolds, Ruskin chanced to hear 'with disgust' in one of the College chapels an anthem by Mendelssohn 'in which the solemn dignity of the Psalms was lowered by the frivolous prettiness of the music'. This was his setting of Psalm LV, whose soprano solo, 'Oh! for the wings of a dove', used once (the saying went) so often to be sung in village churches by 'a boy with the face and the voice of an angel, but no handkerchief'. In one of these lectures Ruskin said:

> Well, you have had another delightful artist lately, much smaller but a true artist, a man with the heart of a lark – Mendelssohn – the sweetest, most animated, most trillingly musical of living creatures – a perpetual warbler; he warbles and trills his way through Italy, sees no more in Italy than a migrating butterfly might, understands no more. Everything is delicious to him – churches and costumes, and conversation and pictures, and music and sentiment. And how beautiful religion is, for a thing to pipe and fiddle about! And how grand *St Paul* is, for majestic recitative! and *Elijah* – what themes of picturesqueness, what pathos, and choral majesty of priests of Baal! and the Psalms – what endless topics in them for musical contrast! He takes up, for instance, the 55th Psalm – quite one of your favourite anthems here in Oxford. Yes, thinks the little man – who never in his life had the least notion of remaining in the wilderness; who never was oppressed by the wicked, but petted by the pretty; who never heard the voice of an enemy, but of innumerable friends – how sweetly pensive may all this be in music.
>
> 'Give ear to my prayer', in softest bass. 'I mourn in my complaint and make a noise' – and a most sweet noise it shall be; and after everybody has been moved to the most delicious melancholy, then – what a lovely psalm it is – to bring in something, deliciously lively, 'Wings of a dove' – all love letters, and dew of course; now we turn on all the trebles, and away we go.

Bibliography

The standard biography of Mendelssohn is that by Eric Werner (see below), a fine work which has been of great value to me. Philip Radcliffe's *Mendelssohn*, in Dent's 'The Master Musicians' series, is an excellent handbook which it would be found helpful to use in conjunction with my own biography. First-rate too, but unfortunately not available in English, is Karl-Heinz Köhler's well-illustrated paperback which contains an amazing amount of information in a small space, and there is also much of interest in the biographies of Jacob, Kupferberg and Marek. The relative value of the earlier material is, I think, indicated in the course of my book.

Other biographies of the last forty or fifty years range from the good to the indifferent – and beyond. Kaufman, for instance, indulges regrettably in fabricated dialogue: 'Oh, Kalkbrenner! I say there, Kalkbrenner! Oo-oo! Good old Kalkbrenner!' and so on; but his *Mendelssohn: A Second Elijah* makes sober reading by comparison with Pierre La Mure's *Beyond Desire – A Novel based on the Life of Felix and Cécile Mendelssohn*, a novelette of such absurdity that it is impossible to understand why its author bothered to mention the Mendelssohns. Take, for example, Mendelssohn's affair with Queen Victoria's Lady-in-Waiting, the lovely Marchioness of Dorsythe, who was not much given to beating about the bush:

> 'A friend, that's what I need,' she sighed. . . . Her fingers, as she spoke, tightened over his thigh. He rested his hand over hers and gave it a gentle pressure. This innocent gesture sent a responsive shudder through her slender body. She drew herself closer to him and he felt the tender resilience of his new friend's breasts, as she nestled against him. . . .

Yet only twenty pages later we find Mendelssohn happily bedded with an Italian prima donna in Carrington Castle, an edifice 'smaller than Windsor, but not much', which she had bought as a sort of week-end country cottage for the two of them. I am very grateful to Mrs Peter Talbot-Willcox for drawing my attention to this gem, which might otherwise have remained unknown to me.

The list which follows contains only a selection of the books which I have read or consulted. Where English translations of German works exist I have quoted them in preference to the original publications; it should, however, be noted that the former are usually abbreviated.

Andrews, Keith Kurt. *The Nazarenes*. Oxford, 1964.

Barzun, Jacques. *Berlioz and the Romantic Century*, 2 vols. London, 1969.

Benedict, Sir Julius. *A Sketch of the Life and Works of the late Felix Mendelssohn-Bartholdy*. London, 1850.

Bennett, J. R. S. *The Life of W. S. Bennett*. London, 1907.

Berlioz, Hector. *Memoirs*, ed. David Cairns. New York, 1970.

Berlioz and the Romantic Imagination. Catalogue of the Arts Council Exhibition. London, 1969.

Bulman, Joan. *Jenny Lind*. London, 1956.

Chopin, Frederick. *Selected Correspondence*, trs. and ed. Arthur Hedley. London, 1962.

Chorley, Henry. *Modern German Music*. London, 1854. *Thirty Years' Musical Recollections*. London, 1862. *Memoir*, by H. G. Hewlett. London, 1873.

Crum, Margaret. *Felix Mendelssohn Bartholdy* (Bodleian Picture Book). Oxford, 1972.

Dahms, W. *Mendelssohn*. Berlin, 1919.

Davison, J. W. *From Mendelssohn to Wagner*. London, 1912.

Devrient, Eduard. *My Recollections of Felix Mendelssohn Bartholdy . . .*, trs. Natalia Macfarren. London, 1869.

Eckardt, Julius. *Ferdinand David und Die Familie Mendelssohn-Bartholdy*. Leipzig, 1888.

Edwards, Frederick George. *The History of Mendelssohn's Oratorio* Elijah. London and New York, 1896.

Erskine, J. *Song Without Words*. New York, 1941.

Gotch, R. B. *Mendelssohn and his Friends in Kensington*. London, 1934.

Grove's Dictionary of Music and Musicians. Articles on Mendelssohn: 3rd edition, by Sir George Grove. London, 1929. 5th edition, by Percy M. Young. London, 1960.

Hallé, Sir Charles. *Life and Letters*. London, 1896.

Hedley, Arthur, *see* Chopin.

Hensel, Sebastian. *The Mendelssohn Family*, 2 vols., trs. Karl Klingemann. London, 1880.

Hiller, Ferdinand. *Mendelssohn, Letters and Recollections*, trs. M. E. von Glehn. London, 1874.

Holland, H. S. and Rockstro, W. S. *Memoir of Jenny Lind Goldschmidt*. London, 1891.

Horsley, *see* Gotch, R. B.

Horton, J. *Mendelssohn's Chamber Music* (BBC publication). London, 1972.

Hoyer, Walter. *Goethe's Life in Pictures*, trs. Edith Anderson. Leipzig, 1963.

Hurd, Michael. *Mendelssohn*. London, 1970.

Jacob, H. E. *Felix Mendelssohn and his Times*, trs. Richard and Clara Winston. London, 1963.

Jacobson, J. 'Mendelssohn Bartholdy', *Year Book VII of the Leo Baeck Institute*. London, 1962.

Kaufman, Schima. *Mendelssohn: A Second Elijah*. New York, 1936.

Kayserling, M. *Moses Mendelssohn*. Leigzig, 1862.

Klingemann, Karl and Mendelssohn Bartholdy, Felix. *Briefwechsel*, ed. Dr Karl Klingemann. Essex, 1909.

Kupferberg, Herbert. *The Mendelssohns*. New York, 1972.

Lampadius, W. A. *Life of Felix Mendelssohn Bartholdy*, trs. W. L. Gage. London, 1876.

La Mure, P. *Beyond Desire* (novel). London, 1956.

Marek, George. *Gentle Genius*. New York, 1972.

Marx, Adolf Bernhard. *Erinnerungen aus meinem Leben*. Berlin, 1865.

Max-Müller, Felix. *Life and Letters*, 2 vols., ed. by his wife. London, 1901.

Mellers, Wilfrid. *Man and his Music*, Vol. 4. London, 1957.

Mendelssohn Bartholdy, Felix. *Andria*, trs. F.M.B., *see* Terence. *Letters from Italy and Switzerland*, trs. Lady Wallace. London, 1862. *Letters, 1833–1847*, trs. Lady Wallace. London, 1863. *Letters . . . to Ignaz and Charlotte Moscheles*. London, 1888. *Souvenirs d'un Voyage en Suisse, 1842*. Basel, 1966. *Album of Swiss water colours* [of 1847], eds. Max F. Schneider and Cécile Hensel. Basel, no date.

Mendelssohn Bartholdy, Felix and Schubring, J. *Briefwechsel*. Leipzig, 1892.

Mendelssohn Bartholdy, Felix and Sutermeister, P. *Briefe einer Reise* und *Lebensbilden* Zürich, 1958.

Mendelssohn-Bartholdy, Karl. *Goethe and Mendelssohn*, trs. M. E. von Glehn. London, 1872.

Moscheles, Ignaz and Charlotte. *Life of Moscheles*, 2 vols., trs. A. D. Coleridge. London, 1873.

Moser, Andreas. *Joseph Joachim*, trs. L. Durham. London, 1901.

Newman, E. *The Life of Richard Wagner*, Vols. 1 and 2. London, 1933–47.

Novello, Clara. *Reminiscences*. London, 1910.

Petitpierre, J. *The Romance of the Mendelssohns*. Lausanne, 1937. New York, 1947.

Pleasants, Henry. *The Great Singers*. London, 1967.

Polko, Elise. *Reminiscences of Felix Mendelssohn-Bartholdy*, trs. Lady Wallace. London, 1869.

Radcliffe, Philip. *Mendelssohn*. London, 1954 (revised 1967).

Reich, W. *Felix Mendelssohn im Spiegel eigener Aussagen und zeitgenossischer Dokumente*. Zürich, 1970.

Reid, Charles, *Thomas Beecham: an Independent Biography*. London, 1961.

Rellstab, Ludwig. *Aus Meinem Leben*. Berlin, 1861.

Rockstro, W. S. *Mendelssohn*. London, 1884.

Scholes, Percy A. *The Oxford Companion to Music*. London, 1938 (latest edition 1950).

Schumann, Robert. *Gesammelte Schriften über Musik und Musiker*. Leipzig, 1891. *On Music and Musicians*, ed. Konrad Wolff. London, 1947.

Shaw, George Bernard *Music in London*, 3 vols. London, 1932.

Sheppard, E. *Charles Auchester* (novel). London, 1853.

Sitwell, Sacheverell. *Liszt*. London, 1934, 1938, 1955.

Stratton, S. S. *Mendelssohn*. London, 1901.

Terence. *Andria*, trs. Felix Mendelssohn Bartholdy. Verona, 1972.

Tiénot, Y. *Mendelssohn – Musicien Complet*. Paris, 1972.

Wagner, Richard. 'Judaism in Music', in *Richard Wagner's Prose Works*, vol. 3, trs. W. E. Ellis. London, 1894. *My Life*, 2 vols. London, 1911.

Werner, Eric. *Mendelssohn*, trs. Dika Newlin. New York, 1963.

Wolff, Ernst. *Mendelssohn-Bartholdy*. Berlin, 1906.

Wulf, J. *Musik im Dritten Reich*. Gütersloh, 1963.

Zelter-Goethe Briefwechsel, 6 vols. Berlin, 1834.

Notes on the Illustrations

Where the following abbreviations appear in the notes, they are intended to indicate the locations of pictures, and to acknowledge permission to reproduce photographs that the museums, art galleries and other institutions (or specifically their governing bodies) have granted in cases where they hold the copyright.

BM: The Trustees of the British Museum, London.
Bodleian: The Curators of the Bodleian Library, Oxford.
Leipzig: Museum fur Geschichte der Stadt Leipzig.
MA: Mendelssohn-Archiv, Staatsbibliothek, West Berlin.
Mansell: The Mansell Collection, London.
NGB: Nationalgalerie, West Berlin.
RTH: Radio Times Hulton Picture Library, London.
Staatsbibliothek: Staatsbibliothek Bildarchiv, West Berlin.
V & A: Victoria and Albert Museum, London.

111 Fenton House, Hampstead. The National Trust
113 French Academy in Rome. Photo: Marianne Adelmann.
114–15 Kunsthalle, Hamburg. Photo: Ralph Kleinhempel.
116 Royal Collection. By gracious permission of Her Majesty the Queen.
119 MA.
123 Bodleian.
125 *Left* NGB. *Right* Mary Evans Picture Library.
131 Bodleian.
132 NGB.
133 *Top* Château de Malmaison. Photo: Giraudon. *Bottom* Bethnal Green Museum. Photo: Derrick Witty.
134–5 NGB.
136 Louvre, Paris. Photo: Giraudon.
139–41 *Letters from Italy and Switzerland, 1830–32* by Felix Mendelssohn-Bartholdy. Longmans, Green & Co. Photos: Robert Harding.
145 Bodleian.
146 George Rainbird Ltd. Photo: Freeman.
148 *Left* Staatsbibliothek. *Right* M. Feilchenfeldt Collection, Zurich.
149 *Left* Staatsbibliothek. *Right* NGB.
153 Mansell.
158 NGB.
159 *The Wilkie Gallery*. Photo: Freeman.
160 By courtesy of the author.
161 NGB.
163 Royal Academy of Music. Photo: Robert Harding.
164 *Top* V & A. Photo: Derrick Witty. *Bottom* Schloss Hohenzollern. Staatsbibliothek.
167 Staatsbibliothek.
168 Staatsbibliothek.
170 Mansell.
177 Leipzig.
178 Staatsbibliothek.
181 Bodleian
182 Library of Congress, Washington, D.C.
184 Staatsbibliothek.
187 NGB.
189 Bodleian.
191 Bodleian.

192 Bodleian.
196 Bodleian.
199 By kind permission of the Countess Bona Gigliucci. Photo: John Ross.
200 Birmingham City Art Gallery.
203 MA.
204 *Autobiography* by Henry Chorley. Richard Bentley & Son, 1873. Photo: Robert Harding.
210 *My Autobiography* by F. Max Müller. Longmans, Green & Co., 1901. Photo: Robert Harding.
212 RTH.
214 Leipzig.
215 MA.
219 *Top* BM. Photo: Freeman. *Bottom* MA.
221 *Punch*, 18 January 1845. Photo: Robert Harding.
225 MA.
226–7 MA.
228 MA.
230 RTH.
231 Mansell.
232 Staatsbibliothek.
233 MA.
237 *Left Journal pour rire*, 27 June 1850. Bibliothèque Municipale Grenoble. *Right* Musée Instrumental de la Conservatoire Nationale de Musique, Paris.
239 Staatsbibliothek.
242 Bodleian.
245 Staatsbibliothek.
250 BM. Photo: Freeman.
253 Stockholm National Museum.
254 V & A. Photo: Derrick Witty.
256 *Illustrated London News*. Photo: Robert Harding.
259 Leipzig.
260 *Illustrated London News*. Mansell.
261 *Illustrated London News*. Photo: Robert Harding.
263 *Illustrated London News*. Photo: Robert Harding.
265 NGB.
269 MA.
271 MA.
272 Albi Rosenthal. Photo: Derrick Witty.
275 Photo: Freeman.
276 MA.

Index